T0202718

Lecture Notes in Computer Science 13035

More information about this subseries at http://www.springer.com/series/7407

Paul C. Bell · Patrick Totzke ·
Igor Potapov (Eds.)

Reachability Problems

15th International Conference, RP 2021
Liverpool, UK, October 25–27, 2021
Proceedings

 Springer

Editors
Paul C. Bell (iD)
Liverpool John Moores University
Liverpool, UK

Patrick Totzke (iD)
University of Liverpool
Liverpool, UK

Igor Potapov (iD)
University of Liverpool
Liverpool, UK

ISSN 0302-9743   ISSN 1611-3349 (electronic)
Lecture Notes in Computer Science
ISBN 978-3-030-89715-4   ISBN 978-3-030-89716-1 (eBook)
https://doi.org/10.1007/978-3-030-89716-1

LNCS Sublibrary: SL1 – Theoretical Computer Science and General Issues

This Springer imprint is published by the registered company Springer Nature Switzerland AG
The registered company address is: Gewerbestrasse 11, 6330 Cham, Switzerland

Preface

This volume contains the papers presented at the 15th International Conference on Reachability Problems (RP 2021), organized by the University of Liverpool and Liverpool John Moores University, UK. Previous events in the series were located at the University of Paris, France (2020), Université Libre de Bruxelles, Belgium (2019), Aix-Marseille University, France (2018), Royal Holloway, University of London, UK (2017), Aalborg University, Denmark (2016), the University of Warsaw, Poland (2015), the University of Oxford, UK (2014), Uppsala University, Sweden (2013), the University of Bordeaux, France (2012), the University of Genoa, Italy (2011), Masaryk University Brno, Czech Republic (2010), École Polytechnique, France (2009), the University of Liverpool, UK (2008), and Turku University, Finland (2007).

The aim of the conference is to bring together scholars from diverse fields with a shared interest in reachability problems, and to promote the exploration of new approaches for the modeling and analysis of computational processes by combining mathematical, algorithmic, and computational techniques. Topics of interest include (but are not limited to) reachability for infinite state systems; rewriting systems; reachability analysis in counter/timed/cellular/communicating automata; Petri nets; computational game theory; computational aspects of semigroups, groups, and rings; reachability in dynamical and hybrid systems; frontiers between decidable and undecidable reachability problems; complexity and decidability aspects; predictability in iterative maps, and new computational paradigms.

We are very grateful to our invited speakers, who gave the following talks:

- Udi Boker, Interdisciplinary Center (IDC), Israel:
  "Quantitative vs. Weighted Automata"
- Clare Dixon, University of Manchester, UK:
  "Theorem Proving Using Clausal Resolution: From Past to Present"
- Javier Esparza, Technische Universität München, Germany:
  "Population Protocols: Beyond Runtime Analysis"
- Damien Woods, Maynooth University, Ireland:
  "Algorithmic Self-assembly and Molecular Robotics: Theory and Practice"
- Georg Zetzsche Max Planck Institute for Software System, Kaiserslautern, Germany:
  "Recent Advances on Reachability Problems for Valence Systems (Invited Talk)"

The conference received 27 submissions (17 regular and 10 presentation only submissions) from which four regular papers were withdrawn. Each submission was carefully reviewed by three Program Committee (PC) members. Based on these reviews, the PC decided to accept six regular papers in addition to four invited speakers contributions. The members of the PC and the list of external reviewers can be found at the end of this preface. We are grateful for the high-quality work produced by the PC and the external reviewers. Overall this volume contains six contributed papers and four papers from invited speakers which cover their talks.

The conference also provided the opportunity to other young and established researchers to present work in progress or work already published elsewhere. This year in addition to six regular submissions, the PC accepted 10 high-quality informal presentations on various reachability aspects in theoretical computer science. A list of accepted presentation-only submissions is given below:

Not All Bugs Are Created Equal, But Robust Reachability Can Tell the Difference

Guillaume Girol, Benjamin Farinier, and Sebastien Bardin

Abstract. This paper introduces a new property called robust reachability which refines the standard notion of reachability in order to take replicability into account. A bug is robustly reachable if a controlled input can make it so the bug is reached whatever the value of uncontrolled input. Robust reachability is better suited than standard reachability in many realistic situations related to security (e.g., criticality assessment or bug prioritization) or software engineering (e.g., replicable test suites and flakiness). We propose a formal treatment of the concept, and we revisit existing symbolic bug finding methods through this new lens. Remarkably, robust reachability allows differentiating bounded model checking from symbolic execution while they have the same deductive power in the standard case. Finally, we propose the first symbolic verifier dedicated to robust reachability: we use it for criticality assessment of four existing vulnerabilities and compare it with standard symbolic execution. Note: this paper has been published in the proceedings of CAV 2021.

Sound Verification Procedures for Temporal Properties of Infinite-State Systems

Quentin Peyras, Jean-Paul Bodeveix, Julien Brunel, and David Chemouil

Abstract. First-order Linear Temporal Logic (FOLTL) is particularly convenient to specify distributed systems, in particular because of the unbounded aspect of their state space. Decidable fragments have recently been exhibited and open the way for tractable verification. However, these fragments are not expressible enough for realistic specifications. In this paper, we propose three abstraction techniques to translate a typical FOLTL specification into two of its decidable fragments. All three abstractions are proved to be sound (the proofs are validated with Coq) and have a high degree of automation. In order to put these techniques into practice, we propose a specification language relying on FOLTL. Our prototype then performs the verification relying on existing model checkers. We successfully verified safety and liveness properties for eight specifications of distributed systems from the literature. Note: this paper has been published in the proceedings of CAV 2021.

Continuous One-counter Automata

Michael Blondin, Tim Leys, Filip Mazowiecki, Philip Offtermatt, and Guillermo Perez

Abstract. We study the reachability problem for continuous one-counter automata, COCA for short. In such automata, transitions are guarded by upper and lower bound tests against the counter value. Additionally, the counter updates associated with taking transitions can be (non-deterministically) scaled down by a nonzero factor between zero and one. Our three main results are as follows: (1) we prove that the reachability problem for COCA with global upper and lower bound tests is in NC2; (2) that, in general, the problem is decidable in polynomial time; and (3) that it is decidable in the polynomial hierarchy for COCA with parametric counter updates and bound tests. Note: this paper has been published in the proceedings of LICS 2021.

Solitaire of Independence

Ville Salo

Abstract. We introduce the solitaire of independence, and ask some questions about it, in particular we state the associated reachability problem and ask about its complexity. We briefly explain the connection to certain invariant measures on TEP subshifts.

Linear-time Model Checking Branching Processes

Stefan Kiefer, Pavel Semukhin, and Cas Widdershoven

Abstract. (Multi-type) branching processes are a natural and well-studied model for generating random infinite trees. Branching processes feature both nondeterministic and probabilistic branching, generalizing both transition systems and Markov chains (but not generally Markov decision processes). We study the complexity of model checking branching processes against linear-time omega-regular specifications: is it the case almost surely that every branch of a tree randomly generated by the branching process satisfies the omega-regular specification? The main result is that for LTL specifications this problem is in PSPACE, subsuming classic results for transition systems and Markov chains, respectively. The underlying general model-checking algorithm is based on the automata-theoretic approach, using unambiguous Büchi automata. Note: this paper has been published in the proceedings of CONCUR 2021.

Depth-first Search in Directed Planar Graphs

Eric Allender, Archit Chauhan, and Samir Datta

Abstract. We present an algorithm for constructing a depth-first search tree in planar digraphs; the algorithm can be implemented in the complexity class AC^1 (UL intersection co-UL), which is contained in AC^2. Prior to this (for more than a quarter-century), the fastest uniform deterministic parallel algorithm for this problem was $O(log^{10}n)$ (corresponding to the complexity class $AC^{10} \subseteq NC^{11}$). We also consider the problem of computing depth-first search trees in other classes of graphs, and obtain additional new upper bounds. Note: this paper has been published in the proceedings of MFCS 2021.

The Pseudo-Skolem Problem is Decidable

Julian D'Costa, Toghrul Karimov, Rupak Majumdar, Joel Ouaknine, Mahmoud Salamati, Sadegh Soudjani, and James Worrell

Abstract. We study fundamental decision problems on linear dynamical systems in discrete time. We focus on pseudo-orbits, the collection of trajectories of the dynamical system for which there is an arbitrarily small perturbation at each step. Pseudo-orbits are generalizations of orbits in the topological theory of dynamical systems. We study the pseudo-orbit problem, whether a state belongs to the pseudo-orbit of another state, and the pseudo-Skolem problem, whether a hyperplane is reachable by an ε-pseudo-orbit for every ε. These problems are analogous to the well-studied orbit problem and Skolem problem on unperturbed dynamical systems. Our main results show that the pseudo-orbit problem is decidable in polynomial time and, surprisingly, the Skolem problem on pseudo-orbits is also decidable. The former extends the seminal result of Kannan and Lipton from orbits to pseudo-orbits. The latter is in contrast to the Skolem problem for linear dynamical systems, which remains open for proper orbits. Note: this paper has been published in the proceedings of MFCS 2021.

The Edit Distance to k-Subsequence Universality

Joel Day, Pamela Fleischmann, Maria Kosche, Tore Ko, Florin Manea, and Stefan Siemer

Abstract. A word u is a subsequence of another word w if u can be obtained from w by deleting some of its letters. In the early 1970s, Imre Simon defined the relation $\sim_k$ (now called Simon-Congruence) as follows: two words having exactly the same set of subsequences of length at most k are $\sim_k$-congruent. This relation was central in defining and analyzing piecewise testable languages, but has found many applications in areas such as algorithmic learning theory, databases theory, or computational linguistics. Recently, it was shown that testing whether two words are $\sim_k$-congruent can be done in optimal linear time. Thus, it is a natural next step to ask, for two words w and u which are not $\sim_k$-equivalent, what is the minimal number of edit operations that we need to perform on w in order to obtain a word which is $\sim_k$-equivalent to u? In this paper, we consider this problem in a setting which seems interesting: when u is a k-subsequence universal word. A word u with alph $(u) = \Sigma$ is called k-subsequence universal if the set of subsequences of length k of u contains all possible words of length k over Σ. As such, our results are a series of efficient algorithms computing the edit distance from w to the language of k-subsequence universal words. In other words, we are interested in optimally editing a word w in order to reach k-universality. The submitted manuscript was an extended version of a paper which was published at STACS 2021.

Matching Patterns with Variables under Hamming Distance

Pawel Gawrychowski, Florin Manea, and Stefan Siemer

Abstract. A pattern α is a string of variables and terminal letters. We say that α matches a word w, consisting only of terminal letters, if w can be obtained by replacing the variables of α by terminal words. The matching problem, i.e., deciding whether a given pattern matches a given word, has been heavily investigated: it is NP-complete in general, but can be solved efficiently for classes of patterns with restricted structure. In this paper, we approach this problem in a generalized setting, by considering approximate pattern matching under Hamming distance. More precisely, we are interested in what is the minimum Hamming distance between w and any word u obtained by replacing the variables of α by terminal words. Firstly, we address the class of regular patterns (in which no variable occurs twice) and propose efficient algorithms for this problem, as well as matching conditional lower bounds. We show that the problem can still be solved efficiently if we allow repeated variables, but restrict the way the different variables can be interleaved according to a locality parameter. However, as soon as we allow a variable to occur more than once and its occurrences can be interleaved arbitrarily with those of other variables, even if none of them occurs more than once, the problem becomes intractable. Note: this paper has been published in the proceedings of MFCS 2021.

Runtime Monitoring for Markov Decision Processes

Sebastian Junges, Hazem Torfah, and Sanjit A. Seshia

Abstract. We investigate the problem of monitoring partially observable systems with nondeterministic and probabilistic dynamics. In such systems, every state may be associated with a risk, e.g., the probability of an imminent crash. During runtime, we obtain partial information about the system state in the form of observations. The monitor uses this information to estimate the risk of the (unobservable) current system state. Our results are threefold. First, we show that extensions of state estimation approaches do not scale due the combination of nondeterminism and probabilities. While convex hull algorithms improve the practical runtime, they do not prevent an exponential memory blowup. Second, we present a tractable algorithm based on model checking conditional reachability probabilities. Third, we provide prototypical implementations and manifest the applicability of our algorithms to a range of benchmarks. The results highlight the possibilities and boundaries of our novel algorithms. Note:

this paper has been published in the proceedings of CAV 2021; the full paper with appendices can be found at https://arxiv.org/abs/2105.12322.

So overall, the conference program consisted of five invited talks, six presentations of contributed papers, and 10 informal presentations in the area of reachability problems, stretching from results on fundamental questions in mathematics and computer science up to efficient solutions of practical problems.

It is a pleasure to thank the team behind the EasyChair system and the Lecture Notes in Computer Science team at Springer, who together made the production of this volume possible in time for the conference. Finally, we thank all the authors and invited speakers for their high-quality contributions, and the participants for making RP 2021 a success. We are also very grateful to Alfred Hofmann for the continuous support of the event in the last decade and to Ronan Nugent for supporting this year's conference, as well as to the London Mathematical Society and Springer for their financial sponsorship.

October 2021

Paul C. Bell
Patrick Totzke
Igor Potapov

Organization

Program Committee

Patrick Totzke (Co-chair)	University of Liverpool, UK
Paul C. Bell (Co-chair)	Liverpool John Moores University, UK
Shaull Almagor	The University of Oxford, UK
Christel Baier	TU Dresden, Germany
Srivathsan B	Chennai Mathematical Institute, India
Olivier Bournez	École Polytechnique, France
Laura Ciobanu	The University of Edinburgh, UK
Lorenzo Clemente	The University of Warsaw, Poland
Thao Dang	CNRS, The University of Grenoble, France
Rayna Dimitrova	Helmholtz Center for Information Security, Germany
Manfred Droste	The University of Leipzig, Germany
Stefan Göller	The University of Kassel, Germany
Matthew Hague	Royal Holloway University, London, UK
Mika Hirvensalo	The University of Turku, Finland
Sang-Ki Ko	Kangwon National University, South Korea
Florin Manea	The University of Göttingen, Germany
Filip Mazowiecki	MPI Saarbrücken, Germany
Anca Muscholl	The University of Bordeaux, France
Igor Potapov	The University of Liverpool, UK
Maria Prandini	The University of Milan, Italy
Krishna S	IIT Bombay, India
Grégoire Sutre	The University of Bordeaux, France
Pavel Semukhin	The University of Oxford, UK

Additional Reviewers

Joel Day
Mitja Kulczynski
Philip Offtermatt

Abstracts of Invited Talks

Quantitative vs. Weighted Automata

Udi Boker

Interdisciplinary Center (IDC) Herzliya, Israel
udiboker@idc.ac.il
https://faculty.idc.ac.il/udiboker

Abstract. Weighted automata are widely researched, but with a variety of different semantics, which mostly fit into either the "quantitative view" or the "algebraic view". We argue that the two views result with incomparable automata families, each providing a different conceptual generalization of Boolean automata and having different natural extensions. We propose to term the former "quantitative automata" and the latter "weighted automata". In both views, transitions are labeled with weights and the value of a path of transitions is given by some value function on the traversed weights. However, the main conceptual difference is in the generalization of nondeterminism and its dual (universality, in alternating automata). Quantitative automata keep the *preference* meaning of *choice* and *obligation* to nondeterminism and universality, interpreted as supremum and infimum, respectively, and accordingly restrict weights and value functions to the totally ordered domain of real numbers. Weighted automata, on the other hand, generalize nondeterminism to an arbitrary *commutative operation* (of a semiring or valuation monoid), and generally have no interpretation of universality. The weights and value functions can be from arbitrary domains. On several aspects the algebraic view generalizes the quantitative one, allowing for richer weight domains and interpretations of nondeterminism, whereas on different aspects the quantitative view is more general, having alternation, inherent compatibility with games and adequacy to approximations. We argue that clarifying the conceptual difference between the two automata families can enlighten their possible future extensions.

Keywords: Quantitative automata · Weighted automata · Nondeterminism · Alternation · Games · Logic

Theorem Proving Using Clausal Resolution: From Past to Present

Clare Dixon (ID)

Department of Computer Science, University of Manchester, Manchester, M13
9PL, UK
clare.dixon@manchester.ac.uk

Abstract. Modal and temporal logics are extensions to classical logic that have
operators that deal with necessity and possibility (modal logics) and such as
sometime, always and next (temporal logics). Models are sets of worlds that are
connected by an accessibility relation. Restrictions imposed on this relation and
the operators allowed give rise to different families of logic. This paper discusses
an approach to theorem proving for temporal and modal logics based on clausal
resolution. The main ideas are the translation to a normal form and the application of resolution rules that relate to the same world. This research initially
focused on propositional linear time temporal logic but has been extended to
computation tree logic, monadic first order temporal logic and normal modal
logics. We describe the approach, explain the adaptations necessary for the
logics mentioned and discuss the results of the provers developed for these
logics.

This work was funded by the Engineering and Physical Sciences Research Council (EPSRC)
under the historic grants GR/K57282, GR/M44859 and GR/M46631 and more recently the Science
of Sensor Systems Software (S4 EP/N007565/1) and by the UK Industrial Strategy Challenge Fund
(ISCF), delivered by UKRI and managed by EPSRC under the grants Future AI and Robotics Hub
for Space (FAIR-SPACE EP/R026092/1) and Robotics and Artificial Intelligence for Nuclear (RAIN
EP/R026084/1)

Population Protocols: Beyond Runtime Analysis

Javier Esparza (ID)

Technical University of Munich, Germany
esparza@in.tum.de

Abstract. Population protocols are a model of computation in which an arbitrary number of indistinguishable finite-state agents interact in pairs to collectively decide if their initial global configuration satisfies a given property. Population protocols were introduced by Angluin et al. to study the theoretical properties of networks of mobile sensors with very limited computational resources, but they are also very strongly related to chemical reaction networks, a discrete model of chemistry in which agents are molecules that change their states due to collisions. We survey our recent work on the verification of population protocols and their state complexity.

The work surveyed in this note was supported by the European Research Council (ERC) under the European Union's Horizon 2020 research and innovation program under grant agreement No 787367 "Parameterized Verification and Synthesis" (PaVeS).

Algorithmic Self-Assembly and Molecular Robotics: Theory and Practice

Damien Woods

Hamilton Institute and Department of Computer Science, Maynooth University,
Ireland
damien.woods@mu.ie
https://dna.hamilton.ie/

Abstract. The field of algorithmic self-assembly is concerned with the theory and practice of designing molecules that perform computations while growing structures, in an autonomous bottom-up fashion. Algorithmic molecular robotics imagines pre-formed structures that actuate and move while performing computational tasks. Significant effort has been invested into defining and studying discrete mathematical models that are close enough to physical reality to be implementable in the wet-lab, yet suitable for mathematical investigation and characterisation. In some cases, theoretical ideas have inspired wet-lab implementations, and in others physical limitations and abilities have inspired model definitions. The presentation will introduce both self-assembly and robotics models, and show what it means to compute in these models. The main directions of theoretical research in the field to date will be covered, along with an overview of the kinds of techniques used in some proofs. Finally, there will be a light overview of how one goes about designing and experimentally implementing algorithmic self-assembling DNA tiles in the wet lab, including some of our latest results on that topic.

Keywords: DNA computing · Self-assembly · Theory of computation

Supported by European Research Council (ERC) award number 772766 and Science foundation Ireland (SFI) grant 18/ERCS/5746 (this abstract reflects only the authors' view and the ERC is not responsible for any use that may be made of the information it contains).

Recent Advances on Reachability Problems for Valence Systems

Georg Zetzsche (iD)

Max Planck Institute for Software Systems (MPI-SWS), Germany

Abstract. Valence systems are an abstract model of computation that consists of a finite-state control and some storage mechanism. In contrast to traditional models, the storage mechanism is not fixed, but given as a parameter. This allows us to precisely state questions like: For which storage mechanisms is the reachability problem decidable? This survey reports on recent results that aim to understand the impact of the storage mechanism on decidability and complexity of several variants of the reachability problem. The considered problems are configuration reachability, model-checking first-order logic with reachability, and reachability under bounded context switching and scope-boundedness.

Contents

Invited Papers

Quantitative vs. Weighted Automata

Udi Boker[(✉)]

Reichman University, Herzliya, Israel
udiboker@idc.ac.il
https://faculty.idc.ac.il/udiboker

Abstract. Weighted automata are widely researched, but with a variety of different semantics, which mostly fit into either the "quantitative view" or the "algebraic view". We argue that the two views result with incomparable automata families, each providing a different conceptual generalization of Boolean automata and having different natural extensions.

We propose to term the former "quantitative automata" and the latter "weighted automata".

In both views, transitions are labeled with weights and the value of a path of transitions is given by some value function on the traversed weights. However, the main conceptual difference is in the generalization of nondeterminism and its dual (universality, in alternating automata).

Quantitative automata keep the *preference* meaning of *choice* and *obligation* to nondeterminism and universality, interpreted as supremum and infimum, respectively, and accordingly restrict weights and value functions to the totally ordered domain of real numbers.

Weighted automata, on the other hand, generalize nondeterminism to an arbitrary *commutative operation* (of a semiring or valuation monoid), and generally have no interpretation of universality. The weights and value functions can be from arbitrary domains.

On several aspects the algebraic view generalizes the quantitative one, allowing for richer weight domains and interpretations of nondeterminism, whereas on different aspects the quantitative view is more general, having alternation, inherent compatibility with games and adequacy to approximations.

We argue that clarifying the conceptual difference between the two automata families can enlighten their possible future extensions.

Keywords: Quantitative automata · Weighted automata · Nondeterminism · Alternation · Games · Logic

1 Introduction

A Bit of History

1959 *Nondeterministic automata* (on finite words) introduced by Michael Rabin and Dana Scott [65].

© Springer Nature Switzerland AG 2021
P. C. Bell et al. (Eds.): RP 2021, LNCS 13035, pp. 3–18, 2021.
https://doi.org/10.1007/978-3-030-89716-1_1

1961 *Weighted automata* (with integer weights on finite words) introduced by Marcel-Paul Schützenberger [67].

1962 *Automata on infinite words* introduced by Julius Richard Büchi [19].

1963 *Probabilistic automata* (on finite words) introduced by Michael Rabin [64].

1970s *Weighted automata over semirings* (on finite words) have evolved (e.g., [41,66]).

1976 *Alternating automata* introduced by Ashok Chandra, Dexter Kozen and Larry Stockmeyer [21,22].

2000s *Weighted automata over semirings on infinite words* have evolved (e.g., [30,36,40]).

2008 *Quantitative automata*, as we refer to them, introduced by Krishnendu Chatterjee, Laurent Doyen, and Thomas Henzinger [23–25].

2010 *Weighted automata over valuation monoids* introduced by Manfred Droste and Ingmar Meinecke [37,38].

Along the years:

- The various automata types were generalized to operate not only on words, but also on trees, graphs, and other structures.
- Counter automata of various types have evolved, which are inherently different from quantitative and weighted automata in the sense that in counter automata the counter value along a run can allow or forbid certain transitions.
- Automata were shown to be closely related to other entities and especially to logic and games, in both the Boolean and weighted settings.
- Automata on infinite words proved very useful in verification and synthesis.
- Alternation was shown to be particularly related to logic and games, and also proved very useful in verification.

The Relations Between Quantitative and Weighted Automata

The main conceptual difference between quantitative and weighted automata is in the interpretation of nondeterminism and its dual (universality). Quantitative automata keep their *preference* meaning with *choice* and *obligation*, respectively, thus considering weights and value functions over the totally ordered domain of real numbers. Weighted automata, on the other hand, allow for an arbitrary commutative interpretation of nondeterminism and generally have no interpretation of universality.

Quantitative automata usually have no acceptance condition, which is generalized by the numerical value of the automaton on the input. Weighted automata generally do have a Boolean acceptance condition, and only the values of accepting runs are considered by the commutative operation.

The automata families are formally defined in Sect. 2 and their relations are illustrated in Fig. 1.

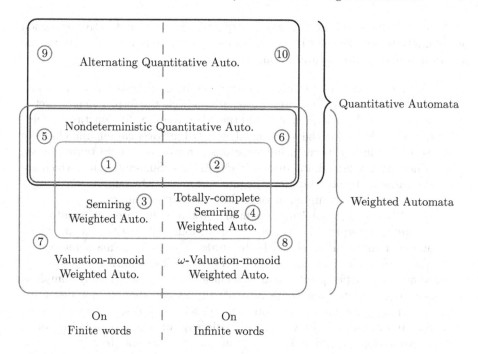

Fig. 1. Quantitative and weighted automata relations. Examples of some automata types that belong to the different (intersection of) automata families, as marked by the circled numbers, are given below.

For a quantitative automaton, one may first consider whether it is nondeterministic, universal, or alternating, and then consider its specific type, which is determined by its *value function*—a function Val from finite or infinite sequences of real numbers to a real number, defining how to value a path of transition weights. For example, an alternating discounted-sum automaton.

For a weighted automaton, one needs to first consider which subfamily it belongs to, depending on the algebraic restrictions on the function $\prod$ to value a path of transition weights and the function $\sum$ to aggregate the values of the accepting paths on an input word. The most common subfamily is of *semiring* weighted automata, operating on finite words and requiring $\prod$ and $\sum$ to correspond to the $\otimes$ and $\oplus$ operations of a semiring. For automata on infinite words, one needs to restrict the semiring to a *totally-complete semiring*, which properly extends $\prod$ and $\sum$ to infinite sequences and sets. In order to extend weighted automata to allow for the value functions that are used by quantitative automata, one needs to replace semirings with the more liberal *valuation monoid* for finite words and ω-valuation monoid for infinite words.

Example of Automata Types in the Different (intersection of) Automata Families. The numbers below correspond to the circled numbers in Fig. 1. Some of the value functions, semirings, and valuation monoids mentioned in the examples are formally defined in Sect. 2. For ④ and ⑧, requiring a commutative operation on infinitely many elements that is different from supremum and infimum, we are not aware of many natural examples in the literature.

1,2. The intersection of [totally-complete] semiring weighted automata and nondeterministic quantitative automata restricts the former to interpret $\oplus$ as max (and $\sum$ as supremum) and the latter to use value functions (which take the role of $\prod$ in the semiring) that distribute over supremum. On finite words (① in Fig. 1), it includes various common automata types, among which are Boolean finite automata (NFAs) and Sum-automata, which are the same as tropical/arctic/max-plus automata. On infinite words (②), there are fewer examples, among which are Sup automata.

3,4. [Totally-complete] semiring weighted automata that are not quantitative automata interpret the $\oplus$ and $\sum$ operations differently from max/min and supremum/infimum. For finite words (③), there are many interesting examples, such as weighted automata over the log semiring.

5,6. Nondeterministic quantitative automata that are not [totally-complete] semiring weighted automata use value functions that do not distribute over max/ supremum. There are many such examples, among which are Avg automata on finite words and LimInfAvg automata on infinite words.

7,8. [ω-]valuation-monoid weighted automata that are not [totally-complete] semiring weighted automata and not quantitative automata interpret the $\oplus$ and $\sum$ operations differently from max/min and supremum/infimum, and their value functions do not distribute over $\sum$. On finite words (⑦), one can take for example the domain of weights to be $\{0, 1\}$, use the value function Avg, and interpret $\oplus$ as multiplication.

9,10. All alternating quantitative automata that indeed use alternation (namely, automata that do not have only nondeterministic or universal transitions) are not [ω-]valuation-monoid weighted automata.

Terminology Mismatch in the Literature. The usage in the literature of "weighted automata" to different automata families can often be confusing. Some papers on "weighted automata" are specific to the tropical/arctic semiring (which is in ① of Fig. 1), for example [3,6,20]; some speak of quantitative automata, for example [24,27]; and a significant segment of them refer to semiring weighted automata on finite words. There are also cases of using "quantitative automata" when referring to the algebraic view, for example [8].

Different Conceptual Views Leading to Different Extensions

As a result of the conceptual differences between the two automata families, they are naturally related to and extended with different notions and entities.

In particular, quantitative automata, which incorporate preference and the dual roles of nondeterminism and universality, naturally relate to two-player turn-based zero-sum games and to formal verification and synthesis, and allow for approximations with respect to standard distance functions over the real numbers.

Weighted automata, on the other hand, having an algebraic structure and a flexible interpretation of nondeterminism, are naturally related to various algebraic areas and have established equivalences with monadic second order logic.

In Sect. 3 we elaborate on several such notions and entities that are differently related to each of the automata families, and put forward possible extensions of the relations with the "less related" family.

We believe that understanding the conceptual difference between the two automata families (and making a terminological distinction between them) can help clarity, and furthermore enlighten the possible future extensions of each family, taking inspiration from natural extensions of the other family.

2   Definitions of Quantitative and Weighted Automata

We start with defining transition-labeled automata[1], and then extend them separately to quantitative automata and to weighted automata.

Remark 1. We describe automata on finite or infinite *words*, while both quantitative and weighted automata have orthogonal generalizations to more involved input structures, such as trees, graphs, and pictures. Likewise, we speak of automata with a *single weight* on each transition, while both automata families have natural extensions that allow for multiple weights on each transition.

Nondeterministic and Alternating Transition-labeled Automata

A *nondeterministic transition-labeled automaton* is a tuple $\mathcal{A} = (\Sigma, Q, I, \delta)$, where Σ is an alphabet set; Q is a finite nonempty set of states; $I \subseteq Q$ is a set of initial states; and $\delta \colon Q \times \Sigma \to 2^{W \times Q}$ is a transition function, where W is a set of labels.

A *transition* is a tuple $(q, \sigma, x, q') \in Q \times \Sigma \times W \times Q$, also written $q \xrightarrow{\sigma:x} q'$. (Note that there might be several transitions with different weights over the same letter between the same pair of states[2].) We write $\gamma(t) = x$ for the *weight* of a transition $t = (q, \sigma, x, q')$.

A *run* (or *path*) of the automaton on a word w is a sequence π of transitions that starts in an initial state and respects the transition function; that is $\pi = t_0, t_1, t_2, \ldots$, such that $t_0 = q \xrightarrow{w[0]:x} q'$ for a transition $t_0 \in \delta$ and $q \in I$, and

---

[1] We define first an automaton without an acceptance-condition/value-function/semi-ring/valuation-monoid, but with initial state(s). Usually, the term 'automaton' refers to an entity with them, while 'semiautomaton' to an entity that also lacks initial state(s).

[2] This extra flexibility of allowing for "parallel" transitions with different weights is often omitted, since it is redundant for some value functions while important for others.

for every $i > 0$, we have $t_{i-1} = q \xrightarrow{w[i-1]:x} q'$ and $t_i = q' \xrightarrow{w[i]:x} q''$, such that $t_{i-1}, t_i \in \delta$.

A nondeterministic automaton is *deterministic* if its set of initial states is a singleton and its transition function maps every state and letter to a singleton (a weight-state pair).

An *alternating transition-labeled automaton* is also a tuple $\mathcal{A} = (\Sigma, Q, \iota, \delta)$, where Σ and Q are as in the nondeterministic case, $\iota \in Q$ is an initial state[3], and $\delta: Q \times \Sigma \to B^+(\mathbb{R} \times Q)$ is a transition function, where $B^+(\mathbb{R} \times Q)$ is the set of positive Boolean formulas (*transition conditions*) over weight-state pairs.

A *transition* is as in the nondeterministic case a tuple $(q, \sigma, x, q') \in Q \times \Sigma \times \mathbb{R} \times Q$. (A transition condition generally yields many transitions.)

A run of the automaton on a word w is intuitively a play between Adam and Eve in a game denoted by $G_{\mathcal{A}}(w)$[4]. It starts in the initial state ι, and in each round, when the automaton is in state q and the next letter of w is σ, Eve resolves the nondeterminism (disjunctions) of the transition condition $\delta(q, \sigma)$ and Adam resolves its universality (conjunctions), yielding a transition $q \xrightarrow{\sigma:x} q'$. The output of a play is thus a path $\pi = t_0 t_1 t_2 \ldots$ of transitions.

A nondeterministic (resp. universal) automaton is a special case of an alternating automaton, in which all transition conditions are disjunctions (resp. conjunctions).

A nondeterministic/alternating automaton is *complete* if for every state $q \in Q$ and letter $\sigma \in \Sigma$, there is at least one transition $q \xrightarrow{\sigma:x} q'$ to some state q'.

2.1   Quantitative Automata

A quantitative automaton is defined with respect to a *value function* $\mathsf{Val}: \mathbb{R}^* \to \mathbb{R}$ or $\mathsf{Val}: \mathbb{R}^\omega \to \mathbb{R}$. It is then called a nondeterministic/alternating Val automaton (e.g., a nondeterministic discounted-sum automaton).

Examples of Common Value Functions Over Sequences of Real Values.[5]
For finite sequences $v = v_0 v_1 \ldots v_{n-1}$:

$$- \; \mathsf{Sum}(v) = \sum_{i=0}^{n-1} v_i \qquad - \; \mathsf{Avg}(v) = \frac{1}{n} \sum_{i=0}^{n-1} v_i \qquad - \; \mathsf{Prod}(v) = \prod_{i=0}^{n-1} v_i$$

For finite and infinite sequences $v = v_0 v_1 \ldots$:

$$- \; \mathsf{Inf}(v) = \inf\{v_n \mid n \geq 0\} \qquad\qquad - \; \mathsf{Sup}(v) = \sup\{v_n \mid n \geq 0\}$$

$$- \; \text{For a discount factor } \lambda \in \mathbb{Q} \cap (0,1), \; {}_\lambda\mathsf{DSum}(v) = \sum_{i \geq 0} \lambda^i v_i$$

---

[3] Nondeterministic automata are also often defined with a single initial state.

[4] An equivalent definition goes via trees instead of games.

[5] There are value functions that are more naturally defined over sequences of tuples of real values (see Remark 1), for example lexicographic-mean-payoff [9] and discounted-summation with multiple discount factors [13].

For infinite sequences $v = v_0v_1 \ldots$:

- $\mathsf{LimInf}(v) = \lim\limits_{n\to\infty} \inf\{v_i \mid i \geq n\}$

- $\mathsf{LimSup}(v) = \lim\limits_{n\to\infty} \sup\{v_i \mid i \geq n\}$

- $\mathsf{LimInfAvg}(v) = \mathsf{LimInf}\left(\dfrac{1}{n}\sum\limits_{i=0}^{n-1} v_i\right)$

- $\mathsf{LimSupAvg}(v) = \mathsf{LimSup}\left(\dfrac{1}{n}\sum\limits_{i=0}^{n-1} v_i\right)$

($\mathsf{LimInfAvg}$ and $\mathsf{LimSupAvg}$ are also called $\underline{\mathsf{MeanPayoff}}$ and $\overline{\mathsf{MeanPayoff}}$.)

A *nondeterministic quantitative automaton* is a complete nondeterministic transition-labeled automaton with labels of real numbers[6] and some value function Val.

The value of a run π is $\mathsf{Val}(\gamma(\pi))$. The value of $\mathcal{A}$ on a word w is the supremum[7] of $\mathsf{Val}(\pi)$ over all runs π of $\mathcal{A}$ on w.

An *alternating quantitative automaton* is a complete alternating transition-labeled automaton with labels of real numbers and some value function Val.

The value of $\mathcal{A}$ on a word w is determined by the game $G_{\mathcal{A}}(w)$, which becomes a Val game: the value of a play (which is a path π of transitions) is $\mathsf{Val}(\gamma(\pi))$; Eve wants to maximize it and Adam wants to minimize it. When this game is determined, which is guaranteed for the considered value functions, the value of $\mathcal{A}$ on w is the value of $G_{\mathcal{A}}(w)$.

Two automata $\mathcal{A}$ and $\mathcal{A}'$ are *equivalent*, denoted by $\mathcal{A} \equiv \mathcal{A}'$, if they realize the same function[8].

2.2 Weighted Automata

A weighted automaton is defined with respect to a semiring or more generally with respect to an [ω-]valuation monoid[9].

A *semiring* is a structure $(D, \oplus, \otimes, \overline{0}, \overline{1})$, where $(D, \oplus, \overline{0})$ is a commutative monoid, $(D, \otimes, \overline{1})$ is a monoid, multiplication distributes over addition, and for every $x \in D$, $\overline{0} \otimes x = x \otimes \overline{0} = \overline{0}$.

A semiring is *complete* if $(D, \oplus, \overline{0})$ is a complete monoid (namely, equipped with a $\sum$ operation that properly extends $\oplus$ to infinite sets of elements), and it is *totally complete* if it is also equipped with a $\prod$ operation that properly extends $\otimes$ to infinite sequences of elements, while preserving distributivity over addition [40,59].

Examples of common semirings.

- The Boolean $(\{0,1\}, \vee, \wedge, 0, 1)$
- The tropical (also known as min-plus) $(\mathbb{N} \cup \{\infty\}, \min, +, \infty, 0)$

---

[6] Considering algorithmic aspects of quantitative automata, labels are usually rational numbers, concretely represented.

[7] It is sometimes defined analogously with infimum instead of supremum. Considering alternating quantitative automata, infimum relates to universal transitions.

[8] A function in this context is called in [23] a "quantitative language".

[9] Automata with multiple weights on transitions can be defined with respect to structure monoids [39].

- The arctic (also known as max-plus) $(\mathbb{N} \cup \{-\infty\}, \max, +, -\infty, 0)$
- The natural numbers $(\mathbb{N}, +, \cdot, 0, 1)$ with the usual addition and multiplication
- The log semiring $(\mathbb{R} \cup \{-\infty, +\infty\}, \oplus, +, -\infty, 0)$ with $x \oplus y = \log(e^x + e^y)$

A *valuation monoid* is a tuple $(D, \oplus, \overline{0}, \mathsf{Val})$, where $(D, \oplus, \overline{0})$ is a commutative monoid and $\mathsf{Val} : D^* \to D$ is a function[10]. An ω-*valuation monoid* is defined analogously, while requiring that $\oplus$ is properly extended to $\sum$ over infinite sets of elements, and having $\mathsf{Val} : D^\omega \to D$.

Examples of common [ω-]valuation monoids

- A semiring, taking its product $\otimes$ to be the valuation function Val.
- $(\mathbb{R} \cup \{-\infty\}, \sup, -\infty, \mathsf{Val})$, where Val is some value function as appears in Sect. 2.1 with a corresponding extension to $\mathbb{R} \cup \{-\infty\}$.

A *weighted automaton* on finite words (resp. infinite words) is a transition-labeled nondeterministic automaton together with a Boolean acceptance condition[11] and a semiring or a valuation-monoid (resp. a totally complete semiring or an ω-valuation-monoid).

A run is accepting if it satisfies the acceptance condition[12].

The value of an accepting run π is $\prod \gamma(\pi)$ with respect to a semiring and $\mathsf{Val}(\gamma(\pi))$ with respect to an [ω-]valuation monoid.

The value of $\mathcal{A}$ on a word w is the semiring's/[ω-]valuation-monoid's summation $(\sum)$ of w's accepting-runs values or $\overline{0}$ if there are no accepting runs.

Two automata $\mathcal{A}$ and $\mathcal{A}'$ are *equivalent*, denoted by $\mathcal{A} \equiv \mathcal{A}'$, if they realize the same function[13].

3   Related Notions and Entities

Automata are closely related to many notions and entities in computer science. We briefly look into how quantitative automata and weighted automata are, often differently, related to some of them, and how to possibly extend each such relation with respect to the "less related" automata family.

---

[10] In [38], the original definition of a valuation monoid has additional restrictions that are loosened in [48].

[11] Semiring weighted automata are sometimes defined with an acceptance condition (e.g., [48]) and sometimes without it, while having instead labels on both transitions and states (e.g., [34]). However, considering infinite words or valuation monoids, weighted automata have an acceptance condition [38].

[12] For finite words, the acceptance condition is a set $F \subseteq Q$ of final states, and a run satisfies it if it ends in a final state. For infinite words there are many acceptance conditions, such as Büchi or Muller. (More details on the different acceptance conditions can be found, for example, in [12]).

[13] A function in this context is often viewed as a formal power series.

3.1 Alternation

Since alternating automata were introduced in [21,22], they were extended to many models (e.g., [31,55]) over various input structures (e.g., [57,58,62]), and shown to be closely related to logic and to games (e.g., [58,74]), very useful in formal verification (e.g., [31,72]), and in general to play a key role in automata theory.

Quantitative automata are naturally generalized from nondeterminism to alternation, having the dual roles of *choice* for nondeterminism and *obligation* for universality, and alternating quantitative automata are often more expressive than nondeterministic ones and allow for better closure properties [24]. (The title of [24] speaks of "weighted automata", but relates to quantitative automata.)

Considering weighted automata, on either a semirings or [ω-]valuation monoids, there is no natural interpretation of alternation, as nondeterminism is interpreted by a general commutative operation $\oplus$, which need not have a dual.

The $\otimes$ or Val functions that are used for valuing a path of transitions have an orthogonal role, and are not generally adequate for the 'universality role'. Yet, in some settings it is interesting to look into an interpretation of an alternating weighted automaton, in which $\otimes$ takes this role, as is done in [4] with respect to the tropical semiring and in [53] with respect to commutative semirings.

It may possibly be interesting to look into extensions of semirings and valuation monoids, as suggested in [53], that add another operator to take the role of universality.

It may also be interesting to look into restrictions of semirings and valuation monoids for which the $\oplus$ operation has a meaningful syntactic dual.

3.2 Games

Two-player turn-based *win-lose* games are closely related to logic and to *Boolean* automata, especially to alternating Boolean automata. For example, deciding the winner of an infinite game over an arena A is the same as deciding whether A, seen as a one-letter alternating automaton with a corresponding acceptance condition, is empty. Other examples are *good-for-games* automata [15,50] (see Sect. 3.4), which are useful in solving games [29,50], and the interplay between automata and games in formal verification and synthesis (see Sect. 3.6).

Analogously, two-player turn-based *zero-sum* games, which generalize win-lose games by having (possibly infinitely) many values to plays, and in which Eve wants to maximize the play's value and Adam wants to minimize it, are closely related to *quantitative* automata.

In particular, the above example of viewing a game as a special case of an alternating automaton over a singleton alphabet generalizes to the quantitative setting—the value of the game, which is the value that Eve can guarantee against any strategy of Adam, is the value of the automaton on the single input word.

Along the same lines, the other examples above are also naturally generalized to the quantitative setting (e.g., [5, 16, 33, 46, 49])[14].

Weighted automata are connected to games via their connection to logics (see Sect. 3.3), which are connected to Ehrenfeucht-Fraïssé games. However, we are not aware of works that directly connect between general weighted automata and games.

3.3 Logic

Automata theory has evolved from logic and remained very related to it. In particular, Büchi, Elgot and Trakhtenbrot established the equivalence of (ω-regular complete) automata and monadic second order (MSO) logic (of order) on words [19, 42, 71], while a series of results provided the equivalence of counter-free (aperiodic) automata and both first order logic (FOL) and linear temporal logic (LTL) on finite and infinite words [47, 52, 56, 61, 63, 68–70] (see a detailed exploration of the latter in [32]).

The result on the equivalence of Boolean automata and MSO was extended by Manfred Droste and Paul Gastin to the equivalence of semiring weighted automata on finite words and a restricted version of a weighted MSO logic that they defined [34]. This result was then further extended to totally-complete semiring weighted automata on infinite words [40], to [ω-]valuation monoid weighted automata on finite and infinite words [38], and to various extensions of weighted automata on various input structures, each corresponding to a variant of weighted MSO. In [48], there is a unifying framework for the equivalence of weighted automata and weighted MSO on finite words.

The result on the equivalence of aperiodic Boolean automata and first-order logic was extended by Droste and Gastin to the equivalence of aperiodic polynomially ambiguous weighted automata on finite words and weighted FOL [35].

As for the connection of quantitative automata and logic, there are various extensions of temporal logic with value functions Val that are related to Val automata, for example [1, 10, 17, 60]. However, we are not aware of general equivalence theorems as in the case of weighted automata.

It may be interesting to look into adaptations of weighted MSO that are equivalent to nondeterministic and alternating quantitative automata, as well as on adaptations of weighted FOL that are equivalent to their aperiodic counterparts. Another interesting direction, in particular for formal verification (see Sect. 2.2), is to establish equivalence between quantitative automata and some weighted temporal logics.

3.4 Between Determinism and Nondeterminism

In general, deterministic automata have better compositional properties than nondeterministic automata, making them better suited for applications such as

---

[14] The "weighted automata" in the title of [49] refer to a variant of Sum automata, defined over infinite words with an acceptance condition on finite prefixes.

synthesis and probabilistic model checking. Yet, deterministic automata are often exponentially bigger than equivalent nondeterministic automata and sometimes lack in expressive power.

This unpleasant trade-off between determinism and nondeterminism motivates formalisms that are in between them, aiming at enjoying, sometimes, the best of both worlds.

Dominant such formalisms are *unambiguity, determinism in the limit* (semideterminism), *history determinism* [28], and *good for gameness* [50].

A Boolean automaton is unambiguous if there is at most one accepting run on each word; it is deterministic in the limit (for Büchi automata) if its continuation from every accepting state is deterministic; it is history deterministic if there is a strategy to resolve its nondeterminism by only considering the prefix of the word read so far (and getting an equivalent automaton); and it is good for games if its product with every game G whose winning condition is the automaton's language provides a game with the same winner as of G.

Unambiguity and determinism-in-the-limit are defined, as is, on weighted automata, based on their acceptance conditions. Observe that unambiguous weighted automata do not need the $\oplus$ operation, as there is at most one accepting run. Hence, the notion is relevant also to quantitative automata if adding an acceptance condition, which can also relate to a *threshold* (see Sect. 3.6 for threshold quantitative automata). For example, requiring at most one run on each word whose value is equal to or bigger than a threshold.

Unambiguity can also be generalized with respect to weighted automata (with no $\oplus$ operation) or quantitative automata (with acceptance conditions) by means of *functional automata* [44]—rather than having at most one accepting run on each word, all accepting runs on a word should have the same value.

History-determinism and good-for-gameness have natural generalizations to quantitative automata, due to the *choice* interpretation of nondeterminism. The definition of history determinism follows as is [16,28], while good-for-gameness relates to zero-sum games rather than to win-lose games [16]. Interestingly, while history determinism and good for gameness are equivalent for Boolean automata [15], they are not equivalent for quantitative automata [16].

Though history-determinism and good-for-gameness look less natural for weighted automata, it might be interesting to analyze such notions. History determinism is technically defined also for a weighted automaton with an arbitrary $\oplus$ operation (requiring a strategy to generate for every word w a single run with the value of the automaton on w), though possibly not very meaningful for a general weighted automaton. As for good for gameness, it might be that certain types of games are adequate to an interesting product with weighted automata.

3.5 Approximations

Quantitative automata, having real values for words, naturally allow for approximations with respect to standard distance functions. Accordingly, there are many works on approximated solutions with quantitative automata (some of them have "weighted automata" in the title), either with respect to a specific distance function, such as difference (e.g., [11,45,51]) or ratio[15] (e.g., [6,7]), or with respect to a general distance function d that respects the order on $\mathbb{R}$, namely having that for every $x \leq y \leq z \in \mathbb{R}$, we have $d(x,y) \leq d(x,z)$ and $d(y,z) \leq d(x,z)$ (e.g., [14]).

These approximated solutions provide a significant added value to the generalization of Boolean automata to quantitative automata, as often an exact solution is impossible or computationally very difficult.

Considering weighted automata, once the domain of values is arbitrary, there is a problem to consider meaningful distance functions. However, restricting the domain to $\mathbb{R}$, or to some other set with meaningful distance functions, allows for analogous approximated solutions.

3.6   Formal Verification and Synthesis

Verification (model checking) asks whether a given system satisfies a given specification, and synthesis asks to automatically generate a system that satisfies a given specification.

Verification and synthesis are traditionally Boolean, having a yes-no value to both the system properties (such as whether or not the system 'serves only coffee') and to the satisfaction level of the specification (for example, 'yes' if the system satisfies the specification of 'serving only coffee' or 'serving only tea').

This Boolean perspective falls short of many verification needs of contemporary systems, concerning performance, robustness, and resource-constraint requirements. One system is often preferred over another, even though they are both correct, since one is, for example, faster than the other, or, if they are both incorrect, one misbehaves less frequently than the other.

As a result, recent years have seen the emergence and rapid development of *quantitative formal verification and synthesis* in an attempt to cope with these needs (e.g., [2,5,9,10,18,26,33,43,46,51]).

According to this approach, both the system properties and the satisfaction values are no longer Boolean. For example, a property of a system can be an 'average response time', and the system can get a satisfaction level of 0.7 to a specification that quantitatively combines requirements on the 'average response time' and the 'power consumption'.

Automata and game theory play a key role in verification and synthesis of reactive systems (see, e.g., [54,73]) and both quantitative and weighted automata are valuable in generalizing them to the quantitative setting.

Considering the generalization of the satisfaction level, quantitative automata are more natural, as satisfaction evaluates to a value from an ordered domain, and we want the system to get a value as high as possible. In this context, and others, it is also common to consider *threshold quantitative automata*, which return a yes-no answer for whether the value of the automaton on an input word

---

[15] As ratio does not satisfy the triangle inequality, it is formally not a distance function, and one may speak instead of $d(x,y) = |\log x - \log y|$.

is equal to or bigger than a threshold. This provides the flexibility of playing back and forth between Boolean and quantitative satisfaction values.

Also for synthesis, which is viewed as a two-player game between the environment, generating the inputs to the system, and the system, interactively responding to these inputs, quantitative automata are more natural (see Sect. 3.2).

As for generalization of system properties, both quantitative and weighted automata are suitable, as such properties might have very general aspects.

Acknowledgments. We thank Nathanaël Fijalkow for raising up the terminology mismatch in the literature, and Shaull Almagor and Karoliina Lehtinen for stimulating discussions on preliminary versions of the paper. Israel Science Foundation grant 1373/16.

References

1. Almagor, S., Boker, U., Kupferman, O.: Discounting in LTL. In: Ábrahám, E., Havelund, K. (eds.) TACAS 2014. LNCS, vol. 8413, pp. 424–439. Springer, Heidelberg (2014). https://doi.org/10.1007/978-3-642-54862-8_37
2. Almagor, S., Boker, U., Kupferman, O.: Formalizing and reasoning about quality. J. ACM **63**(3), 24:1–24:56 (2016)
3. Almagor, S., Boker, U., Kupferman, O.: What's decidable about weighted automata? In: Bultan, T., Hsiung, P.-A. (eds.) ATVA 2011. LNCS, vol. 6996, pp. 482–491. Springer, Heidelberg (2011). https://doi.org/10.1007/978-3-642-24372-1_37
4. Almagor, S., Kupferman, O.: Max and sum semantics for alternating weighted automata. In: Bultan, T., Hsiung, P.-A. (eds.) ATVA 2011. LNCS, vol. 6996, pp. 13–27. Springer, Heidelberg (2011). https://doi.org/10.1007/978-3-642-24372-1_2
5. Almagor, S., Kupferman, O., Ringert, J.O., Velner, Y.: Quantitative assume guarantee synthesis. In: Majumdar, R., Kunčak, V. (eds.) CAV 2017. LNCS, vol. 10427, pp. 353–374. Springer, Cham (2017). https://doi.org/10.1007/978-3-319-63390-9_19
6. Aminof, B., Kupferman, O., Lampert, R.: Reasoning about online algorithms with weighted automata. ACM Trans. Algorithms **6**(2), 28:1–28:36 (2010)
7. Aminof, B., Kupferman, O., Lampert, R.: Rigorous approximated determinization of weighted automata. Theor. Comput. Sci. **480**, 104–117 (2013)
8. Babari, P.: Quantitative Automata and Logic for Pictures and Data Words. Ph.D. thesis, Leipzig University (2017)
9. Bloem, R., Chatterjee, K., Henzinger, T.A., Jobstmann, B.: Better quality in synthesis through quantitative objectives. In: Bouajjani, A., Maler, O. (eds.) CAV 2009. LNCS, vol. 5643, pp. 140–156. Springer, Heidelberg (2009). https://doi.org/10.1007/978-3-642-02658-4_14
10. Boker, U., Chatterjee, K., Henzinger, T.A., Kupferman, O.: Temporal specifications with accumulative values. ACM Trans. Comput. Log. **15**(4), 27:1–27:25 (2014)
11. Boker, U., Henzinger, T.A.: Exact and approximate determinization of discounted-sum automata. Log. Methods Comput. Sci. **10**(1), 1–33 (2014)
12. Boker, U.: Why these automata types? In: Proceedings of the LPAR, pp. 143–163 (2018)

13. Boker, U., Hefetz, G.: Discounted-sum automata with multiple discount factors. In: Proceedings of the CSL. LIPIcs, vol. 183, pp. 12:1–12:23 (2021)
14. Boker, U., Henzinger, T.A.: Approximate determinization of quantitative automata. In: Proceedings of the FSTTCS. LIPIcs, vol. 18, pp. 362–373 (2012)
15. Boker, U., Lehtinen, K.: Good for games automata: from nondeterminism to alternation. In: Fokkink, W.J., van Glabbeek, R. (eds.) Proceedings of the CONCUR. LIPIcs, vol. 140, pp. 19:1–19:16 (2019)
16. Boker, U., Lehtinen, K.: History determinism vs. good for gameness in quantitative automata. In: Proceedings of FSTTCS. pp. 35:1–35:20 (2021)
17. Bouyer, P., Markey, N., Matteplackel, R.: Averaging in LTL. In: Proceedings of the CONCUR, pp. 266–280 (2014)
18. Brenguier, R., et al.: Non-zero sum games for reactive synthesis. In: Dediu, A.-H., Janoušek, J., Martín-Vide, C., Truthe, B. (eds.) LATA 2016. LNCS, vol. 9618, pp. 3–23. Springer, Cham (2016). https://doi.org/10.1007/978-3-319-30000-9_1
19. Büchi, J.R.: On a decision method in restricted second order arithmetic. In: Proceedings of the International Congress on Logic, Method, and Philosophy of Science. 1960, pp. 1–12. Stanford University Press (1962)
20. Buchsbaum, A.L., Giancarlo, R., Westbrook, J.: An approximate determinization algorithm for weighted finite-state automata. Algorithmica 30(4), 503–526 (2001)
21. Chandra, A.K., Kozen, D.C., Stockmeyer, L.J.: Alternation. J. ACM 28(1), 114–133 (1981)
22. Chandra, A.K., Stockmeyer, L.J.: Alternation. In: Proceedings of FOCS, pp. 98–108 (1976)
23. Chatterjee, K., Doyen, L., Henzinger, T.A.: Quantitative languages. In: Kaminski, M., Martini, S. (eds.) CSL 2008. LNCS, vol. 5213, pp. 385–400. Springer, Heidelberg (2008). https://doi.org/10.1007/978-3-540-87531-4_28
24. Chatterjee, K., Doyen, L., Henzinger, T.A.: Alternating weighted automata. In: Proceedings of FCT, pp. 3–13 (2009)
25. Chatterjee, K., Doyen, L., Henzinger, T.A.: Quantitative languages. ACM Trans. Comput. Log. 11(4), 23:1–23:38 (2010)
26. Chatterjee, K., Henzinger, T.A., Jobstmann, B., Singh, R.: QUASY: quantitative synthesis tool. In: Abdulla, P.A., Leino, K.R.M. (eds.) TACAS 2011. LNCS, vol. 6605, pp. 267–271. Springer, Heidelberg (2011). https://doi.org/10.1007/978-3-642-19835-9_24
27. Chatterjee, K., Henzinger, T.A., Otop, J.: Nested weighted automata. ACM Trans. Comput. Log. 18(4), 31:1–31:44 (2017)
28. Colcombet, T.: The theory of stabilisation monoids and regular cost functions, pp. 139–150 (2009)
29. Colcombet, T., Fijalkow, N.: Universal graphs and good for games automata: new tools for infinite duration games. In: Bojańczyk, M., Simpson, A. (eds.) FoSSaCS 2019. LNCS, vol. 11425, pp. 1–26. Springer, Cham (2019). https://doi.org/10.1007/978-3-030-17127-8_1
30. Culik, K., Karhumaki, J.: Finite automata computing real functions. SIAM J. Comput. 23(4), 789–814 (1994)
31. Dickhöfer, M., Wilke, T.: Timed alternating tree automata: the automata-theoretic solution to the TCTL model checking problem. In: Wiedermann, J., van Emde Boas, P., Nielsen, M. (eds.) ICALP 1999. LNCS, vol. 1644, pp. 281–290. Springer, Heidelberg (1999). https://doi.org/10.1007/3-540-48523-6_25
32. Diekert, V., Gastin, P.: First-order definable languages. In: Flum, J., Grädel, E., Wilke, T. (eds.) Logic and Automata: History and Perspectives [in Honor of Wolf-

gang Thomas]. Texts in Logic and Games, vol. 2, pp. 261–306. Amsterdam University Press (2008)

33. Doyen, L.: Games and automata: From Boolean to quantitative verification. Habilitation Thesis, École Normale Supérieure de Cachan (2011)

34. Droste, M., Gastin, P.: Weighted automata and weighted logics. Theor. Comput. Sci. **380**(1–2), 69–86 (2007)

35. Droste, M., Gastin, P.: Aperiodic weighted automata and weighted first-order logic. In: Proceedings of the MFCS. LIPIcs, vol. 138, pp. 76:1–76:15 (2019)

36. Droste, M., Kuske, D.: Skew and infinitary formal power series. In: Baeten, J.C.M., Lenstra, J.K., Parrow, J., Woeginger, G.J. (eds.) ICALP 2003. LNCS, vol. 2719, pp. 426–438. Springer, Heidelberg (2003). https://doi.org/10.1007/3-540-45061-0_35

37. Droste, M., Meinecke, I.: Describing average- and longtime-behavior by weighted MSO logics. In: Proceedings of the MFCS, pp. 537–548 (2010)

38. Droste, M., Meinecke, I.: Weighted automata and weighted MSO logics for average and long-time behaviors. Inf. Comput. **220–221**, 44–59 (2012)

39. Droste, M., Perevoshchikov, V.: Multi-weighted automata and MSO logic. In: Computer Science - Theory and Applications, pp. 418–430 (2013)

40. Droste, M., Rahonis, G.: Weighted automata and weighted logics on infinite words. In: Ibarra, O.H., Dang, Z. (eds.) DLT 2006. LNCS, vol. 4036, pp. 49–58. Springer, Heidelberg (2006). https://doi.org/10.1007/11779148_6

41. Eilenberg, S.: Automata, Languages, and Machines. Academic Press Inc., USA (1974)

42. Elgot, C.: Decision problems of finite-automata design and related arithmetics. Trans. Am. Math. Soc. **98**, 21–51 (1961)

43. Faella, M., Legay, A., Stoelinga, M.: Model checking quantitative linear time logic. Electron. Notes Theor. Comput. Sci. **220**(3), 61–77 (2008)

44. Filiot, E., Gentilini, R., Raskin, J.: Quantitative languages defined by functional automata. Log. Methods Comput. Sci. **11**(3), 1–32 (2015)

45. Filiot, E., Jecker, I., Lhote, N., Pérez, G.A., Raskin, J.: On delay and regret determinization of max-plus automata. In: LICS, pp. 1–12 (2017)

46. Filiot, E., Löding, C., Winter, S.: Synthesis from weighted specifications with partial domains over finite words. In: Saxena, N., Simon, S. (eds.) FSTTCS. LIPIcs, vol. 182, pp. 46:1–46:16. Schloss Dagstuhl - Leibniz-Zentrum für Informatik (2020)

47. Gabbay, D.M., Pnueli, A., Shelah, S., Stavi, J.: On the temporal analysis of fairness. In: Proceedings of the POPL, pp. 163–173 (1980)

48. Gastin, P., Monmege, B.: A unifying survey on weighted logics and weighted automata - core weighted logic: minimal and versatile specification of quantitative properties. Soft. Comput. **22**(4), 1047–1065 (2018)

49. Halava, V., Harju, T., Niskanen, R., Potapov, I.: Weighted automata on infinite words in the context of attacker-defender games. In: Beckmann, A., Mitrana, V., Soskova, M. (eds.) CiE 2015. LNCS, vol. 9136, pp. 206–215. Springer, Cham (2015). https://doi.org/10.1007/978-3-319-20028-6_21

50. Henzinger, T., Piterman, N.: Solving games without determinization, pp. 395–410 (2006)

51. Hunter, P., Pérez, G.A., Raskin, J.-F.: Reactive synthesis without regret. Acta Inform. **54**(1), 3–39 (2016). https://doi.org/10.1007/s00236-016-0268-z

52. Kamp, J.: Tense Logic and the Theory of Order. Ph.D. thesis, UCLA (1968)

53. Kostolányi, P., Misún, F.: Alternating weighted automata over commutative semirings. Theor. Comput. Sci. **740**, 1–27 (2018)

54. Kupferman, O.: Automata theory and model checking. In: Handbook of Model Checking, pp. 107–151. Springer, Cham (2018). https://doi.org/10.1007/978-3-319-10575-8_4

55. Ladner, R., Lipton, R., Stockmeyer, L.: Alternating pushdown and stack automata. SIAM J. Comput. **13**(1), 135–155 (1984)

56. Ladner, R.E.: Application of model theoretic games to discrete linear orders and finite automata. Inf. Control **33**(4), 281–303 (1977)

57. Lindsay, P.A.: On alternating ω-automata. Theoret. Comput. Sci. **43**, 107–116 (1988)

58. Loding, C., Thomas, W.: Alternating automata and logics over infinite words. In: van Leeuwen, J., Watanabe, O., Hagiya, M., Mosses, P.D., Ito, T. (eds.) TCS 2000. LNCS, vol. 1872, pp. 521–535. Springer, Heidelberg (2000). https://doi.org/10.1007/3-540-44929-9_36

59. M. Droste, W.K., Vogler, H.: Handbook of Weighted Automata, 1st edn. Springer Publishing Company, Incorporated, Heidelberg (2009)

60. Mandrali, E.: Weighted LTL with discounting. In: Moreira, N., Reis, R. (eds.) CIAA 2012. LNCS, vol. 7381, pp. 353–360. Springer, Heidelberg (2012). https://doi.org/10.1007/978-3-642-31606-7_32

61. McNaughton, R., Papert, S.: Counter-free Automata. M.I.T Press, Cambridge (1971)

62. Muller, D., Schupp, P.: Alternating automata on infinite trees. In: Automata on Infinite Words. LNCS, vol. 192, pp. 100–107 (1985)

63. Perrin, D., Pin, J.: First-order logic and star-free sets. J. Comput. Syst. Sci. **32**(3), 393–406 (1986)

64. Rabin, M.O.: Probabilistic automata. Inf. Control **6**(3), 230–245 (1963)

65. Rabin, M.O., Scott, D.: Finite automata and their decision problems. IBM J. Res. Dev. **3**(2), 114–125 (1959)

66. Salomaa, A., Soittola, M.: Automata-Theoretic Aspects of Formal Power Series. Texts and Monographs in Computer Science, Springer, Heidelberg (1978)

67. Schützenberger, M.P.: On the definition of a family of automata. Inf. Control **4**(2), 245–270 (1961)

68. Schützenberger, M.P.: On finite monoids having only trivial subgroups. Inf. Control **8**(2), 190–194 (1965)

69. Thomas, W.: Star-free regular sets of omega-sequences. Inf. Control **42**(2), 148–156 (1979)

70. Thomas, W.: A combinatorial approach to the theory of omega-automata. Inf. Control **48**(3), 261–283 (1981)

71. Trakhtenbrot, B.A.: Finite automata and logic of monadic predicates. Doklady Akademii Nauk SSSR (1961). In Russian

72. Vardi, M.Y.: Alternating automata and program verification. In: van Leeuwen, J. (ed.) Computer Science Today. LNCS, vol. 1000, pp. 471–485. Springer, Heidelberg (1995). https://doi.org/10.1007/BFb0015261

73. Vardi, M.: Verification of concurrent programs: the automata-theoretic framework, pp. 167–176 (1987)

74. Wilke, T.: Alternating tree automata, parity games, and modal μ-calculus. Bull. Belgian Math. Soc. Simon Stevin **8**(2), 359 (2001)

Theorem Proving Using Clausal Resolution: From Past to Present

Clare Dixon$^{(\boxtimes)}$ ⓘ

Department of Computer Science, University of Manchester,
Manchester M13 9PL, UK
clare.dixon@manchester.ac.uk

Abstract. Modal and temporal logics are extensions to classical logic that have operators that deal with necessity and possibility (modal logics) and such as sometime, always and next (temporal logics). Models are sets of worlds that are connected by an accessibility relation. Restrictions imposed on this relation and the operators allowed give rise to different families of logic. This paper discusses an approach to theorem proving for temporal and modal logics based on clausal resolution. The main ideas are the translation to a normal form and the application of resolution rules that relate to the same world. This research initially focused on propositional linear time temporal logic but has been extended to computation tree logic, monodic first order temporal logic and normal modal logics. We describe the approach, explain the adaptations necessary for the logics mentioned and discuss the results of the provers developed for these logics.

1 Introduction

Non-classical logics such as temporal or modal logics have been proposed to model situations with a number of worlds connected by a relation representing temporal ordering or representing possible worlds. We discuss a clausal resolution method that was originally proposed for propositional linear time temporal logic (see for example [13,23]) and has been since been adapted to the branching time temporal logic CTL [10], first order temporal logic [16] and normal modal logics [3].

The main features of the method is the translation of formulae to an equi-satisfiable set of formulae (clauses) in a normal form for that logic. This removes operators, restricts formulae to particular formats and introduces new propositional variables to rename subformulae. Resolution rules are then applied to

---

This work was funded by the Engineering and Physical Sciences Research Council (EPSRC) under the historic grants GR/K57282, GR/M44859 and GR/M46631 and more recently the Science of Sensor Systems Software (S4 EP/N007565/1) and by the UK Industrial Strategy Challenge Fund (ISCF), delivered by UKRI and managed by EPSRC under the grants Future AI and Robotics Hub for Space (FAIR-SPACE EP/R026092/1) and Robotics and Artificial Intelligence for Nuclear (RAIN EP/R026084/1).

ⓒ Springer Nature Switzerland AG 2021
P. C. Bell et al. (Eds.): RP 2021, LNCS 13035, pp. 19–27, 2021.
https://doi.org/10.1007/978-3-030-89716-1_2

clauses that apply to the same world. In temporal logics there is a need to identify sets of formulae that ensure a proposition (or its negation) always holds to resolve with a formula that states that its negation must eventually hold. In modal logics care has to be made that any restrictions on the accessibility relation between worlds is correctly modelled.

In Sect. 2 we present this approach applied to propositional linear time temporal logic and in Sects. 3, 4 and 5 discuss how this has been applied to the branching time temporal logic CTL, first order temporal logic and normal modal logics respectively, providing conclusions in Sect. 6.

2   Propositional Temporal Logic

Propositional (discrete) Linear Time Temporal Logic (LTL) can be thought of as classical propositional logic extended with operators to deal with time. The future-time temporal connectives we use include '$\bigcirc$' (in the next moment) and '$\mathcal{U}$' (until). LTL formulae are constructed from the following elements:

- a set, $PROP$, of propositional symbols;
- propositional connectives, **true**, $\neg, \vee$; and
- temporal connectives, $\bigcirc$, and $\mathcal{U}$.

The set of well-formed formulae (WFF) of LTL, is defined as the smallest set satisfying the following:

- any elements of $PROP$ and **true** are in WFF;
- if φ and ψ are in WFF, then so are $\neg\varphi, \varphi \vee \psi, \bigcirc\varphi, \varphi \, \mathcal{U} \, \psi$.

A *literal* is defined as either a proposition symbol or the negation of a proposition symbol.

A model for LTL formulae can be characterised as a *sequence of states*, σ, of the form $\sigma = s_0, s_1, s_2, s_3, \ldots$, where each state s_i is a set of propositional symbols representing those propositions, which are satisfied at the ith moment in time. The notation $(\sigma, i) \models \varphi$ denotes the truth of formula φ in the model σ at the state of index $i \in \mathbb{N}$ and is defined as follows.

$$
\begin{aligned}
(\sigma, i) &\models \textbf{true} \\
(\sigma, i) &\models p &&\text{iff } p \in s_i \text{ where } p \in PROP \\
(\sigma, i) &\models \neg\varphi &&\text{iff it is not the case that } (\sigma, i) \models \varphi \\
(\sigma, i) &\models \varphi \vee \psi &&\text{iff } (\sigma, i) \models \varphi \text{ or } (\sigma, i) \models \psi \\
(\sigma, i) &\models \bigcirc\varphi &&\text{iff } (\sigma, i+1) \models \varphi \\
(\sigma, i) &\models \varphi \mathcal{U} \psi &&\text{iff } \exists k \in \mathbb{N}. \ k \geq i \text{ and } (\sigma, k) \models \psi \text{ and} \\
& &&\quad \forall j \in \mathbb{N}, \text{ if } i \leqslant j < k \text{ then } (\sigma, j) \models \varphi
\end{aligned}
$$

Note we can obtain **false** and the other Boolean operators via the usual equivalences and we define '$\square$' (always in the future), '$\Diamond$' (sometime in the future) and '$\mathcal{W}$' (unless or weak until) operators as follows.

$$\Diamond\varphi \equiv \mathbf{true}\,\mathcal{U}\,\varphi$$
$$\Box\varphi \equiv \neg\Diamond\neg\varphi$$
$$\varphi\,\mathcal{W}\,\psi \equiv (\varphi\,\mathcal{U}\,\psi) \vee (\,\Box\varphi)$$

For any formula φ, model σ, and state index $i \in \mathbb{N}$, either $(\sigma, i) \models \varphi$ holds or $(\sigma, i) \models \varphi$ does not hold, denoted by $(\sigma, i) \not\models \varphi$. If there is some σ such that $(\sigma, 0) \models \varphi$, then φ is said to be *satisfiable*. If $(\sigma, 0) \models \varphi$ for all models, σ, then φ is said to be *valid* and is written $\models \varphi$. A set $\mathcal{N}$ of formulae is *satisfiable* in the model σ at the state of index $i \in \mathbb{N}$ if, and only if, for all $\varphi \in \mathcal{N}, (\sigma, i) \models \varphi$. A formula of the form $\Diamond\varphi$ or $\psi\,\mathcal{U}\,\varphi$ is called an *eventuality*.

2.1 Normal Form

Separated Normal Form (SNF) was first introduced for LTL in [11,12] with clauses having a past implies present or future form. This was later changed to the present implies (non-strict) future form we present here (see [14]). We also use an additional connective 'start' that holds only at the beginning of time, i.e.,

$$(\sigma, i) \models \mathbf{start} \quad \text{iff} \quad i = 0$$

that allows the general form of the clauses of the normal form to be implications. A normal form for LTL is of the form $\Box \bigwedge_h C_h$ where each C_h is an *initial*, *step*, or *sometime* clause:

$$\mathbf{start} \Rightarrow \bigvee_j l_j \qquad \textit{(initial)}$$
$$\bigwedge_i l'_i \Rightarrow \bigcirc \bigvee_j l_j \qquad \textit{(step)}$$
$$\bigwedge_i l'_i \Rightarrow \Diamond l \qquad \textit{(sometime)}$$

where l'_i, l_j and l are literals in the language PROP. We can translate any LTL formula φ into a formula φ' such that φ is satisfiable if and only if φ' is satisfiable [14] with at most a linear increase in the size of the formula. The translation uses standard equivalences from propositional and temporal logic, renames complex subformulae using new propositions linking the new propositions with the satisfaction of the renamed subformula everywhere in the model and unwinding temporal operators into formulae to be satisfied now and in the next moment in time, using their fixpoint definitions. We also assume clauses are kept in their simplest form by performing standard simplifications for classical logic.

2.2 Resolution for Propositional Temporal Logic

The resolution method for LTL based on SNF was introduced in [11] with further details in [14]. Pairs of initial or step clauses may be resolved using the following initial and step resolution rules which can be viewed as the application of the standard classical resolution rule to formulae representing constraints at a particular moment in time (where A and A' are conjunctions of literals, B and B' are disjunctions of literals and p is a proposition).

$$\begin{array}{c} \textbf{start} \Rightarrow B \vee p \\ \textbf{start} \Rightarrow B' \vee \neg p \\ \hline \textbf{start} \Rightarrow B \vee B' \end{array} \qquad \begin{array}{c} A \Rightarrow \bigcirc (B \vee p) \\ A' \Rightarrow \bigcirc (B' \vee \neg p) \\ \hline (A \wedge A') \Rightarrow \bigcirc (B \vee B') \end{array}$$

The following rewrite rule is used to remove clauses which imply **false** in the next moment in time (where A is a conjunction of literals).

$$\{A \Rightarrow \bigcirc \textbf{false}\} \longrightarrow \left\{ \begin{array}{l} \textbf{start} \Rightarrow \neg A \\ \textbf{true} \Rightarrow \bigcirc \neg A \end{array} \right\}$$

Thus, if, by satisfying A, a contradiction is produced in the next moment, then A must never be satisfied.

The eventuality resolution rule resolves a sometime clause and a set of step clauses that together ensure a complementary literal will always hold. In particular, the eventuality resolution rule can be applied between a sometime clause with l on the right hand side and a set of clauses that together imply $\bigvee_i A \Rightarrow \bigcirc \Box \neg l$. This is made up from a conjunction of one or more step clauses $A_i \Rightarrow \bigcirc B_i$ such that for all i, $0 \leq i \leq r$, $B_i \Rightarrow \neg l$ and $B_i \Rightarrow \bigvee_{j=0}^{r} A_j$.

$$\begin{array}{c} \bigvee_i A_i \Rightarrow \bigcirc \Box \neg l \\ A' \Rightarrow \Diamond l \\ \hline A' \Rightarrow \bigwedge_i (\neg A_i) \mathcal{W} l \end{array}$$

The set of clauses $A_i \Rightarrow \bigcirc B_i$ that satisfy these side conditions are together known as *a loop in* $\neg l$. Algorithms to find the loop are described in [7,8]. The resolvent must be translated into SNF before any further resolution steps.

The resolution process terminates when either no new resolvents can be generated or a contradiction is derived by generating the following unsatisfiable formula

$$\textbf{start} \Rightarrow \textbf{false}.$$

Given any temporal formula, φ, to be tested for unsatisfiability, the following steps are performed.

1. Translate φ into SNF, giving φ'.
2. Perform initial and step resolution (including the above rewrite rule, simplification and subsumption) on φ' until either
   (a) **start** $\Rightarrow$ **false** is derived—terminate declaring that φ is unsatisfiable; or
   (b) no new resolvents are generated—continue to step (3).
3. Select an eventuality from the right-hand side of a sometime clause within φ', for example $\Diamond l$. Search for loop-formulae for $\neg l$.
4. Construct loop resolvents for the loop detected and each sometime clause with $\Diamond l$ on the right-hand side. If any new formulae (i.e., that are not subsumed by clauses already present) have been generated, go to step (2).

5. If all eventualities have been resolved, i.e., no new formulae have been generated for any of the eventualities, terminate declaring φ satisfiable; otherwise go to step (3).

The soundness, completeness and termination of the calculus is shown in [14].

The temporal resolution calculus is implemented in the theorem prover TRP++ [18,19]. The initial and step clauses can be translated into first-order logic using a natural arithmetic translation and then initial and step resolution correspond to first-order ordered resolution [2]. As such any first order theorem prover could be used to implement these aspects. However TRP++ uses its own "near propositional" approach. The loop search algorithm can also be implemented by repeated calls to step resolution inferences [9]. Thus there is a need for the efficient performance of the step resolution. A comparison of TRP++ and an earlier version TRP with other tableau-based provers for LTL is made in [18, 20] and is shown to be competitive.

3   Branching-Time Temporal Logics

CTL [10] is a branching time temporal logic using the syntax of LTL in addition to two path operators $\mathbf{A}$ (all paths) and $\mathbf{E}$ (some path). CTL has the restriction that every path operator is paired with a temporal operator. Formulae are interpreted over model structures with sets of states and a serial binary accessibility relation that can be unwound into infinite trees. The temporal resolution method for LTL has been extended to CTL [30,32] based on earlier work [4]. The normal form is of the form $\mathbf{A} \,\square\, \bigwedge_h C_h$ where the clauses C_h differ from the LTL normal form as follows:

- there are two versions of the step clauses one for each path operator paired with the next operator;
- there are two versions of the sometime clauses one for each path operator paired with the sometime operator;
- the step clauses and sometime clauses are labelled with an index identifying a successor state or a path respectively; and
- global clauses of the form $\mathbf{true} \Rightarrow \bigvee_i l_i$ are also used (note this can be used in the LTL variant of the normal form instead using an initial clause $\mathbf{start} \Rightarrow \bigvee_i l_i$ and a step clause $\mathbf{true} \Rightarrow \bigcirc \bigvee_i l_i$ to represent propositional clauses holding everywhere).

There are more initial and step resolution rules to account for the combinations of step clauses with different path operators and the use of global clauses. There are two temporal resolution rules one for each path operator matched with a sometime operator where the resolvent takes the same path operator as the eventuality. Soundness, completeness and termination are shown in [32] as well as that the translation to the normal form preserves satisfiability.

This has been implemented at the prover CTL-RP [31] using the first order prover SPASS [5] with ordered resolution and selection [2] to implement the resolution rules. A comparison with other provers has been carried out in [15,31] the latter stating that that CTL-RP is more stable than other provers.

4   First Order Temporal Logic

First-Order (linear discrete time) Temporal Logic (FOTL) is an extension of classical first-order logic with operators from Sect. 2. The syntax for LTL is extended with syntax for first order formulae, namely with quantifiers, variables, constants and predicate symbols. Formulae are interpreted over sequences of first order structures.

Whilst being expressive, FOTL, in general, is incomplete and the set of valid formulae of FOTL is not recursively enumerable (see for example [1]). A FOTL formula ψ is called *monodic* if any subformulae of the form $T_1\varphi$, where T_1 is one of $\Diamond$, $\Box$, $\bigcirc$, or $\varphi_1 T_2 \varphi_2$, where T_2 is one of $\mathcal{U}$ or $\mathcal{W}$, contains at most one free variable [16]. The set of valid monodic formulae is known to be finitely axiomatisable [16]. Further by restricting the first order part to some decidable fragment of first-order logic, such as the guarded, two-variable or monadic fragments we obtain decidability.

The LTL resolution calculus has been extended to the monodic fragment of FOTL in [6,21]. A normal form, termed Divided Separated Normal Form (DSNF), has been defined for FOTL [6] of the form

$$\mathcal{I} \wedge \Box \mathcal{U} \wedge \Box \forall x \mathcal{S} \wedge \Box \forall x \mathcal{E}.$$

(where the underlying sets of formulae are viewed as conjunctions). This translates the formula into four sets $\mathcal{U}, \mathcal{I}, \mathcal{S}, \mathcal{E}$, namely:

- the initial part, $\mathcal{I}$, finite set of arbitrary closed first-order formulae;
- the universal part, $\mathcal{U}$, a finite set of arbitrary closed first-order formulae;
- the step part, $\mathcal{S}$, a finite set of temporal step clauses of the form $p \Rightarrow \bigcirc l$, or $P(x) \Rightarrow \bigcirc L(x)$ where p is a proposition, l is a literal, $P(x)$ is a unary atom and $L(x)$ is a unary literal; and
- the eventuality part, $\mathcal{E}$, a finite set of clauses of the form $\Diamond L(x)$ and $\Diamond l$ where l is a propositional literal and $L(x)$ is a unary literal.

In this setting

- initial resolution involves finding a contradiction in the sets $\mathcal{U} \cup \mathcal{I}$;
- step resolution involves finding sets of step clauses whose right hand sides along with the set $\mathcal{U}$ give a contradiction; and
- eventuality resolution is extended to the first order case.

The paper [21] provides a more machine-oriented clausal resolution calculus based on that in [6]. Two implementations of this calculus have been carried out TeMP [17] and TSPASS [22]. TeMP uses the kernel of the first order prover Vampire [29] to carry out step resolution and TSPASS uses the first order prover SPASS [5] to carry out step resolution ensuring that derivations are fair. Whilst an experimental analysis has been carried out in these papers this is restricted by a lack of benchmarks and other provers for this logic.

5 Normal Modal Logics

The general approach is applied to modal logics in [24]. Modal logics are evaluated over possible worlds or states with a family of binary relations R_j between worlds such that $(s, t) \in R_j$ if agent j considers world t possible from world s. The operators $\Box_j$ and $\Diamond_j$ associated with each binary relation R_j denote necessity and possibility. Informally $\Box_j \varphi$ is satisfied at world s if φ holds at all the worlds related to s via the R_j relation and $\Diamond_j \varphi$ is satisfied at world s if φ holds at some world related to s via the R_j relation.

The normal form for normal modal logics SNF_K is a conjunction of clauses $\Box^* \bigwedge_h C_h$ where $\Box^*$ is the universal operator and $\Box^* \varphi$ holds if, and only if, φ holds at the current world and at all reachable worlds. Each C_h is as follows:

$$\textbf{start} \Rightarrow \bigvee_i l_i \qquad \textit{(initial)}$$

$$\textbf{true} \Rightarrow \bigvee_i l_i \qquad \textit{(literal)}$$

$$l' \Rightarrow \Box_j l \qquad \textit{(positive j)}$$
$$l' \Rightarrow \Diamond_j l \qquad \textit{(negative j)}$$

where l_i, l and l' are literals.

Several resolution rules are provided that capture the semantics of the modal operators, some involving more than two premises. Other modal logics can be derived by restricting the accessibility relation to be a particular form (reflexive, serial, transitive, Euclidean or symmetric). This is represented in the calculus by adding clauses that capture these restrictions. For example, for reflexive relations, the T axiom $\Box_j \varphi \Rightarrow \varphi$ holds. This is captured by adding the clause $\textbf{true} \Rightarrow \neg l' \vee l$ for any clause $l' \Rightarrow \Box_j l$. These calculi are shown to be sound, complete and terminating [24].

In [25, 27] the normal form is changed to incorporate a modal level (the maximal number of nested occurrences of modal operators that a subformula is in the scope of) for the modal logic K and initial clauses are not required as they can be represented by literal clauses holding at modal level 0. This representation has been implemented in the theorem prover K_SP [26] and has been shown to work well where formulae are distributed across levels. This has been extended to other normal modal logics by providing translations into the normal form with modal levels [28].

6 Conclusion

We have provided an overview to the clausal resolution method first applied to LTL that has been extended to other temporal logics CTL and FOTL and normal modal logics. The key features of the method have been shown applicable to a range of logics, amenable to implementation, resulting in competitive theorem provers.

Acknowledgments. This paper describes the work of many researchers. I would like to thank all of those who collaborated to further this line of research.

References

1. Abadi, M.: The power of temporal proofs. Theor. Comput. Sci. **65**(1), 35–83 (1989)
2. Bachmair, L., Ganzinger, H.: Resolution theorem proving. In: Robinson, J.A., Voronkov, A. (eds.) Handbook of Automated Reasoning (in 2 volumes), pp. 19–99. Elsevier and MIT Press (2001)
3. Blackburn, P., van Benthem, J.F.A.K., Wolter, F. (eds.): Handbook of Modal Logic. Studies in Logic and Practical Reasoning, vol. 3. North-Holland (2007)
4. Bolotov, A., Fisher, M.: A clausal resolution method for CTL branching-time temporal logic. J. Exp. Theor. Artif. Intell. **11**(1), 77–93 (1999)
5. Weidenbach, C., Schmidt, R.A., Hillenbrand, T., Rusev, R., Topic, D.: System description: Spass version 3.0. In: Pfenning, F. (ed.) CADE 2007. LNCS (LNAI), vol. 4603, pp. 514–520. Springer, Heidelberg (2007). https://doi.org/10.1007/978-3-540-73595-3_38
6. Degtyarev, A., Fisher, M., Konev, B.: Monodic temporal resolution. ACM Trans. Comput. Log. **7**(1), 108–150 (2006)
7. Dixon, C.: Search strategies for resolution in temporal logics. In: McRobbie, M.A., Slaney, J.K. (eds.) CADE 1996. LNCS, vol. 1104, pp. 673–687. Springer, Heidelberg (1996). https://doi.org/10.1007/3-540-61511-3_121
8. Dixon, C.: Temporal resolution using a breadth-first search algorithm. Ann. Math. Artif. Intell. **22**, 87–115 (1998)
9. Dixon, C.: Using Otter for temporal resolution. In: Advances in Temporal Logic. Applied Logic Series, vol. 16, pp. 149–166. Kluwer (2000). Proceedings the Second International Conference on Temporal Logic (ICTL). ISBN 0-7923-6149-0
10. Emerson, E.A., Clarke, E.M.: Using branching time temporal logic to synthesize synchronization skeletons. Sci. Comput. Program. **2**(3), 241–266 (1982)
11. Fisher, M.: A resolution method for temporal logic. In: Proceedings of the Twelfth International Joint Conference on Artificial Intelligence (IJCAI), Sydney, Australia, pp. 99–104. Morgan Kaufman, August 1991
12. Fisher, M.: A normal form for temporal logic and its application in theorem-proving and execution. J. Log. Comput. **7**(4), 429–456 (1997)
13. Fisher, M.: An Introduction to Practical Formal Methods Using Temporal Logic. Wiley, Hoboken (2011)
14. Fisher, M., Dixon, C., Peim, M.: Clausal temporal resolution. ACM Trans. Comput. Log. **2**(1), 12–56 (2001)
15. Goré, R., Thomson, J., Widmann, F.: An experimental comparison of theorem provers for CTL. In: Combi, C., Leucker, M., Wolter, F. (eds.) Eighteenth International Symposium on Temporal Representation and Reasoning, TIME 2011, Lübeck, Germany, 12–14 September 2011, pp. 49–56. IEEE (2011)
16. Hodkinson, I., Wolter, F., Zakharyaschev, M.: Decidable fragments of first-order temporal logics. Ann. Pure Appl. Log. **106**(1–3), 85–134 (2000)
17. Hustadt, U., Konev, B., Riazanov, A., Voronkov, A.: **TeMP**: a temporal monodic prover. In: Basin, D., Rusinowitch, M. (eds.) IJCAR 2004. LNCS (LNAI), vol. 3097, pp. 326–330. Springer, Heidelberg (2004). https://doi.org/10.1007/978-3-540-25984-8_23
18. Hustadt, U., Konev, B.: TRP++: a temporal resolution prover. In: 3rd International Workshop on the Implementation of Logics (2002)
19. Hustadt, U., Konev, B.: TRP++ 2.0: a temporal resolution prover. In: Baader, F. (ed.) CADE 2003. LNCS (LNAI), vol. 2741, pp. 274–278. Springer, Heidelberg (2003). https://doi.org/10.1007/978-3-540-45085-6_21

20. Hustadt, U., Schmidt, R.A.: Scientific benchmarking with temporal logic decision procedures. In: Fensel, D., Giunchiglia, F., McGuinness, D., Williams, M.-A. (eds.) Principles of Knowledge Representation and Reasoning: Proceedings of the Eighth International Conference (KR 2002), pp. 533–544. Morgan Kaufmann (2002)

21. Konev, B., Degtyarev, A., Dixon, C., Fisher, M., Hustadt, U.: Mechanising first-order temporal resolution. Inf. Comput. **199**(1–2), 55–86 (2005)

22. Ludwig, M., Hustadt, U.: Implementing a fair monodic temporal prover. AI Commun. **23**(2–3), 68–96 (2010)

23. Manna, Z., Pnueli, A.: The Temporal Logic of Reactive and Concurrent Systems - Specification. Springer, Heidelberg (1992). https://doi.org/10.1007/978-1-4612-0931-7

24. Nalon, C., Dixon, C.: Clausal resolution for normal modal logics. J. Algorithms **62**(3–4), 117–134 (2007)

25. Nalon, C., Dixon, C., Hustadt, U.: Modal resolution: proofs, layers, and refinements. ACM Trans. Comput. Log. **20**(4), 23:1–23:38 (2019)

26. Nalon, C., Hustadt, U., Dixon, C.: K_SP: A resolution-based prover for multimodal K. In: Olivetti, N., Tiwari, A. (eds.) IJCAR 2016. LNCS (LNAI), vol. 9706, pp. 406–415. Springer, Cham (2016). https://doi.org/10.1007/978-3-319-40229-1_28

27. Nalon, C., Hustadt, U., Dixon, C.: K_n: architecture, refinements, strategies and experiments. J. Autom. Reason. **64**(3), 461–484 (2020)

28. Papacchini, F., Nalon, C., Hustadt, U., Dixon, C.: Efficient local reductions to basic modal logic. In: Platzer, A., Sutcliffe, G. (eds.) CADE 2021. LNCS (LNAI), vol. 12699, pp. 76–92. Springer, Cham (2021). https://doi.org/10.1007/978-3-030-79876-5_5

29. Riazanov, A., Voronkov, A.: The design and implementation of Vampire. AI Communications **15**(2,3), 91–110 (2002)

30. Zhang, L., Hustadt, U., Dixon, C.: A refined resolution calculus for CTL. In: Schmidt, R.A. (ed.) CADE 2009. LNCS (LNAI), vol. 5663, pp. 245–260. Springer, Heidelberg (2009). https://doi.org/10.1007/978-3-642-02959-2_20

31. Zhang, L., Hustadt, U., Dixon, C.: CTL-RP: a computational tree logic resolution prover. AI Commun. **23**(2–3), 111–136 (2009)

32. Zhang, L., Hustadt, U., Dixon, C.: A resolution calculus for the branching-time temporal logic CTL. ACM Trans. Comput. Log. **15**(1), 1529–3785 (2014)

Population Protocols: Beyond Runtime Analysis

Javier Esparza[✉] [iD]

Technical University of Munich, Munich, Germany
esparza@in.tum.de

Abstract. We survey our recent work on the verification of population protocols and their state complexity.

1 Introduction

Population protocols are a model of computation in which an arbitrary number of indistinguishable finite-state agents interact in pairs to collectively decide if their initial global configuration satisfies a given property. Population protocols were introduced by Angluin *et al.* in [7,8] to study the theoretical properties of networks of mobile sensors with very limited computational resources, but they are also very strongly related to chemical reaction networks [53], a discrete model of chemistry in which agents are molecules that change their states due to collisions.

Population protocols decide a property by *stable consensus*. Each state of an agent is assigned a binary output (yes/no). At each step, a pair of agents is selected uniformly at random and allowed to interact. In a correct protocol, all agents eventually reach with probability 1 the set of states whose output correctly answers the question "did our initial configuration satisfy the property?" and stay in these states forever.

The *parallel runtime* of a protocol is defined as the expected number of interactions until a stable consensus is reached (i.e. until the property is decided), divided by the number of agents. In recent years, much research on population protocols has focused on the runtime of population protocols, and several landmark results have been obtained. In particular, recent results have studied protocols for majority and leader election in which the number of states grows with the number of agents, and shown that poly-logarithmic time is achievable by protocols without leaders, even for very slow growth functions, see e.g. [3,4,40]. Many of these results have been described in excellent surveys [5,27].

My work on population protocols, carried out with many of my PhD students and postdocs, and in collaboration with other colleagues, has focused on other aspects than runtime analysis, and this is the reason for the title of this note.

The work surveyed in this note was supported by the European Research Council (ERC) under the European Union's Horizon 2020 research and innovation program under grant agreement No 787367 "Parameterized Verification and Synthesis" (PaVeS).

P. C. Bell et al. (Eds.): RP 2021, LNCS 13035, pp. 28–51, 2021.
https://doi.org/10.1007/978-3-030-89716-1_3

I first learned about population protocols at a talk by Paul Spirakis in ICALP 2008. As a researcher working on the theory of Petri nets, I noticed the connection of population protocols to Petri nets, and as a researcher working on automatic verification, I asked myself if the correctness problem—given a population protocol and a property, does the protocol decide the property?—was decidable. The problem consisted of checking whether an infinite collection of finite-state Markov chains, one for each initial configuration of the protocol, satisfies a rather sophisticated liveness property with probability 1. This makes it very hard: liveness properties are harder to verify than safety properties, probabilistic systems are harder than non-probabilistic ones, and parameterized problems, i.e., problems involving families of systems with an arbitrarily large number of agents, are *much* harder to verify than systems with a fixed number of agents. After looking at the problem for some time I could not find an answer, but I kept it at the back of my mind, and in 2015 (seven years later!) I suggested to my colleagues Pierre Ganty, Jérôme Leroux, and Rupak Majumdar to examine it again. This time, thanks to new progress by Leroux on the theory of Petri nets, we proved that the correctness problem is decidable, although as hard as the reachability problem for Petri nets [31]. This was the starting point of a research program devoted to the theory and practice of verifying population protocols, which reached an important milestone in 2020 with the release of PEREGRINE 2.0, a verifier based on new theoretical results [15,32]. The first part of this note surveys this research, adding all the work carried out since 2017 to a brief previous survey [28].

In 2018, Michael Blondin, Stefan Jaax and myself observed that a well-known result of the theory of Petri nets had a surprising application to the theory of population protocols: It showed that an infinite family of predicates of the form $x \geq k$ for certain values of k could be decided by extremely succinct protocols with only $O(\log \log k)$ states. This sparked our interest in the question of how many states are needed to decide a given predicate, or, by analogy to automata theory, the *state complexity* of the predicate. The question is relevant. For example, the fast protocol for majority implicitly described in [10] has tens of thousands of states. This is an obstacle to implementations of protocols in chemistry, where the number of states corresponds to the number of chemical species participating in the reactions. The number of states is also important because it plays the role of memory in sequential computational models. Indeed, the total memory available to a population protocol is the logarithm of the number of states multiplied by the number of agents.

To the best of our knowledge, we are the first group to study the state complexity of predicates. While we do not have a complete characterization yet, we have already proved several results. In 2018 the only bounds on state complexity were the ones derived from the synthesis procedures of [9,10]. The input to these procedures is a boolean combination of atomic predicates of the form $\sum_{i=1}^{k} a_i x_i \sim b$, where a_i and b are integers, and $\sim$ is either $<$ or $\equiv_m$, the latter denoting congruence modulo m. (It is known that every predicate decidable by population protocols is of this form.) The bounds of [9,10] are exponential in both the number of atomic predicates, and in their size, with numbers written in binary. Since 2018 we have shown that every predicate has a protocol with a polynomial number of states both in the number and the size of the atomic predicates [14,16], and that, as mentioned above, some predicates have much smaller protocols [16]. Very recently, we have also obtained lower bounds for the state complexity [24]. The second part of the note surveys this work.

The note is structured as follows. Section 2 introduces terminology, and Sects. 3 and 4 survey our work on verification and state complexity, respectively.

2   Some Terminology

We assume that the reader is familiar with the basics of the population protocol model; here we just fix some terminology.

Population Protocols. A population protocol has a set of states and transitions, with a distinguished set of initial states. Every state also has an associated output, 1 or 0. Transitions model interactions between two agents. They have the form $q_1, q_2 \mapsto q_1', q_2'$, meaning that two agents in states q_1 and q_2 interact and move to states q_1' and q_2'. We assume that there is exactly one transition for each pair of states, but transitions can also be silent, meaning that the states of the agents do not change. A configuration of a protocol is a mapping assigning to each state a number of agents. Initial configurations put arbitrarily many agents in the initial states, and 0 agents elsewhere. A protocol starts at some initial configuration, and executes steps by repeatedly picking two agents uniformly at random and applying the corresponding transition. A run is an infinite sequence of configurations obtained by executing infinitely many steps.

A configuration has consensus 1 resp. 0 if all its agents occupy states with output 1 resp. 0. We also say that the configuration is a 1-consensus, resp. a 0-consensus, or just a consensus when we are not specific. A configuration is a *stable* 1-consensus if every configuration reachable from it, including itself, is a 1-consensus. A protocol is *well specified* if for every initial configuration C there is $b \in \{0, 1\}$ such that runs starting at C eventually reach a stable b-consensus with probability 1 (abbreviated as w.p.1 in this note); in this case, we say that the protocol *outputs* b for the initial configuration C. A well specified protocol with initial states $q_1, \ldots, q_k$ *decides* the predicate $\varphi(x_1, \ldots, x_k)$ defined by: $\varphi(n_1, \ldots, n_k) = b$ iff the protocol outputs b for the initial configuration that puts $n_1, \ldots, n_k$ agents in $q_1, \ldots, q_k$.

We also consider protocols *with (one or more) leaders.* Intuitively, this is a population protocol with a set of distinguished agents. Formally, a protocol with leaders only differs from a normal population protocol in the definition of the set of initial configurations. The initial configurations of normal protocols put arbitrarily many agents in the initial states, and 0 agents elsewhere. In a protocol with leaders the initial configurations also put a fixed number of agents, the same for every initial configuration, in other states.

Population protocols can be seen as special classes of Petri nets or Vector Addition Systems [51,52]. For the purposes of this note, it suffices to say that, like a protocol, a Petri net has a set of states (called *places* in Petri net jargon) and transitions. However, transitions have the form $q_1, \ldots, q_n \mapsto q'_1, \ldots, q'_m$ for arbitrary $n, m \geq 0$. So, intuitively, transitions of a Petri net can represent interactions between more than two agents, and they can create or destroy agents. The theory of Petri nets has produced numerous results about the properties of their reachability graphs, i.e., the graphs with the configurations as nodes, and the steps as transitions. Such results can be immediately translated to population protocols.

Presburger Arithmetic, Presburger Predicates, and Presburger Sets. A fundamental result of the theory of population protocols is that they decide precisely the Presburger predicates, i.e., the predicates expressible in Presburger arithmetic [11]. We briefly recall the definition of Presburger arithmetic and some results, and refer to [41] for more details.

Atomic formulas of Presburger arithmetic are of the form $\sum_{i=1}^{k} a_i x_i \sim b$, where a_i and b are integers, x_i are variables, and $\sim$ is either $<$ or $\equiv_m$, the latter denoting the congruence modulo m for some $m \geq 2$. We call these atomic formulas *threshold* and *remainder* (or *modulo*) formulas, respectively. The formulas of Presburger arithmetic are the result of closing atomic formulas under Boolean operations and first-order existential or universal quantification. For example,

$$\varphi(x, y) = \forall z \, \exists u \colon 3x - u \leq 0 \wedge 2z - y + u \geq 4 \wedge (x + y) \equiv_5 3$$

is a formula of Presburger arithmetic with free variables x and y.

A formula $\varphi(x_1, \ldots, x_n)$ is interpreted over $\mathbb{N}^n$ in the expected way. A set of vectors $S \subseteq \mathbb{N}^n$ is a *Presburger set* if there is a Presburger formula φ such that a vector belongs to S iff it satisfies φ, and a predicate over $\mathbb{N}^n$ is a *Presburger predicate* if the set of vectors satisfying the predicate is a Presburger set. So Presburger formulas are finite representations of the Presburger sets and predicates. *Semilinear sets* are another representation of the Presburger sets, that is, a set is semilinear iff it is Presburger. In this note we do not need any specific properties of the semilinear representation.

Presburger arithmetic has a quantifier-elimination procedure, meaning that every formula can be transformed into an equivalent boolean combination of threshold and remainder predicates. The satisfiability problem for full Presburger arithmetic is decidable, but its complexity is high, it lies between 2-NEXP and 2-EXPSPACE. For quantifier-free formulas the problem is NP-complete, and there exist SMT-solvers efficient in practice. The tools PEREGRINE 1.0 and 2.0 described later in this note are implemented on top of the Z3 solver [50].

3   Verification of Population Protocols

The design of population protocols is quite error prone. In our experience, it is hardly ever the case that the first design for a protocol computing a predicate is correct. The problem is accentuated by the lack of a suitable high-level programming language for protocols, which makes their design akin to writing machine code.

In this context, the limited expressive power of population protocols also has a positive side: the correctness problem is not trivially undecidable, as happens with many other models of computation. In this section we show that the problem is in fact decidable, and survey our work leading from the first decidability result to the current decision procedures and to their practical implementation.

3.1   Decidability and Complexity

In [31] we proved that the two central verification problems for population protocols are decidable:

- Well-specification: Given a population protocol, is it well specified?
- Correctness: Given a population protocol and a Presburger predicate (represented as a Presburger formula), does the protocol compute the predicate?

The results were extended to decidability of more general properties in [30]. The proofs proceed by reduction to the reachability problem for Petri nets, which is decidable [43, 47]. We also showed that well-specification and correctness are recursively equivalent to the reachability problem for Petri nets. More precisely:

- The reachability problem for Petri nets can be reduced to well-specification or correctness in polynomial time;
- Given an oracle for the reachability problem for Petri nets, well-specification and correctness can be decided in elementary time, i.e., in time bounded by a finite tower of exponentials.

It has been shown recently that the reachability problem for Petri nets is Ackermann-complete, meaning that its complexity is bounded from below and from above by non-primitive recursive fast growing functions related to the Ackermann function [25, 26, 46]. Therefore, well-specification and correctness are not primitive recursive either, that is, no algorithm running in time bounded by a primitive recursive function can solve them.

The very high complexity of the correctness problem leads to the question whether the problem could be more tractable for special protocol classes. In [11] Angluin *et al.* not only characterized the expressive power of population protocols, but also of other models with more restricted communication mechanisms. In [33, 36] we conducted a complete analysis of the complexity of the correctness problem for the models of [11]. We showed that for models based on immediate and delayed observation the correctness problem is PSPACE-complete and complete at the second level of the polynomial hierarchy, respectively. *Immediate observation* protocols have transitions of the form $q_1, q \mapsto q_2, q$. Intuitively, an agent in state q_1 *observes* that the other process is in state q, which allows it to immediately move to state q_2. Intuitively, in such protocols if an agent at q_1 can execute the transition, then every agent at q_1 can take it as well, which greatly simplifies the verification task. In *delayed observation* protocols the observer in q_1 may move to q_2 at a later point.

3.2   A First Attempt at a Verification Tool

In [18], published in 2017, we addressed the problem of developing an algorithm that would be efficient enough to automatically prove correctness for a class of protocols satisfying three conditions:

(a) No loss of expressive power: the class should compute all Presburger predicates.
(b) Naturality: the class should contain many of the protocols discussed in the literature.
(c) Feasible membership problem: deciding if a protocol belongs to the class should have reasonable complexity.

In the paper we introduced the class of *Well-Specified Strongly Silent* protocols (WSSS). Intuitively, a protocol is silent if an execution reaches a terminal configuration with probability 1, where a configuration is terminal if cannot reach any other configuration. (Observe that a protocol correctly deciding a property need not be silent; indeed, the definition of when a protocol decides a property only requires that an execution reaches a *consensus* w.p.1. Reaching a consensus is a weaker property, because it allows the protocol to keep visiting different configurations, as long as in all of them the agents agree on the same value.) Further, a protocol is strongly silent if, loosely speaking, its transitions are organized in layers such that transitions of higher layers cannot be enabled by executing transitions of lower layers. In particular, if the protocol reaches a configuration of the highest layer that does not enable any transition, then this configuration is terminal. We showed that WSSS protocols satisfy (a) and (b), and proved that the membership problem for the class is in the complexity class DP. Recall that DP is the class of languages L such that $L = L_1 \cap L_2$ for some languages $L_1 \in$ NP and $L_2 \in$ coNP; in view of the Ackermannian complexity of the general case, this result shows that WSSS satisfies (c). The proof that the problem is in DP reduces membership to checking satisfiability resp. unsatisfiability of two quantifier-free formulas of Presburger arithmetic. The procedure was implemented in PEREGRINE 1.0 [17], a tool for the verification of population protocols built on top of the constraint solver Z3, and the first tool able to automatically prove well-specification for *all* initial configurations.

While WSSS protocols decide all Presburger predicates, PEREGRINE 1.0 had several limitations, which will be subject of the next section. From the most conceptual to the most practical:

- The verification algorithm of [18] was dissociated from the decidability results proved in [31]. To put it bluntly, the theoretical result was not guiding the design of a practical algorithm.
- The tool did not produce correctness certificates; if the tool returned "correct", the user had to trust the result.
- Many protocols designed to be fast, or to use few states, are not in WSSS. Examples include the average-and-conquer protocol of [6] (for fixed values of the parameters), or the compact threshold protocols of [14]. In particular,

many protocols that perform a "random search", like the second protocol in Example 1 below, are non-silent.

Example 1. The following two (very slow) protocols decide whether the number of blue agents minus the number of red agents is at least 2^k for a given $k \geq 1$. These protocols are also of interest in the next section on state complexity.

First Protocol. Each agent has a bag that can hold up to 2^k pebbles and a flag that can be up or down (corresponding to output 1 and 0, respectively). Initially, each agent has one pebble and its flag is down. When two agents meet they update their bags and flags depending on their colors:

- Two red agents. No change.
- One blue and one red agent. If none of the two bags is empty, then both agents throw one pebble away and lower their flags; we call this interaction a *cancellation*. Else, if the bag of the blue agent is full (that is, if it has 2^k pebbles) or if both flags were up before the interaction, then both agents raise their flags. Else, both agents lower their flags.
- Two blue agents. One agent gives the other as many pebbles as the other agent's bag can still hold. If this fills the other agent's bag, or if both flags were up before the interaction, then both agents raise their flags; otherwise they lower them.

Let us prove correctness. Let x and y be the numbers of blue and red agents, respectively. W.p.1 cancellations keep occurring until a configuration C is reached in which only blue or only red agents have pebbles (or no agent has pebbles). If $x - y \geq 2^k$, then no red agents have pebbles at C, and in runs from C some blue agent fills its bag and raises its flag w.p.1. The bag remains full forever, and w.p.1 this agent eventually meets all other agents *without any other interaction happening in-between*, after which all flags are up, and stay up forever. If $x - y < 2^k$, then after C no bag is ever full, and so any flag that is lowered stays down forever. Moreover, at C the flag of the blue agent that participated in the last cancellation is down, and this agent brings down the flag of any agent it meets. So eventually all flags stay down w.p.1.

Second Protocol. Again, agents have bags and flags. The following updates ensure that the number of pebbles in each bag is always 0 or a power of 2:

- Two red agents. No change.
- One blue and one red agent. If both agents have *exactly one pebble*, they throw their pebbles away and lower their flags. Else, if the bag of the blue agent is full or both flags were up before the interaction, then both agents raise their flags. Else, both agents lower their flags.
- Two blue agents. If both agents hold *the same number of pebbles*, then one of them gives to the other as many pebbles as the other's bag can still hold; if one agent has no pebbles, then it receives from the other half its pebbles; otherwise no pebbles are exchanged. If after this some bag is full, or if both flags were up before the interaction, then both agents raise their flags, else they lower them.

This protocol is also correct. Intuitively, blue agents can distribute pebbles among them into any combination of powers of 2 (up to 2^k). For example, if $k = 2$ the blue agents can partition 5 pebbles among them as 1+1+1+1+1 (5 agents get one pebble each); 2+1+1+1; 2+2+1; or 4+1. Randomness ensures that all these partitions are visited infinitely often, and so that cancellations keep occurring until a configuration C is reached in which only blue or only red agents have pebbles (or no agent has pebbles).

If $x - y \geq 2^k$, then runs from C eventually execute the following sequence of interactions w.p.1: first, some blue agent fills its bag and raises its flag; this agent then proceeds to meet all red agents, and then all blue agents whose bag is not empty; after that, the agent meets each blue agent with empty bag, sharing its pebbles with it, but only to recover them immediately. After this sequence all flags are up, and remain so forever. If $x - y < 2^k$, then the argument is as for the first protocol.

The first protocol is silent. If $x \geq y$, then w.p.1 it eventually reaches and stays in the configuration in which $\lfloor (x - y)/2^k \rfloor$ blue agents have 2^k pebbles, one blue agent has $(x - y) \bmod 2^k$ pebbles each, all other agents have 0 pebbles, and all flags are up or down, depending on whether $x - y \geq 2^k$ holds or not. If $x \leq y$, the protocol reaches and stays in the configuration in which $y - x$ red agents have one pebble each, all other agents have 0 pebbles, and all flags are down. The second protocol needs exponentially fewer states, but is not silent. Indeed, when $x \geq y$ the blue agents keep visiting all partitions of $x - y$ forever.

3.3   A New Proof Methodology: Stage Graphs

Finding theoretical and algorithmic answers to the limitations of PEREGRINE 1.0 took three years. Initially we did not even have a clear picture of these limitations. They emerged when we started to investigate how to automatically compute an upper bound on the expected runtime of a protocol. This work, published in [19], introduced stage graphs, a notion that, after many rewrites, finally led to the stage graph proof methodology of [15], which we describe now.

Stage graphs reduce correctness to checking that certain assertions are inductive invariants, and that certain ranking functions decrease in appropriate ways. For standard sequential programs these checks are still undecidable problems, but for population protocols they turn out to be decidable.

Certificates of Correctness. The *reachability graph* of a population protocol has all possible configurations as nodes, and an edge from C to C' whenever C' is reachable from C in one step. It is an infinite graph, but every configuration has finitely many descendants. (A consequence of the fact that transitions do not change the number of agents). We call graphs with this property *weakly finite* [29]. An edge of the graph corresponds to executing one transition of the protocol. The probability of executing a transition at configuration C is the fraction of the pairs of agents at C that enable the transition. Equipped with these notions, let us briefly review how to certify different kinds of properties.

Certifying Safety. Safety properties can be certified using inductive invariants. An inductive invariant is just a set of configurations closed under the reachability relation, i.e., if a configuration belongs to the set, then so do all its successors. Given a set I of initial configurations and some set D of dangerous configurations, an inductive invariant Int satisfying $I \subseteq Int$ and $Int \cap D = \emptyset$ certifies that D is not reachable from I.

Certifying Termination. Liveness properties, like termination, can be certified by ranking functions assigning to each configuration an element of a set with a well-founded order, like the natural numbers. Termination for *all* runs of the program starting at I is certified by an inductive invariant Int containing I, and a *strictly decreasing* ranking function over Int, i.e., a ranking function that strictly decreases whenever the protocol takes a step.

Certifying Termination w.p.1. Termination *with probability 1* can also be certified by an inductive invariant Int containing I, and a ranking function f. However, the ranking function only needs to be *weakly decreasing*, meaning that for every non-terminal configuration $C \in Int$, some configuration C' reachable from C in one or more steps satisfies $f(C') < f(C)$. Indeed, if such a function exists, then for every non-terminal configuration of $C \in Int$ there is a positive probability of taking a path that stays within Int by inductivity, and decreases the ranking function. Since the reachability graph is weakly finite, this probability is bounded from below by some $\epsilon > 0$ independent of C. So runs reach and stay at terminal configurations w.p.1.

Certifying Stable Consensus w.p.1. In order to certify that a run starting at a given set I eventually reaches stable consensus b w.p.1, for some given $b \in \{0, 1\}$, we need two inductive invariants Int_1, Int_2 and a ranking function f satisfying three properties:

- Int_1 contains I (and so, by inductivity, also all configurations reachable from I) and Int_2;
- Int_2 contains only b-consensus configurations (and so, by inductivity, any run reaching Int_2 reaches stable consensus); and
- f is weakly decreasing on $Int_1 \setminus Int_2$, i.e., for every $C \in Int_1 \setminus Int_2$, some C' reachable from C in one or more steps satisfies $f(C') < f(C)$.

The same argument as above shows that runs starting at $C \in Int_1 \setminus Int_2$ eventually reach Int_2 w.p.1, and, since Int_2 is inductive, get trapped in Int_2. Since Int_2 only contains configurations with consensus b, runs starting at I reach stable consensus b w.p.1.

This proof technique is *complete*, meaning that if a run starting at I eventually reaches stable consensus b w.p.1, then we can always find a suitable Int_1 and Int_2, and f. Indeed, it suffices to choose Int_1 as the set of all configurations reachable from I; Int_2 as the set of all configurations of Int_1 with stable consensus b; and f as the function assigning 0 to the configurations of Int_2, and 1 to the configurations of $Int_1 \setminus Int_2$.

Stage Graphs. It is useful to split stable consensus proofs into a small steps. For this one can exhibit a finite, directed, and acyclic graph, whose nodes are pairs $v = (Int, f)$, where Int is an inductive invariant, and f is a ranking function certifying that runs starting at Int eventually get trapped in $Int_1 \cup \ldots \cup Int_n$ w.p.1, where $Int_1, \ldots, Int_n$ are the invariants of the children of v. Further, the invariants of the bottom nodes of the graph only contain consensus configurations. In [15] we call these objects *stage graphs*, and their nodes *stages*. A stage graph proves that runs starting at a stage "travel down the graph w.p.1" until they reach a bottom stage, and so stable consensus. Intuitively, stages correspond to "milestones" towards stable consensus.

To prove a protocol correct, we produce two stage graphs proving that runs starting at initial configurations that satisfy the predicate eventually reach stable consensus 1, and the corresponding property for stable consensus 0. The stage graphs have an initial stage containing the initial configurations satisfying or not satisfying the predicate, respectively. Observe that, since stages are inductive the initial stages also contain every reachable configuration. Let us examine stage graphs in more detail with the help of a well-known example.

Example 2. Consider the following majority protocol, whose purpose is to decide if the initial configuration contains more blue agents than red agents. Apart from red or blue, agents can also be active of passive, yielding four possible states $Q = \{\mathrm{B}, \mathrm{R}, \mathrm{b}, \mathrm{r}\}$ (uppercase for active agents, lowercase for passive ones). The initial states are B and R, and so initially all agents are active. The protocol has four transitions:

$$t_1 : \mathrm{B}, \mathrm{R} \mapsto \mathrm{b}, \mathrm{r} \qquad\qquad t_2 : \mathrm{B}, \mathrm{r} \mapsto \mathrm{B}, \mathrm{b}$$
$$t_3 : \mathrm{R}, \mathrm{b} \mapsto \mathrm{R}, \mathrm{r} \qquad\qquad t_4 : \mathrm{b}, \mathrm{r} \mapsto \mathrm{b}, \mathrm{b}$$

The blue states B, b have output 1, and the red states R, r output 0. So in this case, for better visualization, we call the outputs "blue" and "red", instead of 1 and 0. The protocol is correct if it satisfies the following property: for every initial configuration C, i.e., every configuration C satisfying $C(\mathrm{b}) = C(\mathrm{r}) = 0$, if $C(\mathrm{B}) < C(\mathrm{R})$, eventually all agents stay forever in the red states $\{\mathrm{R}, \mathrm{r}\}$ w.p.1, and if $C(\mathrm{B}) \geq C(\mathrm{R})$ eventually all agents stay forever in the blue states $\{\mathrm{B}, \mathrm{b}\}$ w.p.1.

Figure 1 shows two stage graphs for the protocol. Stages are given as constraints over variables $\underline{\mathrm{B}}, \underline{\mathrm{R}}, \underline{\mathrm{b}}, \underline{\mathrm{r}}$, describing the number of agents in states $\mathrm{B}, \mathrm{R}, \mathrm{b}, \mathrm{r}$, respectively. For example, the constraint $\underline{\mathrm{B}} < \underline{\mathrm{R}}$ represents the set of all configurations C satisfying $C(\mathrm{B}) < C(\mathrm{R})$. Ranking functions are described as functions of $\underline{\mathrm{B}}, \underline{\mathrm{R}}, \underline{\mathrm{b}}, \underline{\mathrm{r}}$. For example, the function $\underline{\mathrm{B}} + \underline{\mathrm{R}}$ assigns to every configuration C the number $C(\mathrm{B}) + C(\mathrm{R})$.

The stage graph on the left of Fig. 1 proves that runs starting at any configuration satisfying $\underline{\mathrm{B}} < \underline{\mathrm{R}}$ reaches stable consensus red with probability 1. The "human" proof goes as follows: because of transition t_1, from any configuration satisfying $\underline{\mathrm{B}} < \underline{\mathrm{R}}$ the protocol eventually reaches a configuration satisfying

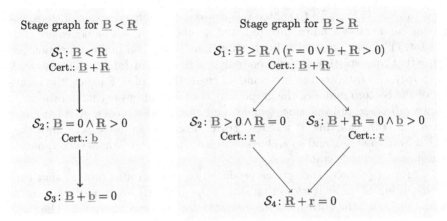

Fig. 1. Stage graphs for the protocol of Example 2

$\underline{B} = 0$, and then transition t_3 eventually changes all remaining blue agents into red agents. The stage graph reflects this proof structure:

- The initial stage $\mathcal{S}_1$ contains exactly the configurations satisfying $\underline{B} < \underline{R}$. The ranking function $f(\underline{B}, \underline{R}, \underline{b}, \underline{r}) = \underline{B} + \underline{R}$ certifies that runs starting at a configuration of $\mathcal{S}_1$ eventually get trapped in $\mathcal{S}_2$, the set of configurations satisfying $\underline{R} > 0 \wedge \underline{B} = 0$, w.p.1. Indeed, consider any configuration $C \in \mathcal{S}_1 \backslash \mathcal{S}_2$, i.e., a configuration satisfying $0 < \underline{B} < \underline{R}$. Then C enables transition t_1. Letting $C \xrightarrow{t_1} C'$ we have

$$f(C') = \underline{B}' + \underline{R}' = (\underline{B} - 1) + (\underline{R} - 1) < \underline{B} + \underline{R} = f(C) \ .$$

  So f is weakly decreasing.
- Similarly, the ranking function $g(\underline{B}, \underline{R}, \underline{b}, \underline{r}) = \underline{b}$ certifies that runs starting at a configuration of $\mathcal{S}_2 \backslash \mathcal{S}_3$ eventually get trapped in $\mathcal{S}_3$. Since $\mathcal{S}_3$ is the set of configurations without blue agents, we are done. Observe that not every transition decreases $\underline{b}$; actually, transition t_4, which is enabled at some configurations of $\mathcal{S}_2 \backslash \mathcal{S}_3$, increases it. However, g is weakly decreasing because of transition t_3.
- Observe that $\mathcal{S}_1, \mathcal{S}_2, \mathcal{S}_3$ are inductive invariants. For example, if a configuration satisfies $\underline{B} < \underline{R}$, then so does any configuration reached by applying any of the four transitions of the protocol.

Let us now consider the stage graph on the right. It proves that runs starting at initial configurations satisfying $\underline{B} \geq \underline{R}$ (that is, at the set of configurations satisfying $\underline{B} \geq \underline{R}$ and $b = 0 = r$) reach stable consensus blue w.p.1. The choice of the initial stage $\mathcal{S}_1$ is not completely trivial. $\mathcal{S}_1$ must satisfy three conditions: (a) contain all configurations satisfying $\underline{B} \geq \underline{R}$ and $b = 0 = r$; (b) contain only configurations with a majority of blue agents or a tie, because only those configurations reach stable consensus blue; (c) be inductive. We cannot choose

$\mathcal{S}_1 = \underline{\mathbf{B}} \geq \underline{\mathbf{R}}$ because it violates (b); for example, the configuration given by $\mathbf{B} = 1$, $\mathbf{R} = 1$, $\underline{\mathbf{b}} = 1$, $\underline{\mathbf{r}} = 2$ has a majority of red agents. We cannot choose $\mathcal{S}_1 = \underline{\mathbf{B}} \geq \underline{\mathbf{R}} \wedge \mathbf{b} = 0 = \mathbf{r}$ either, because it violates (c). One has to find the right set between these two.

The "human" proof uses as milestone the configurations at which there are no agents left in state $\mathbf{R}$. These configurations can be of three kinds, corresponding to the stages $\mathcal{S}_2$, $\mathcal{S}_3$, and $\mathcal{S}_4$:

- if there are no red agents left (stage $\mathcal{S}_4$), then the run has already reached stable consensus blue;
- if there are agents left in B (stage $\mathcal{S}_2$), then any agents in state $\mathbf{r}$ are eventually turned blue by transition t_2;
- if there are agents left in b (stage $\mathcal{S}_3$), then any agents in state $\mathbf{r}$ are eventually turned blue by transition t_4.

Decidability of Correctness. If we are given stage graphs and told they prove that a protocol correctly decides a given property, we can in principle check this statement. We need to check that the initial stages contain the initial configurations satisfying and violating the property, respectively; that all stages are inductive and all ranking functions weakly decreasing; and that the bottom stages only contain configurations with the right consensus. However, since stages are infinite sets, the problem of carrying out such checks might be undecidable. The main theorem of [15] proves that, if a protocol is correct, then there exist stage graphs for which the checks reduce to proving satisfiability of formulas of Presburger arithmetic, which is decidable. More precisely, the theorem proves that every correct protocol has *Presburger stage graphs*, i.e., stage graphs satisfying the following properties:

- Stages are Presburger sets of configurations, i..e, sets expressible in Presburger arithmetic.
- Ranking functions are *Presburger functions*.
  A ranking function f is *Presburger* if there is a formula $\varphi(\mathbf{C}, \mathbf{n})$ of Presburger arithmetic with free variables $\mathbf{C}$ and $\mathbf{n}$ such that for every configuration C and every number n we have $f(C) = n$ iff $\varphi(C, n)$ holds.
- Each ranking function f comes equipped with a bound B such that for every configuration C in the domain of f, some configuration C' reachable from C *in at most B steps* satisfies $f(C') < f(C)$. So, strictly speaking, a Presburger stage graph consists not only of stages and ranking functions, but also of bounds for these functions.

Let us now see why checking that a stage graph is Presburger reduces to the satisfiability problem of Presburger arithmetic. Checking that the initial stages contain all initial configurations, and that the bottom stages only contain configurations with the right consensus is easy, because the sets of initial configurations and consensuses are Presburger. Let us consider the other two checks.

Checking that a Stage is Inductive. Since stages are Presburger sets, given a stage S there is a formula $S(\mathbf{C})$ expressing it. Further, for every transition t it is easy to construct a formula $step_t(\mathbf{C}, \mathbf{C}')$ that holds iff $C \xrightarrow{t} C'$. For example, for our majority protocol we have

$$step_{t_1}(\mathbf{C}, \mathbf{C}') := \mathbf{C} \geq (1, 1, 0, 0) \wedge \mathbf{C}' = \mathbf{C} + (-1, -1, 1, 1)$$

So inductivity is expressed by the formula

$$\forall \mathbf{C}, \mathbf{C}' : \left(S(\mathbf{C}) \wedge \bigvee_{t \in T} step_t(\mathbf{C}, \mathbf{C}') \right) \to S(\mathbf{C}')$$

where T is the set of transitions of the protocol.

Checking that a Ranking Function is Weakly Decreasing. If the reachability relation of population protocols would be expressible in Presburger arithmetic, i.e., if there were a Presburger formula $reach(\mathbf{C}, \mathbf{C}')$ such that $reach(C, C')$ holds iff $C \xrightarrow{*} C'$, then the weakly-decreasing property for arbitrary ranking functions would be expressible by the formula

$$\exists \mathbf{C}', \mathbf{n}, \mathbf{n}' : reach(\mathbf{C}, \mathbf{C}') \wedge \varphi_f(\mathbf{C}, \mathbf{n}) \wedge \varphi_f(\mathbf{C}', \mathbf{n}') \wedge \mathbf{n}' \geq \mathbf{n}$$

However, this is not the case; it is well known that the reachability relation of Petri nets may not be Presburger, and the result easily transfers to population protocols. This is the reason for the restriction to bounded ranking functions. It is easy to construct by induction a formula $reach_B(\mathbf{C}, \mathbf{C}')$ that holds if there exists a configuration C' reachable from C in at most B steps. Just take

$$reach_1(\mathbf{C}, \mathbf{C}') := \mathbf{C} = \mathbf{C}' \vee \bigvee_{t \in T} step_t(\mathbf{C}, \mathbf{C}')$$

$$reach_{k+1}(\mathbf{C}, \mathbf{C}') := \exists \mathbf{C}'' : reach_1(\mathbf{C}, \mathbf{C}'') \wedge reach_k(\mathbf{C}'', \mathbf{C}')$$

Now we can express the weakly decreasing property as above, replacing *reach* by $reach_B$.

As we mentioned before, the proof of existence of Presburger stage graphs is based on deep results on the theory of Petri nets, which can also be applied to population protocols. The main one is Leroux's theorem [45], stating the following. Let X and Y be Presburger sets of configurations of a Petri net, and let $reach(X)$ be the set of configurations reachable from X. The theorem states that if $reach(X) \cap Y = \emptyset$ holds, then there exists a Presburger inductive invariant that certifies this fact, i.e., there exists a Presburger set S closed under the reachability relation such that $reach(X) \subseteq S$ and $S \cap Y = \emptyset$. Observe that if $reach(X)$ were always itself a Presburger set, then we could just take $S = reach(X)$. Intuitively, Leroux's theorem shows that, while $reach(X)$ is not always a Presburger set, it is always very close to it (in fact, Leroux's proof shows that $reach(X)$ always belongs to a class of sets called *almost semilinear*).

3.4   Population Protocols Decide Exactly the Presburger Predicates

Angluin *et al.* proved in [11] that population protocols compute exactly the Presburger predicates. The difficult part is to show that population protocols *only* compute Presburger predicates. Let us show that this is a simple corollary of the fact that correctness can always be certified by Presburger stage graphs.

Consider a protocol that decides a predicate, say φ. Let I be the set of initial configurations of the protocol, and let I_1 and I_0 be a partition of I into the set of initial configurations that satisfy and do not satisfy φ, respectively. Our theorem shows that there exists a Presburger stage graph with initial stage S such that $I_1 \subseteq S$. This stage graph proves that a run starting at any configuration of S eventually reaches stable consensus 1 w.p.1. Since the protocol decides φ, no configuration of I_0 belongs to S, i.e., we have $S \cap I_0 = \emptyset$. Together with $I_1 \subseteq S$, we have $S \cap I = I_1$. But S is Presburger, and so is I (indeed, I is just the set of configurations with 0 agents in non-initial states). Since Presburger sets are closed under intersection, I_1 is also Presburger.

3.5   Automatic Computation of Stage Graphs

We have developed a practical approach to the computation of stage graphs, implemented in the tool PEREGRINE 2.0 [32]. The design of the tool is guided by the theoretical results on stage graphs, and by the notion of *dead transitions*. A transition t is *dead at a configuration* C if no run starting at C executes t, and t is *dead at a stage* S if t is dead at every $C \in S$. Population protocols designed by humans usually run in phases. Initially, all transitions are alive, and the end of each phase is marked by the "death" of one or more transitions, i.e., by reaching a configuration at which these transitions become dead. Runs of the protocol keep "killing transitions" until they reach a consensus configuration whose consensus cannot be broken by any of the transitions still alive. This consensus is then stable. When applied to the majority protocol, PEREGRINE 2.0 computes automatically two stage graphs very similar to those of Fig. 1 in a couple of seconds.

Like PEREGRINE 1.0, PEREGRINE 2.0 is built on top of the Z3 constraint solver. More precisely, it uses Z3 to check satisfiability of formulas of the existential fragment of Presburger arithmetic. The existential fragment is as expressive as full Presburger arithmetic, but can be handled much more efficiently.

Given a protocol and a Presburger predicate, PEREGRINE 2.0 computes two stage graphs, proving that runs starting at every initial configuration of the protocol satisfying (resp. violating) the predicate eventually reach stable consensus 1 (resp. stable consensus 0) w.p.1. Let I_1 be the set of initial configurations satisfying the predicate, the other case being similar. PEREGRINE 2.0 maintains a worklist of Presburger stages, finitely represented by Presburger formulas. Initially, the worklist contains only one stage, namely an inductive Presburger overapproximation $PotReach(I_1)$ (for "potentially reachable") of the configurations reachable from I_1. The procedure computing $PotReach(I_1)$ is the result of many years of research on tractable "relaxations" of the reachability relation of Petri nets [13, 20, 34, 35, 39].

In its main loop, PEREGRINE 2.0 repeatedly picks a Presburger stage S from the worklist, and processes it. First, the tool checks whether S is terminal, i.e., if all its configurations are a 1-consensus. (Since S is inductive by construction, an affirmative answer implies that all configurations of S are stable 1-consensuses.) Checking that every configuration of S is a 1-consensus reduces to checking unsatisfiability of a simple formula. If S is not terminal, the tool attempts to construct one or more successor stages with strictly more dead transitions than S. For this, the tool computes a set of *eventually dead transitions*: transitions that are alive at one or more configurations of S, but will become dead w.p.1 in any run starting at those configurations. Again, the procedure to compute U makes heavy use of results of Petri net theory [42], but also of the theory of well-quasi-orders [1, 38].

If PEREGRINE 2.0 finds a nonempty set of eventually dead transitions, then it constructs a successor stage of S by overapproximating the configurations reachable from S, underapproximating the configurations at which the transitions of U are dead, and intersecting the results. If PEREGRINE 2.0 fails to find eventually dead transitions, it heuristically splits S into different stages and adds them to the worklist to be processed. Indeed, it could be the case that no transition becomes eventually dead from *every* configuration of S, but this no longer holds after a split; for example, imagine that transition t_1 eventually becomes dead from every configuration of $S_1 \subset S$, and another transition t_2 becomes eventually dead from every configuration of $S_2 = S \setminus S_1$. In this case, after splitting S into S_1 and S_2 the tool can find nonempty sets of eventually dead transitions for both S_1 and S_2.

PEREGRINE 2.0 has successfully proved correct a large variety of protocols, including majority and approximate majority protocols (Example 2, [19, Ex. 3], [6, 21], [44, *coin game*], [49]), various *flock-of-birds* protocol families ([22], [16, Sect. 3], [23, *threshold-n*]) for the family of predicates $x \geq k$ for some constant $k \geq 0$; or protocols for threshold and remainder predicates of [7, 16]. For all these examples PEREGRINE 2.0 computes stage graphs with a few stages. Currently, the main limitation of the tool is the size of the systems of linear constraints involved, which limits the tool to protocols with up to some dozens of states and some thousands of transitions.

4   Succinct Predicates and State Complexity

After writing our first papers on the verification of population protocols, we observed that the theory of Petri nets was also relevant for a problem that, perhaps surprisingly, had not been studied yet: the *state complexity* of predicates decidable by population protocols. Informally, the state complexity of a predicate is the minimal number of states of the protocols that decide it, and, given a number η, one defines the function $STATE(\eta)$ as the maximum state state complexity of all predicates of size at most η. But what is the size of a predicate? This requires us to fix a representation. Since population protocols compute exactly the predicates expressible in Presburger arithmetic [11], we must choose a representation of the Presburger sets. There are three natural representations: formulas of Presburger arithmetic, quantifier-free formulas of Presburger arithmetic, and semilinear sets [41]. Semilinear sets are difficult to parse by humans, and no paper on population protocols uses them to describe predicates. Full Presburger arithmetic is very succinct, but the complexity of its satisfiability problem lies between 2-NEXP and 2-EXPSPACE [41], and so it can lead to results in which a predicate requires very few states, but only because of a representation that is very difficult to compute. This leaves quantifier-free Presburger arithmetic. This representation also has two advantages of its own. First, standard predicates for which numerous protocols have been given in the literature (like majority, threshold, or remainder predicates) are naturally expressed without quantifiers. Second, the procedures given so far to construct population protocols for any given Presburger predicate explicitly use the fact that Presburger arithmetic has a quantifier elimination procedure, i.e., they first construct protocols for all threshold and remainder predicates, and then show that the predicates computed by protocols are closed under negation and conjunction.

4.1   State Complexity: Upper Bounds

The first synthesis procedure for the construction of a protocol deciding a given Presburger predicate was presented in [9]. The procedure is simple and elegant, but it yields large protocols. Given a quantifier-free Presburger formula φ, i.e., a boolean combination of atomic formulas, the number of states of the synthesized protocol grows exponentially in both the number of bits of the largest coefficient of φ in absolute value, and the number of atomic formulas. In terms of $|\varphi|$ (defined as the number of bits needed to write φ, with coefficients written in binary) they have $\Omega(2^{\mathsf{poly}(|\varphi|)})$ states. This raises the question whether protocols with $O(\mathsf{poly}(|\varphi|))$ states, which we call *succinct*, exist. We gave an affirmative answer in [14], completing first partial results obtained in [16]. We describe how to avoid both exponential dependencies.

Handling Large Coefficients. In order to prevent having the exponential dependence on the coefficients, we design protocols for threshold and remainder predicates that, loosely speaking, represent numbers in binary. A very easy case is described in Example 1: the first predicate for $x - y \geq 2^k$ has $\Theta(2^k)$ states, because agents can hold any number of pebbles between 0 and 2^k, but the second has only $\Theta(k)$ states, because the number of pebbles is always a power of 2. The construction of [14] proceeds in two steps: first we construct a succinct protocol in which the agents are assisted by *helpers*, additional agents that are not part of the input, and initially occupy a distinguished state, say H; then we give an equivalent protocol without helpers. Helpers are similar to leaders, but with the property (guaranteed by the design of the protocol) that if the protocol works correctly with a certain number of helpers, then it also works correctly for any larger number. This property is crucial when dealing with boolean combinations.

Consider a predicate like $13x - 9y \geq 5$. Protocols for this predicate have two initial states, for x and y. Since $13 = 2^3 + 2^2 + 2^0$, the protocol has a transition that moves an agent in the initial state for x and two helpers into states 2^3, 2^2, and 2^0, respectively. (Transitions that move multiple agents to new states in one single step can be easily simulated by the usual protocol transitions with a very low cost in terms of states.) Similarly, another transition for each agent in the initial state for y, the protocol moves this agent and one helper into states -2^3 and -2^1. Pairs of agents in states 2^l and -2^l can "cancel", meaning that they both move to state H, and so become helpers ready to continue assisting.

In [14] we show that this idea can be applied to every threshold or remainder predicate, resulting in a succinct protocol with a *fixed* number of helpers, cubic in the size of the predicate, but independent of the size of the input. But how do we go from this protocol to another one without helpers? For large inputs in which the number of agents exceeds this number of helpers, we can let each agent take two jobs: act as a regular agent *and* a helper. Let us show how to do for h helpers. In a first phase, the protocol assigns to each agent a number between 1 and h, ensuring that each number is assigned to at least one agent (this is the point at which we need a sufficiently large input with at least h agents). More precisely, at the end of this phase each agent is in a state of the form (x, i), meaning that the agent initially represented one unit of input for variable x, and that it has been assigned number i. For this, initially every agent is placed in state $(x, 1)$. Transitions of the form $(x, i), (x, i) \mapsto (x, i + 1), (x, i)$ for every $1 \leq i \leq h - 1$ guarantee that all but one agent is promoted to $(x, 2)$, all but one to $(x, 3)$, etc. In other words, at each step one agent is "left behind", and so the protocol has at least h helpers.

However, the protocol must be correct for all inputs, not only for those with at least h agents. In [14] this is solved by designing a second family of protocols for small inputs, which works in a completely different way. It is then easy to combine the protocols for large and small inputs into a protocol for all inputs.

Handling Large Boolean Combinations of Atomic Formulas. The second problem of the synthesis procedure of [9] is the exponential dependence of the number of states on the number of atomic formulas. The dependence comes from the fact that, given protocols $\mathcal{P}_1, \ldots, \mathcal{P}_k$ with $n_1, \ldots, n_k$ states deciding formulas $\varphi_1, \ldots, \varphi_k$, respectively, the synthesis procedure yields a protocol $\mathcal{P}$ for deciding $\varphi_1 \wedge \cdots \wedge \varphi_k$ with $n_1 \cdot n_2 \cdot \ldots \cdot n_k$ states (and similarly for $\varphi_1 \vee \cdots \vee \varphi_k$). Intuitively, in $\mathcal{P}$ each agent carries out k jobs: act as an agent of $\mathcal{P}_1$, of $\mathcal{P}_2$, $\ldots$, and of $\mathcal{P}_k$. The state of an agent is a k-tuple of states of the $\mathcal{P}_1, \ldots, \mathcal{P}_k$, and when two agents meet, they compare their states in each protocol $\mathcal{P}_i$, and apply the corresponding transition. In other words: the new protocol executes all of $\mathcal{P}_1, \ldots, \mathcal{P}_k$ synchronously.

We need a new succinct construction for a boolean combination of atomic predicates with $O(n_1 + \cdots + n_k)$ instead of $\Omega(n_1 \cdot \ldots \cdot n_k)$ states. A naive first idea is to let $\mathcal{P}$ execute $\mathcal{P}_1, \ldots, \mathcal{P}_k$ asynchronously in parallel, instead of synchronously, and combine the results. However, this does not work. Assume $\varphi_1, \ldots, \varphi_k$ have arity m. In order to compute $(\varphi_1 \wedge \cdots \wedge \varphi_k)(\boldsymbol{x})$, where $\boldsymbol{x} = (x_1, \ldots, x_m)$, the protocol $\mathcal{P}$ would have to dispatch x agents to (the input states of) each $\mathcal{P}_i$, giving a total of $k \cdot x$ agents, but the protocol only has the agents of the input, i.e. x agents. But couldn't we use $(k-1) \cdot x$ helpers, and then obtain an equivalent protocol without helpers? No, this does not work either, because in this case the number of helpers depends on the size of the input, and the technique we used above only allows us to simulate a fixed number of helpers. The solution is to use a more sophisticated construction for parallel asynchronous computation. Again, we need to consider separately the cases of large and small inputs, but the former is more interesting, and so we only describe protocols for large inputs.

Given an arbitrary threshold or modulo predicate $\psi(\boldsymbol{x})$ of arity m, it is easy to construct a predicate $\widetilde{\psi}(\boldsymbol{y}, \boldsymbol{z})$ of arity $2m$ satisfying

$$\widetilde{\psi}(\boldsymbol{y}, \boldsymbol{z}) = \psi(k\boldsymbol{y} + \boldsymbol{z})$$

For instance, if $\psi(x_1, x_2) = (3x_1 - 2x_2 > 6)$ and $k = 4$, then we can choose $\widetilde{\psi}(y_1, y_2, z_1, z_2) = (12y_1 + 3z_1 - 8y_2 - 2z_2 > 6)$.

Intuitively, the idea is to let $\mathcal{P}$ compute $\widetilde{\varphi}_1(\boldsymbol{y}, \boldsymbol{z}), \ldots, \widetilde{\varphi}_k(\boldsymbol{y}, \boldsymbol{z})$ instead of $\varphi_1(\boldsymbol{x}), \ldots, \varphi_k(\boldsymbol{x})$ for some $\boldsymbol{y}$ and $\boldsymbol{z}$ satisfying $\boldsymbol{x} = k\boldsymbol{y} + \boldsymbol{z}$. Then $\mathcal{P}$ only needs to dispatch a total of

$$k \left(\sum_{i=1}^{m} y_i + z_i \right) = k \left(\sum_{i=1}^{m} y_i + (x_i - ky_i) \right) \leq \sum_{i=1}^{m} x_i + m \cdot (k-1)^2$$

agents to compute all of $\widetilde{\varphi}_1, \ldots, \widetilde{\varphi}_k$. So $\mathcal{P}$ only needs $m \cdot (k-1)^2$ helpers, a fixed number independent of the number of agents.

Let us now describe how $\mathcal{P}$ computes $\widetilde{\varphi}_i(\boldsymbol{y}, \boldsymbol{z})$ for some $\boldsymbol{y}$ and $\boldsymbol{z}$ satisfying $\boldsymbol{x} = k\boldsymbol{y} + \boldsymbol{z}$. Let $\widetilde{\mathcal{P}}_1, \ldots, \widetilde{\mathcal{P}}_k$ be protocols computing $\widetilde{\varphi}_1, \ldots, \widetilde{\varphi}_k$, let $x_1, \ldots, x_m$ be the input states of $\mathcal{P}$, and let $y_1^j, \ldots, y_m^j$ and $z_1^j, \ldots, z_m^j$ be the input states of $\widetilde{\mathcal{P}}_j$ for every $1 \leq j \leq k$. Protocol $\mathcal{P}$ repeatedly chooses an index $1 \leq i \leq m$, and executes one of these two actions, which can be implemented with some effort using only binary interactions: take k agents from x_i, and dispatch them to $y_i^1, \ldots, y_i^k$ (one agent to each state); or take one agent from x_i and $(k-1)$ helpers, and dispatch them to $z_i^1, \ldots, z_i^k$. If all agents of x_i are dispatched for every $1 \leq i \leq m$, then we say that the *dispatch is correct*. Observe that a correct dispatch satisfies $\boldsymbol{x} = k\boldsymbol{y} + \boldsymbol{z}$.

The problem is that the dispatch may or may not be correct. Assume, e.g., that $k = 5$ and $m = 1$. Consider the input $x_1 = 17$, and assume that $\mathcal{P}$ has $m \cdot (k-1)^2 = 16$ helpers. $\mathcal{P}$ may correctly dispatch $y_1 = 3$ agents to each of $y_1^1, \ldots, y_5^1$ and $z_1 = 2$ to each of $z_1^1, \ldots, z_5^1$; this gives a total of $(3 + 2) \cdot 5 = 25$ agents, consisting of the 17 agents for the input plus 8 helpers. However, it may also wrongly dispatch 2 agents to each y_i^1 and 4 agents to each z_i^1, with a total of $(2 + 4) \cdot 5 = 30$ agents, consisting of 14 input agents plus 16 helpers. In the second case, each $\mathcal{P}_j$ wrongly computes $\widetilde{\varphi}_j(2, 4) = \varphi_j(2 \cdot 5 + 4) = \varphi_j(14)$, instead of the correct value $\varphi_j(17)$.

To solve this problem we ensure that $\mathcal{P}$ can always recall agents already dispatched to $\widetilde{\mathcal{P}}_1, \ldots, \widetilde{\mathcal{P}}_k$ as long as the dispatch is not yet correct. This allows

$\mathcal{P}$ to "try out" dispatches until it dispatches correctly, which happens eventually w.p.1. For this we design $\mathcal{P}$ so that the atomic protocols $\widetilde{\mathcal{P}}_1, \ldots, \widetilde{\mathcal{P}}_k$ can work with agents that arrive to the initial states over time (*dynamic initialization*), and can always return to their initial states and go back to $\mathcal{P}$, unless the dispatch is correct (*reversibility*). To ensure that $\mathcal{P}$ stops recalling agents after a correct dispatch, we modify the dispatch transitions so that they become disabled when $x_1, \ldots, x_m$ are not populated.

4.2   State Complexity: Lower Bounds

In [16,24] we have also studied the problem of obtaining lower bounds for $STATE(\eta)$. This question turns out be surprisingly hard, and so we have focused on obtain lower bounds for the state complexity of a particularly simple family of predicates, namely those of of the form $x \geq k$. This amounts to finding a lower bound for the number n of states needed to decide $x \geq k$, or, equivalently, an upper bound for the largest number k such that $x \geq k$ can be decided by a protocol with n states. We prefer the latter formulation due to its analogy with the busy beaver function. Recall that the busy beaver function assigns to a number n the largest η such that a Turing machine with at most n states, started on a blank tape, writes η consecutive 1s on the tape and halts. Analogously, the busy beaver function for population protocols assigns to n the largest η such that a population protocol with at most n states decides the predicate $x \geq \eta$. Intuitively, η is the largest number "recognizable" by protocols with at most n states.

We have obtained results for protocols with and without leaders. It is known that the time complexity of predicates is different for population protocols with and without leaders: While the first can decide any Presburger predicate in polylogarithmic parallel time [10], the latter need linear parallel time for majority [4]. Is the same true for state complexity? The question is still open, but we have made some progress.

Let $BB, BB_L \colon \mathbb{N} \to \mathbb{N}$ be the busy beaver functions for leaderless protocols and for protocols with leaders, respectively. A protocol similar to the second one of Example 1, only simpler, decides $x \geq 2^n$ with $O(n)$ states, showing that $BB(n) \in \Omega(2^n)$. In [16] we prove $BB_L(n) \in \Omega(2^{2^n})$. This result is quite surprising: for certain numbers k, there are population protocols that decide $x \geq k$ even though an agent does not have enough memory to index even one bit of k. The proof follows from a theorem by Mayr and Meyer on presentations of commutative semigroups [48], which can be reformulated in protocol terms as follows: for every $n \geq 1$, there exists a protocol with $O(n)$ states and three distinguished states *start, end, counter* such that from an initial configuration that puts one agent in *start* and k agents in *counter*, respectively, it is possible to reach a configuration putting at least one agent in state *end* if and only if $k \geq 2^{2^n}$. By adding transitions that allow an agent in state *end* to attract all other agents to *end*, it is easy to obtain a protocol deciding $x \geq 2^{2^n}$.

Can we also obtain upper bounds on $BB(n)$ and $BB_L(n)$, and so lower bounds on the state complexity? After some years investigating this question without progress, we have recently made a breakthrough [24]. Our first result is that $BB_L(n)$ is bounded by a variant of the Ackermann function. The result is proved by means of a pumping technique. We first show that if a protocol with n states answers 0 for two inputs $a < b$ satisfying certain conditions, then it also answers 0 for every input $a + \lambda(b - a)$, and so the protocol cannot compute any predicate of the form $x \geq \eta$. Then we find a function $F(n)$ such that if a protocol with at most n states rejects all inputs with at most $F(n)$ agents, then there are inputs $a < b < F(n)$ satisfying the conditions. The function is obtained using results from the theory of controlled sequences, an area of mathematics related to well-quasi-orders [2, 12, 37].

An Ackermannian upper bound may seem extremely weak. However, it follows from recent results in the theory of Petri nets that functions similar to $BB_L(n)$ have an Ackermannian *lower* bound. To give an example, say that a protocol *weakly decides* the predicate $x \geq k$ if the following holds: for every initial configuration with at least k agents there exists a run leading to a configuration with consensus 1; for every initial configuration with less than k agents, no such configuration is reachable. Then the largest k such that $x \geq k$ is weakly computable with n states is an Ackermannian function of n.

The main result of [24] is a triple exponential bound on $BB(n)$. That is, leaderless protocols with at most n states can recognize numbers at most triple exponential in n. The proof technique is again a pumping lemma. The key property of leaderless protocols that we use to obtain an elementary bound is that, loosely speaking, the set of initial configurations of a leaderless protocol is closed under addition. To understand this, observe that initial configurations of a leaderless protocol deciding $x \geq k$ put k agents in the initial state and 0 agents in all others. Therefore, the sum of two initial configurations with k_1 and k_2 agents is the initial configuration with $k_1 + k_2$ agents. This does no longer hold for protocols with a leader, whose initial configurations also put one agent in the initial state of the leader; in this case, the sum of two initial configurations with a leader is a configuration with *two* leaders.

In an unpublished result obtained together with Jérôme Leroux, we have improved the bound for leaderless protocols to double exponential; we conjecture that the optimal upper bound is single exponential, matching the lower bound. But currently we do not even have a line of attack to obtain an elementary bound for protocols with a leader.

5   Conclusions and Future Work

We have surveyed our recent work on the verification of population protocols, and on their state complexity. This work has produced PEREGRINE, the first automatic tool able to verify correctness of protocols for all inputs. In the verification area, there are many open directions for future work:

- Protocols are often designed parametrically, for example, one gives a construction that yields a protocol deciding $ax - by \geq c$ for arbitrary coefficients a, b, c. Our methods cannot yet prove that the construction is correct for every

a, b, c. It is easy to show that verifying infinite families of protocols is an undecidable problem, even for very restricted cases, but it should be possible to design procedures that perform well in practice.

- As mentioned in the introduction, in the last years families of protocols that decide one single predicate, but where the number of states increases with the number of agents, have been intensely investigated, see e.g. [5,27]. Again, we do not have any verification technique for them.
- The work initiated in [19] on the automatic verification of the expected runtime of a protocol is still in its infancy.

Our work on the state complexity problem is tightly linked to difficult problems of the theory of Petri nets. The obvious future direction is closing the current gaps between the upper and lower bounds for the busy beaver functions in the leaderless case, and the case with leaders. We consider this a fundamental problem in the theory of population protocols. Intuitively, it measures quantitatively the relation between the microscopic scale of agents and the macroscopic scale of the predicates they decide.

References

1. Abdulla, P.A., Cerans, K., Jonsson, B., Tsay, Y.: General decidability theorems for infinite-state systems. In: LICS, pp. 313–321. IEEE Computer Society (1996)
2. Abriola, S., Figueira, S., Senno, G.: Linearizing well quasi-orders and bounding the length of bad sequences. Theor. Comput. Sci. **603**, 3–22 (2015)
3. Alistarh, D., Aspnes, J., Eisenstat, D., Gelashvili, R., Rivest, R.L.: Time-space trade-offs in population protocols. In: SODA, pp. 2560–2579. SIAM (2017)
4. Alistarh, D., Aspnes, J., Gelashvili, R.: Space-optimal majority in population protocols. In: SODA, pp. 2221–2239. SIAM (2018)
5. Alistarh, D., Gelashvili, R.: Recent algorithmic advances in population protocols. SIGACT News **49**(3), 63–73 (2018)
6. Alistarh, D., Gelashvili, R., Vojnovic, M.: Fast and exact majority in population protocols. In: PODC, pp. 47–56. ACM (2015)
7. Angluin, D., Aspnes, J., Diamadi, Z., Fischer, M.J., Peralta, R.: Computation in networks of passively mobile finite-state sensors. In: PODC, pp. 290–299. ACM (2004)
8. Angluin, D., Aspnes, J., Diamadi, Z., Fischer, M.J., Peralta, R.: Computation in networks of passively mobile finite-state sensors. Distrib. Comput. **18**(4), 235–253 (2006)
9. Angluin, D., Aspnes, J., Eisenstat, D.: Stably computable predicates are semilinear. In: PODC, pp. 292–299. ACM (2006)
10. Angluin, D., Aspnes, J., Eisenstat, D.: Fast computation by population protocols with a leader. Distrib. Comput. **21**(3), 183–199 (2008)
11. Angluin, D., Aspnes, J., Eisenstat, D., Ruppert, E.: The computational power of population protocols. Distrib. Comput. **20**(4), 279–304 (2007)
12. Balasubramanian, A.R.: Complexity of controlled bad sequences over finite sets of $\mathbb{N}^d$. In: LICS, pp. 130–140. ACM (2020)
13. Blondin, M.: The ABCs of Petri net reachability relaxations. ACM SIGLOG News **7**(3), 29–43 (2020)

14. Blondin, M., Esparza, J., Genest, B., Helfrich, M., Jaax, S.: Succinct population protocols for presburger arithmetic. In: STACS. LIPIcs, vol. 154, pp. 40:1–40:15. Schloss Dagstuhl - Leibniz-Zentrum für Informatik (2020)
15. Blondin, M., Esparza, J., Helfrich, M., Kučera, A., Meyer, P.J.: Checking qualitative liveness properties of replicated systems with stochastic scheduling. In: Lahiri, S.K., Wang, C. (eds.) CAV 2020. LNCS, vol. 12225, pp. 372–397. Springer, Cham (2020). https://doi.org/10.1007/978-3-030-53291-8_20
16. Blondin, M., Esparza, J., Jaax, S.: Large flocks of small birds: on the minimal size of population protocols. In: STACS. LIPIcs, vol. 96, pp. 16:1–16:14. Schloss Dagstuhl - Leibniz-Zentrum für Informatik (2018)
17. Blondin, M., Esparza, J., Jaax, S.: Peregrine: a tool for the analysis of population protocols. In: Chockler, H., Weissenbacher, G. (eds.) CAV 2018. LNCS, vol. 10981, pp. 604–611. Springer, Cham (2018). https://doi.org/10.1007/978-3-319-96145-3_34
18. Blondin, M., Esparza, J., Jaax, S., Meyer, P.J.: Towards efficient verification of population protocols. In: PODC, pp. 423–430. ACM (2017)
19. Blondin, M., Esparza, J., Kucera, A.: Automatic analysis of expected termination time for population protocols. In: CONCUR. LIPIcs, vol. 118, pp. 33:1–33:16. Schloss Dagstuhl - Leibniz-Zentrum für Informatik (2018)
20. Blondin, M., Finkel, A., Haase, C., Haddad, S.: The logical view on continuous Petri nets. ACM Trans. Comput. Log. (TOCL) 18(3), 24:1–24:28 (2017)
21. Cardelli, L., Csikász-Nagy, A.: The cell cycle switch computes approximate majority. Sci. Rep. 2(1), 656 (2012)
22. Chatzigiannakis, I., Michail, O., Spirakis, P.G.: Algorithmic verification of population protocols. In: Dolev, S., Cobb, J., Fischer, M., Yung, M. (eds.) SSS 2010. LNCS, vol. 6366, pp. 221–235. Springer, Heidelberg (2010). https://doi.org/10.1007/978-3-642-16023-3_19
23. Clément, J., Delporte-Gallet, C., Fauconnier, H., Sighireanu, M.: Guidelines for the verification of population protocols. In: ICDCS, pp. 215–224. IEEE Computer Society (2011)
24. Czerner, P., Esparza, J.: Lower bounds on the state complexity of population protocols. In: PODC, pp. 45–54. ACM (2021)
25. Czerwinski, W., Lasota, S., Lazic, R., Leroux, J., Mazowiecki, F.: The reachability problem for Petri nets is not elementary. J. ACM 68(1), 7:1–7:28 (2021)
26. Czerwinski, W., Orlikowski, L.: Reachability in vector addition systems is Ackermann-complete. CoRR abs/2104.13866 (2021)
27. Elsässer, R., Radzik, T.: Recent results in population protocols for exact majority and leader election. Bull. EATCS 126, 32–64 (2018)
28. Esparza, J.: Advances in parameterized verification of population protocols. In: Weil, P. (ed.) CSR 2017. LNCS, vol. 10304, pp. 7–14. Springer, Cham (2017). https://doi.org/10.1007/978-3-319-58747-9_2
29. Esparza, J., Gaiser, A., Kiefer, S.: Proving termination of probabilistic programs using patterns. In: Madhusudan, P., Seshia, S.A. (eds.) CAV 2012. LNCS, vol. 7358, pp. 123–138. Springer, Heidelberg (2012). https://doi.org/10.1007/978-3-642-31424-7_14
30. Esparza, J., Ganty, P., Leroux, J., Majumdar, R.: Model checking population protocols. In: FSTTCS. LIPIcs, vol. 65, pp. 27:1–27:14. Schloss Dagstuhl - Leibniz-Zentrum für Informatik (2016)
31. Esparza, J., Ganty, P., Leroux, J., Majumdar, R.: Verification of population protocols. Acta Inf. 54(2), 191–215 (2016). https://doi.org/10.1007/s00236-016-0272-3

32. Esparza, J., Helfrich, M., Jaax, S., Meyer, P.J.: Peregrine 2.0: explaining correctness of population protocols through stage graphs. In: Hung, D.V., Sokolsky, O. (eds.) ATVA 2020. LNCS, vol. 12302, pp. 550–556. Springer, Cham (2020). https://doi.org/10.1007/978-3-030-59152-6_32

33. Esparza, J., Jaax, S., Raskin, M., Weil-Kennedy, C.: The complexity of verifying population protocols. Distrib. Comput. **34**(2), 133–177 (2021). https://doi.org/10.1007/s00446-021-00390-x

34. Esparza, J., Ledesma-Garza, R., Majumdar, R., Meyer, P., Niksic, F.: An SMT-based approach to coverability analysis. In: Biere, A., Bloem, R. (eds.) CAV 2014. LNCS, vol. 8559, pp. 603–619. Springer, Cham (2014). https://doi.org/10.1007/978-3-319-08867-9_40

35. Esparza, J., Melzer, S.: Verification of safety properties using integer programming: beyond the state equation. Formal Methods Syst. Des. **16**(2), 159–189 (2000)

36. Esparza, J., Raskin, M., Weil-Kennedy, C.: Parameterized analysis of immediate observation Petri nets. In: Donatelli, S., Haar, S. (eds.) PETRI NETS 2019. LNCS, vol. 11522, pp. 365–385. Springer, Cham (2019). https://doi.org/10.1007/978-3-030-21571-2_20

37. Figueira, D., Figueira, S., Schmitz, S., Schnoebelen, P.: Ackermannian and primitive-recursive bounds with Dickson's lemma. In: LICS, pp. 269–278. IEEE Computer Society (2011)

38. Finkel, A., Schnoebelen, P.: Well-structured transition systems everywhere! Theoret. Comput. Sci. **256**(1–2), 63–92 (2001)

39. Fraca, E., Haddad, S.: Complexity analysis of continuous Petri nets. Fundam. Inf. **137**(1), 1–28 (2015)

40. Gasieniec, L., Stachowiak, G.: Enhanced phase clocks, population protocols, and fast space optimal leader election. J. ACM **68**(1), 2:1–2:21 (2021)

41. Haase, C.: A survival guide to Presburger arithmetic. SIGLOG News **5**(3), 67–82 (2018)

42. Jancar, P., Purser, D.: Structural liveness of Petri nets is EXPSPACE-hard and decidable. Acta Inf. **56**(6), 537–552 (2019)

43. Kosaraju, S.R.: Decidability of reachability in vector addition systems (preliminary version). In: STOC, pp. 267–281. ACM (1982)

44. Lengál, O., Lin, A.W., Majumdar, R., Rümmer, P.: Fair termination for parameterized probabilistic concurrent systems. In: Legay, A., Margaria, T. (eds.) TACAS 2017. LNCS, vol. 10205, pp. 499–517. Springer, Heidelberg (2017). https://doi.org/10.1007/978-3-662-54577-5_29

45. Leroux, J.: Vector addition systems reachability problem (a simpler solution). In: Turing-100. EPiC Series in Computing, vol. 10, pp. 214–228. EasyChair (2012)

46. Leroux, J.: The reachability problem for Petri nets is not primitive recursive. CoRR abs/2104.12695 (2021)

47. Mayr, E.W.: An algorithm for the general Petri net reachability problem. In: STOC, pp. 238–246. ACM (1981)

48. Meyer, E.W., Meyer, A.R.: The complexity of the word problems for commutative semigroups and polynomial ideals. Adv. Math. **46**(3), 305–329 (1982)

49. Moran, P.A.P.: Random processes in genetics. Math. Proc. Camb. Philos. Soc. **54**(1), 60–71 (1958)

50. de Moura, L., Bjørner, N.: Z3: an efficient SMT solver. In: Ramakrishnan, C.R., Rehof, J. (eds.) TACAS 2008. LNCS, vol. 4963, pp. 337–340. Springer, Heidelberg (2008). https://doi.org/10.1007/978-3-540-78800-3_24

51. Murata, T.: Petri nets: properties, analysis and applications. Proc. IEEE **77**(4), 541–580 (1989)

52. Reisig, W.: Petri Nets: An introduction. EATCS Monographs on Theoretical Computer Science, vol. 4. Springer, Heidelberg (1985). https://doi.org/10.1007/978-3-642-69968-9

53. Soloveichik, D., Cook, M., Winfree, E., Bruck, J.: Computation with finite stochastic chemical reaction networks. Nat. Comput. **7**(4), 615–633 (2008)

Recent Advances on Reachability Problems for Valence Systems (Invited Talk)

Georg Zetzsche[✉] [ID]

Max Planck Institute for Software Systems (MPI-SWS), Saarbrücken, Germany
georg@mpi-sws.org

Abstract. Valence systems are an abstract model of computation that consists of a finite-state control and some storage mechanism. In contrast to traditional models, the storage mechanism is not fixed, but given as a parameter. This allows us to precisely state questions like: For which storage mechanisms is the reachability problem decidable?

This survey reports on recent results that aim to understand the impact of the storage mechanism on decidability and complexity of several variants of the reachability problem. The considered problems are configuration reachability, model-checking first-order logic with reachability, and reachability under bounded context switching and scope-boundedness.

1 Introduction

Reachability problems play a central role in automata theory, particularly in applications to verification. The most prominent example is safety verification, where we have some system model and we want to establish algorithmically that in this model it is not possible to reach certain undesirable configurations.

Therefore, during the last few decades, an extensive research effort has aimed to understand, for various kinds of abstract system models, whether reachability is decidable and with which computational complexity. Many of the results in this space consider abstract system models that consist of some *finite-state control* and some *storage mechanism*. This is because when we want to verify a particular program, the finite-state control allows us to describe the control flow of the program, whereas the storage mechanism can be used to store memory contents.

Well-known examples of such models are *vector addition systems with states (VASS)* and *pushdown systems*. In a VASS, the storage mechanism consists of several $\mathbb{N}$-counters: These assume values in the natural numbers that can be *incremented* and *decremented* (but not tested for zero). In a pushdown system, the storage consists of a stack that can be manipulated with *push* and *pop* instructions. In addition to these basic types of storage mechanisms, there exists a rich variety of extensions both of $\mathbb{N}$-counters (resets [7,11], transfers [11], lossiness [24], just to name a few) and of pushdowns (e.g. higher-order stacks [28], additional counters [15,21], etc.).

© The Author(s) 2021
P. C. Bell et al. (Eds.): RP 2021, LNCS 13035, pp. 52–65, 2021.
https://doi.org/10.1007/978-3-030-89716-1_4

A large part of the questions studied in this space are of the following form: For a concrete storage mechanism, is a certain reachability problem decidable, and if so, what is the complexity?

This survey presents a line of work that takes a slightly different perspective. Instead of studying concrete storage mechanisms, can we obtain general insights into how the structure of the storage mechanism impacts decidability and complexity of reachability problems? To this end, one considers an abstract model in which the storage mechanism appears as a parameter. Then, one can ask: For which storage mechanism is a particular problem decidable, tractable, etc.?

A Too General Question. To set the stage, we start with a question that is likely too general to answer. Suppose we have a storage mechanism whose (finite) set of instructions is an alphabet X. The set of all sequences of instructions that bring the storage into an accepting configurations is a language $L \subseteq X^*$. We consider the following decision problem REACH(L):

Given A regular language $R \subseteq X^*$.
Question Is $R \cap L$ non-empty?

For example, suppose $X_d = \{a_1, \ldots, a_d, \bar{a}_1, \ldots, \bar{a}_d\}$ and let $V_d \subseteq X_d^*$ be the set of all words where for every i: (1) there are just as many a_i as $\bar{a}_i$ and (2) in every prefix, there are at least as many a_i as there are $\bar{a}_i$. Then, REACH(V_d) is just the reachability problem in d-dimensional VASS.

Another example is the language $d_2 \subseteq X_2$, where $w \in P_d$ if and only if w can be obtained from the empty word by repeatedly inserting the words $a_i \bar{a}_i$ with $i \in \{1, \ldots, d\}$. Then, REACH(P_d) is just the reachability problem (of the empty-stack configuration) for pushdown systems with d stack symbols.

Furthermore, suppose $Z_d \subseteq X_d^*$ is the set of words that contain, for each i, the same number of a_i as $\bar{a}_i$. Then REACH(Z_d) is the reachability problem for automata with d separate $\mathbb{Z}$-counters, which can assume values in $\mathbb{Z}$ and have to be zero in the end. This corresponds to the model of $\mathbb{Z}$-VASS [13] (which are also known as blind counter automata [12] and are in most contexts equivalent to reversal bounded counter machines [16]).

This raises the following question:

Question 1.1. *For which languages L is* REACH(L) *decidable?*

Of course, understanding this would be extremely useful for designing abstract system models for reasoning about programs. Unfortunately, Question 1.1 currently appears out of reach. In fact, it even seems unlikely that there exists an illuminating characterization.

However, there is a more restricted setting that still covers many storage mechanisms from the literature and, as it turned out during the last few years, several variants of the reachability problem admit simple characterizations in terms of decidability and complexity.

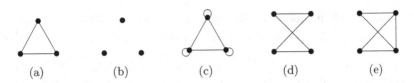

Fig. 1. Example graphs

Graphs. In this setting, the storage mechanism is defined by an undirected graph $\Gamma = (V, E)$ where self-loops are allowed. Hence, V is a finite set of *vertices* and $E \subseteq \{e \subseteq V \mid 1 \le |e| \le 2\}$ is its set of *edges*. A vertex v is *looped* if $\{v\} \in E$, otherwise it is *unlooped*. We say that Γ is a *clique* if there is an edge between any two distinct vertices. A graph is *looped* (*unlooped*) if all its vertices are looped (unlooped). A graph $\Gamma_0 = (V_0, E_0)$ is an *induced subgraph* of $\Gamma_1 = (V_1, E_1)$ if Γ_0 is isomorphic to a restriction of Γ_1 onto some vertex set. Formally, this means there there is an injective map $f\colon V_0 \to V_1$ such that for $u, v \in V_0$, we have $\{f(u), f(v)\} \in E_1$ if and only if $\{u, v\} \in E_0$.

To a graph Γ, we associate the alphabet $X_\Gamma = \{v, \bar{v} \mid v \in V\}$, which we think of as a set of instructions as above. Intuitively, $\bar{v}$ will be the inverse instruction of v, as in the examples above. Moreover, the edges of Γ tell us whether the respective instructions should commute. Thus, we obtain a rewriting relation $\twoheadrightarrow$ on the set of words X_Γ^*:

$$rv\bar{v}s \twoheadrightarrow rs \qquad \text{for } r, s \in X_\Gamma^* \text{ and } v \in V, \text{ and} \tag{R1}$$

$$rxys \twoheadrightarrow ryxs \quad \text{for } r, s \in X_\Gamma^* \text{ and } x \in \{u, \bar{u}\},\ y \in \{v, \bar{v}\},\ \{u, v\} \in E \tag{R2}$$

In particular, if v has a self-loop ($\{v\} \in E$), then we have $r\bar{v}vs \twoheadrightarrow rv\bar{v}s \twoheadrightarrow rs$.

This allows us to define a language that can play a similar role as the languages above:

$$L(\Gamma) = \{w \in X_\Gamma^* \mid w \overset{*}{\twoheadrightarrow} \varepsilon\},$$

where $\varepsilon \in X_\Gamma^*$ is the empty word and $\overset{*}{\twoheadrightarrow}$ is the reflexive transitive closure of $\twoheadrightarrow$.

Examples. Let us see how to realize storage mechanisms with graphs. If Γ is one of the graphs from Figs. 1a to 1c, then, up to renaming letters, $L(\Gamma)$ is V_3, P_3, or Z_3 from above.

If Γ is the graph from Fig. 1d, then $L(\Gamma)$ is the language corresponding to two pushdowns. This is because the vertices on the left together behave like one pushdown; the same is true for the two vertices on the right. Moreover, Γ has an edge from any left vertex to any right vertex. Hence, these two pushdowns can be used independently. It is well-known that such systems can simulate Turing machines, so that the reachability problem is undecidable.

Let Γ be the graph from Fig. 1e. The two vertices on the left together realize a pushdown (with two stack symbols). The two vertices on the right are adjacent and thus behave like two $\mathbb{N}$-counters. Furthermore, as in Fig. 1d, there are edges everywhere from left to right. Thus, Γ realizes a storage consisting of one pushdown and two $\mathbb{N}$-counters. Thus, we have a two-dimensional pushdown VASS [21].

Suppose Γ is the *direct product* of graphs Γ_1 and Γ_2. This means, Γ is obtained from the disjoint union of Γ_1 and Γ_2 by adding an edge from every vertex of Γ_1 to every vertex of Γ_2. Then Γ realizes a storage mechanism that consists of both the storage mechanisms of Γ_1 and Γ_2, and they can be used independently. An instance of this which will be used frequently is that of *adding an $\mathbb{N}$-counter* or *adding a $\mathbb{Z}$-counter*. This means, we take the direct product with an unlooped (resp. looped) vertex.

If Γ is obtained from Γ_0 by adding an isolated vertex v with no self-loop, then Γ behaves like a stack whose entries are configurations of the storage mechanism of Γ_0. Hence, with Γ, we have the instructions of Γ_0, which act on the top-most entry in the stack. Moreover, using v, we can start a new stack entry. With $\bar{v}$, we pop the top-most entry. The latter can only succeed if the top-most entry (which is a configuration of Γ_0) is final according to Γ_0. Thus, we think of the storage mechanism of Γ as obtained from that of Γ_0 by *building stacks*.

Valence Systems. Given a graph $\Gamma = (V, E)$, we can now define a formal machine model that uses Γ as its storage mechanism. A *valence system over Γ* is a pair $\mathcal{A} = (Q, T)$, where Q is a finite set of *states* and $T \subseteq Q \times X_\Gamma \times Q$ is its set of *transitions*. A *pre-configuration* of $\mathcal{A}$ is a pair (q, w) with $q \in Q$ and $w \in X_\Gamma^*$. Then (q, w) can *reach* (q', w') *in one step* if there is a transition (q, u, q') with $w' = wu$. In this case, we write $(q, w) \to (q', w')$.

The *reachability problem for valence systems over Γ*, short REACH(Γ) is the following:

Given A valence system $\mathcal{A} = (Q, T)$ over Γ and states $s, t \in Q$

Question Is there some $w \in X_\Gamma^*$ such that $(s, \varepsilon) \xrightarrow{*} (t, w)$ with $w \xrightarrow{*} \varepsilon$?

Now clearly, REACH(Γ) is essentially the same as REACH($L(\Gamma)$). This allows us to formulate a more manageable version of Question 1.1:

Question 1.2. *For which graphs Γ is REACH(Γ) decidable?*

This question is clearly much more restricted in scope than Question 1.1. Therefore, there is hope that we can understand this class of graphs. And in fact, while Question 1.2 is still not settled, at least a partial answer is available (see Theorem 2.1).

Outline. This survey reports on results about variations of Question 1.2. In other words, we focus on decidability and complexity results concerning reachability-type problems for valence systems. In Sect. 2, we consider Question 1.2 itself. In Sect. 3, we turn to the complexity of REACH(Γ) depending on Γ. In Sect. 4, we look at a harder problem, namely model-checking first-order logic with a reachability predicate for the configuration space of a valence system. Finally, in Sects. 5 and 6, we consider underapproximations of the set of all runs in which reachability is decidable for every Γ.

Historical Notes. Some remarks on the history of the notion of valence systems are in order. The origin of this concept is the idea to study finite automata in which each edge is labeled (in addition to some input) by an element of a (typically infinite) monoid. This type of model has been studied under various names by several authors, either defining acceptance by producing the identity element of the monoid [10, 17–19, 26] or a prescribed target set [33]. The earliest (although implicit) use of this is probably the Chomsky-Schützenberger theorem, stating that every context-free language can be obtained using a rational transduction from the word problem of the free group [2]. The term *valence automaton* (and thus valence system) originates from the theory of regulated rewriting (see [5] for a general overview), where it was first used for *valence grammars* [29], in which each grammar rule has an associated monoid element. Afterwards, the term was also applied to automata (e.g. in [10]).

The graphs Γ above, together with their interpretation as storage mechanisms, were introduced in [36] and used there to define monoids, which were then used in valence automata. For this survey, it turned out that avoiding the terminology of monoids simplified the exposition.

2 Reachability

We begin with the partial answer that exists for Question 1.2. As we have seen in the examples above (Fig. 1e), there are graphs that realize the storage mechanism of a pushdown with additional $\mathbb{N}$-counters. Systems with such a storage are called *pushdown VASS (PVASS)* in the literature [8, 21]. Whether reachability is decidable for these is a long-standing open problem in the area of infinite-state systems [8, 21]. In fact, even for PVASS with a single counter (i.e. one-dimensional PVASS), the decidability status is open. Thus, determining the decidability status of REACH for the graph •——•——• would amount to a solution to this problem. Aside from this, there are two other graphs that realize a one-dimensional PVASS: We say that Γ is a *PVASS-graph* if it is isomorphic to one of the following three graphs:

The fact that the left and the middle graph represent a (one-dimensional) PVASS can be seen as for Fig. 1e. For the graph on the right, this follows from the classical Chomsky-Schützenberger theorem [2, 18].

We say that the graph Γ is *PVASS-free* if it has no PVASS-graph as an induced subgraph. Observe that a graph Γ is PVASS-free if and only if in the neighborhood of each unlooped vertex, any two vertices are adjacent.

To state the result, we need a further notion. We define the class of *transitive forests* inductively. First, every isolated vertex is a transitive forest. Moreover, if Γ_1 and Γ_2 are transitive forests, then (i) the disjoint union of Γ_1 and Γ_2 is a transitive forest and (ii) if Γ is the graph obtained by adding one vertex v to Γ_1 so that v is adjacent to every vertex in Γ_1, then Γ is also a transitive forest.

We are now ready to state the partial answer to Question 1.2.

Theorem 2.1 ([38]). *Let Γ be PVASS-free. Then* REACH(Γ) *is decidable if and only if Γ is a transitive forest.*

By $\mathsf{SC}^{\pm}$, we denote the class of PVASS-free transitive forests. Intuitively, the storage mechanisms in $\mathsf{SC}^{\pm}$ are obtained as follows. In the simplest case, they are unlooped cliques (hence a set of $\mathbb{N}$-counters). In addition to this, we can *build stacks* and *add $\mathbb{Z}$-counters*. In this notation, "$\pm$" stands for the two types of counters: We start with $\mathbb{N}$-counters ($+$), but after building stacks once, we can then only add $\mathbb{Z}$-counters ($-$).

In contrast, let SC^{+} consist of all graphs that are transitive forests and contain a PVASS-graph. One can show that if Γ is not a transitive forest, then REACH(Γ) is undecidable [38]. Thus, SC^{+} is the class of graphs for which decidability remains open. Intuitively, the corresponding storage mechanisms are obtained by starting with a set of $\mathbb{N}$-counters and then alternating (1) building stacks and (2) adding $\mathbb{N}$-counters.

Open Problem 2.2. *Is* REACH(Γ) *decidable for every Γ in* SC^{+}?

Of course, the simplest case of Open Problem 2.2 is the reachability problem in one-dimensional PVASS.

3   Complexity

Let us now turn to the complexity of REACH(Γ). What we know so far is confined to the class SC^{-}, which consists of all graphs in $\mathsf{SC}^{\pm}$ that do not have ●——● as an induced subgraph. Hence, intuitively, the corresponding storage mechanisms are obtained by starting from a pushdown and then alternating (1) adding $\mathbb{Z}$-counters and (2) building stacks. (Thus, they are the same as $\mathsf{SC}^{\pm}$, but all the counters are $\mathbb{Z}$-counters, which explains the "$-$".) This is an important subclass, because according to a characterization in [1], these are exactly those graphs for which valence automata (i.e. valence systems that can read input and accept languages) have semilinear Parikh images.

Among the graphs in SC^{-}, the complexity landscape is understood.

Theorem 3.1 ([14]). *Let Γ be a graph in* SC^{-}. *Then* REACH(Γ) *is*

1. *NL-complete if Γ is a looped clique.*
2. *P-complete if Γ is a disjoint union of at least two cliques, and*
3. *NP-complete otherwise.*

Strictly speaking, the proof in [14] is only about the case where Γ has a self-loop on every vertex (in this case, REACH(Γ) is the rational subset membership problem for graph groups, see also [22]). However, the proof works essentially the same for all of SC⁻. Moreover, it follows from [14] that if the graph Γ is part of the input, then reachability is NEXP-complete. In order to show these results, the paper [14] introduces an extension of existential Presburger arithmetic inspired by [30] and determines its complexity.

However, the complexity of reachability for the graphs in SC± is far from being understood.

Open Problem 3.2. *Describe the complexity landscape of* REACH *for the graphs in* SC±.

Until a few years ago, Open Problem 3.2 seemed out of reach. However, given the recent stunning resolution of the complexity of reachability in VASS [3,4,20] and the fact that decidability for SC± is shown in [38] using a reduction to reachability in VASS with nested zero tests, there is hope to obtain new insights into Open Problem 3.2.

4   First-Order Logic with Reachability

We now consider a decision problem that is computationally significantly harder than traditional reachability. Instead of asking whether a particular configuration can reach another, we want to decide a given first-order sentence that can mention configurations and express reachability (either in a single step or in a finite run).

Configuration Graphs of Valence Systems. Let us make this precise. With a valence system $\mathcal{A} = (Q, T)$ over a graph $\Gamma = (V, E)$ we define its configuration space as follows. Its universe consists of the configurations of $\mathcal{A}$, which we define next. It is not appropriate to define pre-configurations (recall that those are pairs $(q, w) \in Q \times X_\Gamma^*$) as elements of the configuration space. This is because, in all the examples mentioned above, the configurations of the realized storage mechanism correspond rather to certain equivalence classes of words in X_Γ^*. For example, if Γ is the graph in Fig. 1a, the set of configurations should be $Q \times \mathbb{N} \times \mathbb{N} \times \mathbb{N}$ and if Γ is the graph in Fig. 1b with vertices a, b, c, then the configuration graph should be $Q \times \{a, b, c\}^*$. In general, the equivalence relation is given by the rewriting relation $\rightarrowtail$. We define the equivalence relation $\equiv$ to be the reflexive, symmetric, and transitive closure of $\rightarrowtail$. It is not difficult to show that then we have $w \equiv \varepsilon$ if and only if $w \overset{*}{\rightarrowtail} \varepsilon$ (this is because $\rightarrowtail$ is terminating and confluent, see [37, Equation (8.2)]). The equivalence class of $w \in X_\Gamma^*$ is denoted $[w]$. We shall define configurations of $\mathcal{A}$ as certain equivalence classes with respect to $\equiv$.

Recall that in a valence system, we consider a run arriving in (q, w) to be valid if $w \overset{*}{\rightarrowtail} \varepsilon$. Therefore, we define an equivalence class $[u]_\equiv$ is *admissible (for configurations)* if there is some $v \in X_\Gamma^*$ with $uv \overset{*}{\rightarrowtail} \varepsilon$ (equivalently, $[uv] = [\varepsilon]$). This leads to the following definition.

A *configuration* of $\mathcal{A}$ is a pair $(q, [w])$ with $q \in Q$ and $w \in X_\Gamma^*$ such that w is admissible. Observe that in all the examples given above, this definition yields a notion of configuration that fits with the realized storage mechanism.

On configurations, it is now natural to define a step relation: Whenever we have $(q, w) \rightarrow (q', w')$, then we also have $(q, [w]) \rightarrow (q', [w'])$.

The Logical Structure. With the valence system $\mathcal{A}$, we associate the following logical structure $\mathcal{S}(\mathcal{A})$. Its universe is the set of configurations of $\mathcal{A}$. Moreover, it has the following predicates:

1. For each configuration, it has a constant.
2. For each $q \in Q$, there is a unary predicate $\text{state}_q(\cdot)$, which is true if the finite-state component of a configuration is q.
3. A binary one-step relation $\text{step}(\cdot, \cdot)$, which states that one configuration can reach the other in exactly one step.
4. A binary reachability relation $\text{reach}(\cdot, \cdot)$, with expresses reachability with an arbitrary run.

We are now interested in the model checking problem of first-order sentences over the structure $\mathcal{S}(\mathcal{A})$:

Given A first-order formula φ over the above signature.
Question Does φ hold in $\mathcal{S}(\mathcal{A})$?

Since this problem consists in deciding first-order sentences that involve reachability, we call this problem briefly FO[R] for Γ.

In order to state the result on decidability of FO[R], we need some terminology on graphs. We call a graph an $\mathbb{N}^2$-*triangle* if it is isomorphic to one of the following two graphs:

In other words, the graph realizes either (1) three $\mathbb{N}$-counters or (2) two $\mathbb{N}$-counters and one $\mathbb{Z}$-counter. We say that Γ is $\mathbb{N}^2$-*triangle-free* if it does not contain an $\mathbb{N}^2$-triangle as an induced subgraph. We are now ready to state the result about FO[R].

Theorem 4.1 ([6]). *Let Γ be a graph. Then* FO[R] *is decidable for Γ if and only if Γ is a disjoint union of $\mathbb{N}^2$-triangle-free cliques.*

5 Underapproximation I: Bounded Context Switching

A well-known example of a storage mechanism for which reachability is undecidable is a *multipushdown*: Two or more stacks that can be used independently. Here, undecidability is unfortunate, because this problem is equivalent to deciding safety properties of multithreaded recursive programs with shared memory [32]. However, it turned out that many bugs in such programs already manifest in runs where the program switches between its threads a small number of times [23,27]. Checking whether such runs exist is called *context-bounded model-checking* [31]. On the side of multipushdown systems, this corresponds to a small number of switches between its stacks. Moreover, given a small bound $k \geq 0$, it is NP-complete to decide if a multipushdown system has a run reaching a given configuration with at most k switches between its stacks [9,31].

Given the sharp drop in complexity from undecidable to NP, it would be useful to have a more abstract notion of bounded context switching that also applies to other storage mechanisms. Such a concept was developed in [25].

Contexts. To define this concept, we begin with the notion of contexts. In the case of a multipushdown system, a context is a segment of the run in which only one stack is used. Observe that a multipushdown consisting of r stacks, with s stack letters each, corresponds to a graph $\mathsf{MP}_{r,s}$, which is a direct product of r separate unlooped anticliques, each having s vertices. Here, an *anticlique* is a graph in which no two distinct vertices have an edge. Thus, if $\Gamma = \mathsf{MP}_{r,s}$, then a context corresponds to a word over X_Γ where the occurring vertices form an anti-clique. This motivates the following definition.

Let Γ be any graph and $w \in X_\Gamma^*$. Then the factorization of w into its *contexts* is obtained as follows. Take the maximal prefix of w whose set of vertices forms an anticlique. This prefix is the first (left-most) context in the factorization. Then, recursively factorize the remaining suffix of w. By $\|w\|$, we denote the number of contexts in its context factorization.

Context-Bounded Reachability. Given the notion of contexts, we can now define the problem of *context-bounded reachability for valence systems over Γ*, which we denote by $\mathsf{BCREACH}(\Gamma)$:

Given A valence system $\mathcal{A} = (Q, T)$, $s, t \in Q$, and $k \geq 0$ (encoded in unary)

Question Is there a $w \in X_\Gamma^*$ such that $(s, \varepsilon) \xrightarrow{*} (t, w)$ with $w \xrightarrow{*} \varepsilon$ and $\|w\| \leq k$?

It turns out that this notion of context bounding yields decidability, and even membership in NP, for every graph Γ.

Theorem 5.1 ([25]). *For every graph Γ, $\mathsf{BCREACH}(\Gamma)$ is in NP. If Γ is a transitive forest, then $\mathsf{BCREACH}(\Gamma)$ is in P.*

However, the exact set of graphs for which $\mathsf{BCREACH}$ is in P remains unclear:

Open Problem 5.2. *Describe the complexity landscape of $\mathsf{BCREACH}$. In particular, what is the complexity of $\mathsf{BCREACH}$ for the graph ●——●——●——● ?*

As mentioned in [25], if one could show NP-hardness for the graph ●——●——●——● and every version of it obtained by placing self-loops, then this would yield the complete landscape: This would imply that $\mathsf{BCREACH}(\Gamma)$ is in P for transitive forests and NP-complete otherwise.

6   Underapproximation II: Scope Boundedness

Aside from bounding the number of contexts, there exist a number of other underapproximations of the set of runs of multipushdown systems that lead to decidable reachability. One such underapproximation that covers a relatively large portion of the set of all runs is obtained by *scope-bounding* [35]. The idea is, instead of bounding the number of *all* contexts, we just bound the number of contexts between each push instruction and its matching pop. A run of a multipushdown system is said to be k-scoped if every letter pushed onto some stack i will be popped within at most k visits to the same stack i. Thus a run with at most k contexts is also k-scoped. However, the price of this higher coverage is that the complexity of k-scoped reachability goes up to PSPACE [35].

As in the case of bounded context switching, this motivates the study of analogues of scope boundedness for more general storage mechanisms. In [34], such an analogue was found.

Weak Dependence Classes. In the notion of scope-boundedness, we first need an analogue of two contexts "belonging to the same stack". This is achieved by the notion of weak dependency. Observe that in the case of multipushdowns, i.e. graphs $\mathsf{MP}_{r,s}$, two instructions belong to the same pushdown if they belong to the same anticlique. However, "the same anticlique" may not be well-defined in a general graph: It is possible that for vertices u, v, w, there is an edge from u to v and from v to w, but no edge from u to w. In that case, do u and w to the same anticlique?

Instead, we generalize this in a different way. Note that two vertices in $\mathsf{MP}_{r,s}$ belong to the same stack if and only if there is a path between them in the complement graph of $\mathsf{MP}_{r,s}$. This also makes sense in the general case: We say that vertices u, v of Γ are *weakly dependent* if there is a path between u and v in the complement of Γ. Here, the complement of Γ is the graph with the same set of vertices, but the opposite set of edges. Clearly, weak dependency is an equivalence relation. Moreover, each context in a word $w \in X_\Gamma^*$ belongs to a well-defined weak dependence class.

Greedy Reductions. The next step is to find a generalization of "matching push and pop instructions". It is natural to define this based on which letters cancel in a reduction $w \overset{*}{\twoheadrightarrow} \varepsilon$. However, to avoid some corner cases in the algorithms, we define this with respect to a particular type of reduction. Instead of the rules in (R1) and (R2), consider the slightly different relation defined by

$$rv\bar{v}s \hookrightarrow rs \qquad \text{for } r, s \in X_\Gamma^* \text{ and } v \in V, \text{ and} \tag{R1'}$$

$$r\bar{v}vs \hookrightarrow rs \qquad \text{for } r, s \in X_\Gamma^* \text{ and } v \in V, \{v\} \in E, \text{ and} \tag{R2'}$$

$$rxys \hookrightarrow ryxs \qquad \text{for } r, s \in X_\Gamma^* \text{ and } x \in \{u, \bar{u}\},\ y \in \{v, \bar{v}\},\ \{u, v\} \in E \tag{R3'}$$

Then of course, we have $w \overset{*}{\hookrightarrow} \varepsilon$ if and only if $w \overset{*}{\twoheadrightarrow} \varepsilon$. A word $w \in X_\Gamma^*$ is *irreducible* if none of the rules (R1) and (R2) (equivalently, none of the rules

(R1′) to (R3′)) are applicable to w. A *reduction* of w is a sequence of applications of (R1′) to (R3′) to obtain ε. We call this reduction *greedy* if it begins with a sequence of applications of (R1′) and (R2′) that turn each each context of w into an irreducible word. Since the relation $\twoheadrightarrow$ and thus $\hookrightarrow$ is confluent, we have $w \stackrel{*}{\twoheadrightarrow} \varepsilon$ if and only if w admits a greedy reduction.

Matching Relation. A reduction $\pi\colon w \stackrel{*}{\hookrightarrow} \varepsilon$ naturally defines a matching relation between positions of w: Two positions are related if they are cancelled using (R3′) (after possibly being transported using (R1′) and (R2′)). This binary relation on the set of positions of w, induced by π, is called the *matching relation*.

Scope Boundedness. We are now ready to formulate the notion of scope boundedness. We say that $w \in X_\Gamma^*$ is *k-scoped* if there exists a greedy reduction $\pi\colon w \stackrel{*}{\hookrightarrow} \varepsilon$ such that: for any two matched positions i and j, there are at most $k-1$ contexts strictly between the contexts of i and j that belong to the same weak dependence class as i and j. It is an easy exercise to observe that in the special case $\Gamma = \mathsf{MP}_{r,s}$, this notion coincides exactly with the original notion of scope boundedness.

This leads to the problem of *bounded scope reachability for valence systems over Γ*, briefly BSREACH(Γ):

Given A valence system $\mathcal{A} = (Q, T)$, $s, t \in Q$, and $k \geq 0$ (encoded in unary)

Question Is there a k-scoped $w \in X_\Gamma^*$ with $(s, \varepsilon) \stackrel{*}{\to} (t, w)$ and $w \stackrel{*}{\twoheadrightarrow} \varepsilon$?

We will also consider the problem BSREACH$_k$(Γ), where k is not part of the input, but fixed.

This notion of scope-boundedness does indeed yield decidable reachability for every graph. Moreover, in contrast to the case of bounded contexts, the complexity landscape is well understood.

Theorem 6.1 ([34]). *Let Γ be a graph. Then* BSREACH(Γ) *is*

1. *NL-complete if Γ has at most one vertex,*
2. *P-complete if Γ is an anti-clique with ≥ 2 vertices,*
3. *PSPACE-complete otherwise.*

Note that the complexity of BSREACH is always PSPACE, except for those cases where scope-bounded reachability is merely classical reachability in one-counter machines (namely, the first case above) or in pushdown automata (the second case). Therefore, the paper [34] also studies the case of fixed k.

Theorem 6.2 ([34]). *Let Γ be a graph and $k \geq 1$. Then* BSREACH$_k$(Γ) *is*

1. *NL-complete if Γ is a clique, and*
2. *P-complete otherwise.*

Since the complexity is well-understood for individual graphs, the paper [34] also studies the case where Γ is part of the input, and drawn from a class of graphs. It then gives partial results on the complexity landscape in terms of the possible graph classes. In this setting, the are many cases where the complexity is not understood yet. We refer to [34] for details.

References

1. Buckheister, P., Zetzsche, G.: Semilinearity and context-freeness of languages accepted by valence automata. In: Chatterjee, K., Sgall, J. (eds.) MFCS 2013. LNCS, vol. 8087, pp. 231–242. Springer, Heidelberg (2013). https://doi.org/10.1007/978-3-642-40313-2_22

2. Chomsky, N., Schützenberger, M.P.: The algebraic theory of context-free languages. In: Computer Programming and Formal Systems, pp. 118–161. North-Holland, Amsterdam (1963). https://doi.org/10.1016/S0049-237X(08)72023-8

3. Czerwinski, W., Lasota, S., Lazic, R., Leroux, J., Mazowiecki, F.: The reachability problem for Petri nets is not elementary. In: Proceedings of the 51st Annual ACM SIGACT Symposium on Theory of Computing (STOC 2019), pp. 24–33. ACM (2019). https://doi.org/10.1145/3313276.3316369

4. Czerwinski, W., Orlikowski, L.: Reachability in vector addition systems is Ackermann-complete. CoRR abs/2104.13866 (2021). https://arxiv.org/abs/2104.13866

5. Dassow, J., Păun, G.: Regulated Rewriting in Formal Language Theory. Springer, Heidelberg (1989)

6. D'Osualdo, E., Meyer, R., Zetzsche, G.: First-order logic with reachability for infinite-state systems. In: Proceedings of the 31st Annual ACM/IEEE Symposium on Logic in Computer Science (LICS 2016), pp. 457–466. ACM (2016). https://doi.org/10.1145/2933575.2934552

7. Dufourd, C., Finkel, A., Schnoebelen, P.: Reset nets between decidability and undecidability. In: Larsen, K.G., Skyum, S., Winskel, G. (eds.) ICALP 1998. LNCS, vol. 1443, pp. 103–115. Springer, Heidelberg (1998). https://doi.org/10.1007/BFb0055044

8. Englert, M., et al.: A lower bound for the coverability problem in acyclic pushdown VAS. Inf. Process. Lett. **167**, 106079 (2021). https://doi.org/10.1016/j.ipl.2020.106079

9. Esparza, J., Ganty, P., Poch, T.: Pattern-based verification for multithreaded programs. ACM ToPLaS **36**(3), 9:1–9:29 (2014)

10. Fernau, H., Stiebe, R.: Sequential grammars and automata with valences. Theoret. Comput. Sci. **276**, 377–405 (2002). https://doi.org/10.1016/S0304-3975(01)00282-1

11. Finkel, A., Sutre, G.: Decidability of reachability problems for classes of two counters automata. In: Reichel, H., Tison, S. (eds.) STACS 2000. LNCS, vol. 1770, pp. 346–357. Springer, Heidelberg (2000). https://doi.org/10.1007/3-540-46541-3_29

12. Greibach, S.A.: Remarks on blind and partially blind one-way multicounter machines. Theor. Comput. Sci. **7**, 311–324 (1978). https://doi.org/10.1016/0304-3975(78)90020-8

13. Haase, C., Halfon, S.: Integer vector addition systems with states. In: Ouaknine, J., Potapov, I., Worrell, J. (eds.) RP 2014. LNCS, vol. 8762, pp. 112–124. Springer, Cham (2014). https://doi.org/10.1007/978-3-319-11439-2_9

14. Haase, C., Zetzsche, G.: Presburger arithmetic with stars, rational subsets of graph groups, and nested zero tests. In: Proceeding of the 34th Annual ACM/IEEE Symposium on Logic in Computer Science (LICS 2019), pp. 1–14. IEEE (2019). https://doi.org/10.1109/LICS.2019.8785850
15. Hague, M., Lin, A.W.: Model checking recursive programs with numeric data types. In: Gopalakrishnan, G., Qadeer, S. (eds.) CAV 2011. LNCS, vol. 6806, pp. 743–759. Springer, Heidelberg (2011). https://doi.org/10.1007/978-3-642-22110-1_60
16. Ibarra, O.H.: Reversal-bounded multicounter machines and their decision problems. J. ACM 25(1), 116–133 (1978). https://doi.org/10.1145/322047.322058
17. Ibarra, O.H., Sahni, S.K., Kim, C.E.: Finite automata with multiplication. Theoret. Comput. Sci. 2(3), 271–294 (1976). https://doi.org/10.1016/0304-3975(76)90081-5
18. Kambites, M.: Formal languages and groups as memory. Comm. Algebra 37, 193–208 (2009). https://doi.org/10.1080/00927870802243580
19. Kambites, M., Silva, P.V., Steinberg, B.: On the rational subset problem for groups. J. Algebra 309, 622–639 (2007). https://doi.org/10.1016/j.jalgebra.2006.05.020
20. Leroux, J., Schmitz, S.: Reachability in vector addition systems is primitive-recursive in fixed dimension. In: Proceeding of the 34th Annual ACM/IEEE Symposium on Logic in Computer Science (LICS 2019), pp. 1–13. IEEE (2019). https://doi.org/10.1109/LICS.2019.8785796
21. Leroux, J., Sutre, G., Totzke, P.: On the coverability problem for pushdown vector addition systems in one dimension. In: Halldórsson, M.M., Iwama, K., Kobayashi, N., Speckmann, B. (eds.) ICALP 2015. LNCS, vol. 9135, pp. 324–336. Springer, Heidelberg (2015). https://doi.org/10.1007/978-3-662-47666-6_26
22. Lohrey, M., Steinberg, B.: The submonoid and rational subset membership problems for graph groups. J. Algebra 320(2), 728–755 (2008)
23. Lu, S., Park, S., Seo, E., Zhou, Y.: Learning from mistakes: A comprehensive study on real world concurrency bug characteristics. In: Proceedings of the 13th International Conference on Architectural Support for Programming Languages and Operating Systems (ASPLOS 2008), pp. 329–339. ACM (2008). https://doi.org/10.1145/1346281.1346323
24. Mayr, R.: Undecidable problems in unreliable computations. Theoret. Comput. Sci. 297(1–3), 337–354 (2003). https://doi.org/10.1016/S0304-3975(02)00646-1
25. Meyer, R., Muskalla, S., Zetzsche, G.: Bounded context switching for valence systems. In: Proceeding of the 29th International Conference on Concurrency Theory (CONCUR 2018). LIPIcs, vol. 118, pp. 12:1–12:18. Schloss Dagstuhl - Leibniz-Zentrum für Informatik (2018). https://doi.org/10.4230/LIPIcs.CONCUR.2018.12
26. Mitrana, V., Stiebe, R.: Extended finite automata over groups. Discret. Appl. Math. 108(3), 287–300 (2001). https://doi.org/10.1016/S0166-218X(00)00200-6
27. Musuvathi, M., Qadeer, S.: Iterative context bounding for systematic testing of multithreaded programs. In: Proceedings of the 2007 ACM SIGPLAN Conference on Programming Language Design and Implementation (PLDI 2007), pp. 446–455. ACM (2007). https://doi.org/10.1145/1273442.1250785
28. Ong, L.: Higher-order model checking: an overview. In: Proceeding of the 30th Annual ACM/IEEE Symposium on Logic in Computer Science (LICS 2015), pp. 1–15. IEEE Computer Society (2015). https://doi.org/10.1109/LICS.2015.9
29. Păun, G.: A new generative device: Valence grammars. Rev. Roumaine Math. Pures Appl. 25, 911–924 (1980)
30. Piskac, R., Kuncak, V.: Linear arithmetic with stars. In: Gupta, A., Malik, S. (eds.) CAV 2008. LNCS, vol. 5123, pp. 268–280. Springer, Heidelberg (2008). https://doi.org/10.1007/978-3-540-70545-1_25

31. Qadeer, S., Rehof, J.: Context-bounded model checking of concurrent software. In: Halbwachs, N., Zuck, L.D. (eds.) TACAS 2005. LNCS, vol. 3440, pp. 93–107. Springer, Heidelberg (2005). https://doi.org/10.1007/978-3-540-31980-1_7

32. Ramalingam, G.: Context-sensitive synchronization-sensitive analysis is undecidable. ACM Transactions on Programming languages and Systems (TOPLAS) **22**(2), 416–430 (2000). https://doi.org/10.1145/349214.349241

33. Red'ko, V., Lisovik, L.: Regular events in semigroups. Probl. Cybern. **37**, 155–184 (1980). in Russian

34. Shetty, A.K., Krishna, S.N., Zetzsche, G.: Scope-bounded reachability in valence systems. In: Proceeding of the 32nd International Conference on Concurrency Theory (CONCUR 2021). LIPIcs, vol. 203, pp. 29:1–29:19. Schloss Dagstuhl - Leibniz-Zentrum für Informatik (2021). https://doi.org/10.4230/LIPIcs.CONCUR.2021.29

35. Torre, S.L., Napoli, M., Parlato, G.: Reachability of scope-bounded multistack pushdown systems. Inf. Comput. **275**, 104588 (2020). https://doi.org/10.1016/j.ic.2020.104588

36. Zetzsche, G.: Silent transitions in automata with storage. In: Fomin, F.V., Freivalds, R., Kwiatkowska, M., Peleg, D. (eds.) ICALP 2013. LNCS, vol. 7966, pp. 434–445. Springer, Heidelberg (2013). https://doi.org/10.1007/978-3-642-39212-2_39

37. Zetzsche, G.: Monoids as Storage Mechanisms. Ph.D. Thesis, Technische Universität Kaiserslautern (2016). https://kluedo.ub.uni-kl.de/frontdoor/index/index/docId/4400

38. Zetzsche, G.: The emptiness problem for valence automata over graph monoids. Inf. Comput. **277**, 104583 (2021). https://doi.org/10.1016/j.ic.2020.104583

Regular Papers

Improvements in Unfolding of Colored Petri Nets

Alexander Bilgram, Peter G. Jensen, Thomas Pedersen, Jiří Srba[✉],
and Peter H. Taankvist

Department of Computer Science, Aalborg University, Aalborg, Denmark
srba@cs.aau.dk

Abstract. Colored Petri nets offer a compact and user friendly representation of the traditional P/T nets and colored nets with finite color ranges can be unfolded into the underlying P/T nets, however, at the expense of an exponential explosion in size. We present two novel techniques based on static analyses in order to reduce the size of unfolded colored nets. The first method identifies colors that behave equivalently and groups them into equivalence classes, potentially reducing the number of used colors. The second method overapproximates the sets of colors that can appear in places and excludes colors that can never be present in a given place. Both methods are complementary and the combined approach allows us to significantly reduce the size of multiple colored Petri nets from the Model Checking Contest benchmark. We compare the performance of our unfolder with state-of-the-art techniques implemented in the tools MCC, Spike and ITS-Tools, and while our approach remains competitive w.r.t. unfolding time, it outperforms the existing approaches both in the size of unfolded nets as well as in the number of answered model checking queries from the 2020 Model Checking Contest.

1 Introduction

Petri nets [22], also known as P/T nets, are a powerful modelling formalism supported by a rich family of verification techniques [20]. However, P/T nets often become too large and incomprehensible for humans to read. Therefore, colored Petri nets (CPN) [14] were introduced to allow for high level modelling of distributed systems. In CPNs, each place is assigned a color domain and each token in that place has a color from its domain. Arcs have expressions that define what colored tokens to consume or produce, and transitions have guard expressions that restrict transition enabledness.

A CPN can be translated into an equivalent P/T net, provided that every color domain is finite, through a process called *unfolding*. This allows us to use efficient verification tools already developed for P/T nets. When unfolding a CPN, each place is unfolded into a new place for each color that a token can take in that place; a naive approach is to create a new place for each color in the color domain of the place. Transitions are unfolded such that each binding of variables to colors, satisfying the guard, is unfolded into a new transition copy in

© Springer Nature Switzerland AG 2021
P. C. Bell et al. (Eds.): RP 2021, LNCS 13035, pp. 69–84, 2021.
https://doi.org/10.1007/978-3-030-89716-1_5

the unfolded net. The size of an unfolded net can be exponentially larger than the colored net and the unfolding process therefore requires optimizations in order to finish in realistic time and memory. Several types of improvements were proposed that analyse transition guards and arc expressions [6,19,23]. However, even with these optimizations, there still exist CPNs that cannot be unfolded. As an example, the largest instances of the nets *FamilyReunion* [5,12] and *DrinkVending-Machine* [11,21] from the Model Checking Contest [18] have not been unfolded yet.

We propose two novel methods for statically analysing a CPN to reduce the size of the unfolded P/T net. The first method called *color quotienting* uses the fact that sometimes multiple colors behave equivalently throughout the colored net. If such colors exist in the net, we can create equivalence classes that represent the colors with similar behaviour. As such, we can reduce the amount of colors that we need to consider when unfolding. The second method called *color approximation* overapproximates which colors can possibly be present in any given place s.t. we only unfold places for the colors that can exist. This method also allows for invalidating bindings that are dependent on unreachable colors, thus reducing the amount of transitions that are unfolded.

Our two methods are implemented in the model checker TAPAAL [7,13] and an extensive experimental evaluation shows convincing performance compared to the state-of-the-art tools for CPN unfolding.

Related Work. Heiner et al. [19] analyse the arc and guard expressions to reduce the amount of bindings by collecting *patterns*. The pattern analysis is implemented in the tool Snoopy [9] and our color approximation method further extends this method. In [23] the same authors present a technique for representing the patterns as Interval Decision Diagrams. This technique is used in the tools Snoopy [9], MARCIE [10] and Spike [3] and performs better compared to [19]; it also allows to unfold a superset of colored nets compared to the format adopted by the Model Checking Contest benchmark [18].

In [6] (MCC) Dal-Zilio describes a method called *stable places*. A stable place is a place that never changes from the initial marking, i.e. every time a token is consumed from this place an equivalent token is added to the place. This method is especially efficient on the net BART from the Model Checking Contest [18], however, it does not detect places that deviate even a little from the initial marking. Our color approximation method includes a more general form of the stable places. In the unfolder MCC [6], a *component analysis* is introduced and it detects if a net consists of a number of copies of the same component. MCC is used in the TINA toolchain [1] and to our knowledge in the latest release of the LoLA tool [27]. GreatSPN [8] is another tool for unfolding CPNs, however, in [6] it is demonstrated that MCC is able to greatly outperform GreatSPN and as such we omit GreatSPN from later experiments.

ITS-Tools [24] has an integrated unfolding engine. The tool uses a technique of *variable symmetry identification*, in which it is analyzed whether variables x and y are permutable in a binding. Furthermore, they use stable places during the binding and they apply analysis to choose the binding order of parameters to simplify false guards as soon as possible. After unfolding, ITS-Tools applies further post-unfolding reductions that remove orphan places/transitions and behaviourally equivalent transitions [25]. Our implementation includes a variant of the symmetric variables reduction as well. In [26] Thierry-Mieg et al. present a technique for automatic detection of symmetries in high level Petri nets used to construct symbolic reachability graphs in the GreatSPN tool. This detection of symmetries is reminiscent of the color quotienting method presented in this paper, although our color quotienting method is used for unfolding the colored Petri net instead of symbolic model checking.

In [17] Klostergaard presents a simple unfolding method implemented in TAPAAL [7,13], which is the base of our implementation. The implementation is efficient but there are several nets which it cannot unfold. Both unfolding methods introduced in this paper are advanced static analyses techniques and all of the above mentioned techniques, except symmetric variables and component analysis, are captured by color approximation and/or color quotienting.

2 Preliminaries

Let $\mathbb{N}^{>0}$ be the set of positive integers and $\mathbb{N}^0$ the set of nonnegative integers. A Labeled Transition System (LTS) is a triple $(Q, Act, \rightarrow)$ where Q is a set of states, Act is a finite, nonempty set of actions, and $\rightarrow \subseteq Q \times Act \times Q$ is the transition relation. A binary relation R over the set of states of an LTS is a *bisimulation* iff for every $(s_1, s_2) \in R$ and $a \in Act$ it holds that if $s_1 \xrightarrow{a} s_1'$ then there is a transition $s_2 \xrightarrow{a} s_2'$ s.t. $(s_1', s_2') \in R$, and if $s_2 \xrightarrow{a} s_2'$ then there is a transition $s_1 \xrightarrow{a} s_1'$ s.t. $(s_1', s_2') \in R$. Two states s and s' are *bisimilar*, written $s \sim s'$, iff there is a bisimulation R s.t. $(s, s') \in R$.

A finite *multiset* over some nonempty set A is a collection of elements from A where each element occurs in the multiset a finite amount of times; a multiset S over a set A can be identified with a function $S : A \rightarrow \mathbb{N}^0$ where $S(a)$ is the number of occurrences of element $a \in A$ in the multiset S. We shall represent multisets by a formal sum $\sum_{a \in A} S(a)'(a)$ such that e.g. $1'(x) + 2'(y)$ stands for a multiset containing one element x and two elements y. We assume the standard multiset operations of membership ($\in$), inclusion ($\subseteq$), equality ($=$), union ($\uplus$), subtraction ($\backslash$) and by $|S|$ we denote the cardinality of S (including the repetition of elements). By $\mathcal{S}(A)$ we denote the set of all multisets over the set A. Finally, we also define the function *set* as a way of reducing multisets of colors to sets of colors given by $set(S) \stackrel{\text{def}}{=} \{a \mid a \in S\}$ where $set(S)$ is the set of all colors with at least one occurrence in S.

2.1 Colored Petri Nets

Colored Petri nets (CPN) are an extension of traditional P/T nets introduced by Kurt Jensen [14] in 1981. In CPNs, places are associated with color domains where colors represent the values of tokens. Arc expressions describe what colors to consume and add to places depending on a given binding (assignment of variables to colors). Transitions may contain guards restricting which bindings are valid. There exist several different definitions of CPNs from the powerful version defined in [16] that includes the ML language for describing arcs expressions and guards to less powerful ones such as the one used in the Model Checking Contest [18]. We shall first give an abstract definition of a CPN.

Definition 1. *A colored Petri net is a tuple* $\mathcal{N} = (P, T, \mathbb{C}, \mathbb{B}, C, G, W, W_I, M_0)$ *where*

1. *P is a finite set of places,*
2. *T is a finite set of transitions s.t. $P \cap T = \emptyset$,*
3. *$\mathbb{C}$ is a nonempty set of colors,*
4. *$\mathbb{B}$ is a nonempty set of bindings,*
5. *$C : P \to 2^{\mathbb{C}} \setminus \emptyset$ is a place color type function,*
6. *$G : T \times \mathbb{B} \to \{true, false\}$ is a guard evaluation function,*
7. *$W : ((P \times T) \cup (T \times P)) \times \mathbb{B} \to \mathcal{S}(\mathbb{C})$ is an arc evaluation function s.t. $set(W((p, t), b)) \subseteq C(p)$ and $set(W((t, p), b)) \subseteq C(p)$ for all $p \in P$, $t \in T$ and $b \in \mathbb{B}$,*
8. *$W_I : P \times T \to \mathbb{N}^{>0} \cup \{\infty\}$ is an inhibitor arc weight function, and*
9. *M_0 is the initial marking where a marking M is a function $M : P \to \mathcal{S}(\mathbb{C})$ s.t. $set(M(p)) \subseteq C(p)$ for all $p \in P$.*

Notice that G, W and W_I are semantic functions which are in different variants of CPN defined by a concrete syntax. The set of all markings on a CPN $\mathcal{N}$ is denoted by $\mathbb{M}(\mathcal{N})$. In order to avoid the use of partial functions, we allow $W((p, t), b) = W((t, p), b) = \emptyset$ and $W_I(p, t) = \infty$, meaning that if the arc evaluation function returns the empty multiset then the arc has no effect on transition firing and if the inhibitor arc function returns infinity then it never inhibits the connected transition.

Let $\mathcal{N} = (P, T, \mathbb{C}, \mathbb{B}, C, G, W, W_I, M_0)$ be a fixed CPN for the rest of this section. Let $B(t) \stackrel{\text{def}}{=} \{b \in \mathbb{B} \mid G(t, b) = true\}$ be the set of all bindings that satisfy the guard of transition $t \in T$. Let $\ell : T \to Act$ be a transition labeling function. The semantics of a CPN $\mathcal{N}$ is defined as an LTS $L(\mathcal{N}) = (\mathbb{M}(\mathcal{N}), Act, \to)$ where $\mathbb{M}(\mathcal{N})$ is the set of states defined as all markings on $\mathcal{N}$, Act is the set of actions, and $M \xrightarrow{a} M'$ iff there exists $t \in T$ where $\ell(t) = a$ and there is $b \in B(t)$ s.t.

$$W((p, t), b) \subseteq M(p) \text{ and } W_I(p, t) > |M(p)| \text{ for all } p \in P, \text{ and}$$
$$M'(p) = (M(p) \setminus W((p, t), b)) \uplus W((t, p), b) \text{ for all } p \in P.$$

We denote the firing of a transition $t \in T$ in marking M reaching M' as $M \xrightarrow{t} M'$. Let $\to = \bigcup_{t \in T} \xrightarrow{t}$ and let $\to^*$ be the reflexive and transitive closure of $\to$.

Remark 1. To reason about model checking of CPNs, we need to have a finite representation of colored nets that can be passed as an input to an algorithm. One way to enforce such a representation is to assume that all color domains are finite and the semantic functions C, G, W and W_I are effectively computable.

Finally, let us define the notion of postset and preset of $p \in P$ as $p^\bullet = \{t \in T \mid \exists b \in \mathbb{B}. \ W((p,t),b) \neq \emptyset\}$ and $^\bullet p = \{t \in T \mid \exists b \in \mathbb{B}. \ W((t,p),b) \neq \emptyset\}$. Similarly, for a transition $t \in T$ we define $t^\bullet = \{p \in P \mid \exists b \in \mathbb{B}. \ W((t,p),b) \neq \emptyset\}$ and $^\bullet t = \{p \in P \mid \exists b \in \mathbb{B}. \ W((p,t),b) \neq \emptyset\}$. We also define the preset of inhibitor arcs as $^\circ t = \{p \in P \mid W_I(p,t) \neq \infty\}$.

2.2   P/T Nets

A Place/Transition (P/T) net is a CPN $\mathcal{N} = (P, T, \mathbb{C}, \mathbb{B}, C, G, W, W_I, M_0)$ with one color $\mathbb{C} = \{\bullet\}$ and only one binding $\mathbb{B} = \{b_\epsilon\}$ s.t. every guard evaluates to true i.e. $G(t, b_\epsilon) = true$ for all $t \in T$ and every arc evaluates to a multiset over $\{\bullet\}$ i.e. $W((p,t), b_\epsilon) \in \mathcal{S}(\{\bullet\})$ and $W((t,p), b_\epsilon) \in \mathcal{S}(\{\bullet\})$ for all $p \in P$ and $t \in T$.

2.3   Integer Colored Petri Nets

An integer CPN (as used e.g. in the Model Checking Contest [18]) is a CPN $\mathcal{N} = (P, T, \mathbb{C}, \mathbb{B}, C, G, W, W_I, M_0)$ where all colors are integer products i.e. $\mathbb{C} = \bigcup_{k \geq 1}(\mathbb{N}^0)^k$. We use interval ranges to describe sets of colors s.t. a tuple of ranges $([a_1, b_1], ..., [a_k, b_k])$ where $a_i, b_i \in \mathbb{N}^0$ for $i, 1 \leq i \leq k$, describes the set of colors $\{(c_1, ..., c_k) \mid a_i \leq c_i \leq b_i$ for all $1 \leq i \leq k\}$. If the interval upperbound is smaller than the lowerbound, the interval range denotes the empty set and by $[a]$ we denote the singleton interval $[a, a]$. We use the set of variables $\mathcal{V} = \{x_1, ..., x_n\}$ to represent colors. Variables can be present on arcs and in guards. A binding $b : \mathcal{V} \to \mathbb{C}$ assigns colors to variables. We write $b \equiv \langle x_1 = c_1, ..., x_n = c_n \rangle$ for a binding where $b(x_i) = c_i$ for all $i, 1 \leq i \leq n$. We now introduce the syntax of arc/guard expressions and its intuitive semantics by an example.

Figure 1 shows an integer CPN where places (circles) are associated with ranges. The initial marking contains five tokens (two of color 0 and three of color 2) in p_1 and two tokens of color 5 in place p_2. There is a guard on transition t (rectangle) that compares x with the integer 1 and restricts the valid bindings. We can see that the arc from t to p_3 creates a product of the integers x and y, where the value of x is decremented by one. We assume that all ranges are cyclic, meaning that the predecessor of 0 in the color set A is 2. Figure 1 also shows an example of transition firing. Markings are written as formal sums showing how many tokens of what colors are in the different places. The transition t can fire only once, as the inhibitor arc (for unlabelled inhibitor arcs we assume the default weight 1) from place p_3 to transition t inhibits the second transition firing.

The CPN model used in Model Checking Contest [18] further uses color types called dots and cyclic enumerations—these can be easily translated to integer ranges. All examples in this paper are expressed in integer CPN syntax.

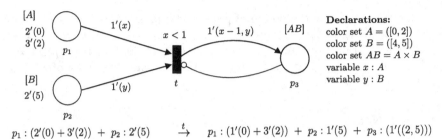

$$p_1 : (2'(0) + 3'(2)) + p_2 : 2'(5) \quad \xrightarrow{t} \quad p_1 : (1'(0) + 3'(2)) + p_2 : 1'(5) + p_3 : (1'((2,5)))$$

Fig. 1. Integer CPN and transition firing under the binding $\langle x = 0, y = 5 \rangle$

2.4   Unfolding

CPNs with finite color domains can be *unfolded* into an equivalent P/T net [15]. Each place p is unfolded into $|C(p)|$ places, a transition is made for each legal binding and we translate the multiset of colors on the arc to a multiset over •. We now provide a formal definition of unfolding in our syntax, following the approach from [4,17].

For each place connected to an inhibitor arc, we create a fresh summation place that contains the sum of tokens across the rest of the unfolded places. The summation places is created to ensure that inhibitor arcs functions correctly after unfolding.

Definition 2 (Unfolding). *Let* $\mathcal{N} = (P, T, \mathbb{C}, \mathbb{B}, C, G, W, W_I, M_0)$ *be a CPN. The unfolded P/T net* $\mathcal{N}^u = (P^u, T^u, \mathbb{C}^u, \mathbb{B}^u, C^u, G^u, W^u, W_I^u, M_0^u)$ *is given by*

1. $P^u = \{p(c) \mid p \in P \wedge c \in C(p)\} \cup \{p(\boldsymbol{sum}) \mid t \in T, p \in {}^\circ t\}$,
2. $T^u = \bigcup_{t \in T} \bigcup_{b \in B(t)} t(b)$,
3. $\mathbb{C}^u = \{\bullet\}$,
4. $\mathbb{B}^u = \{b_\epsilon\}$,
5. $C^u(p(c)) = \{\bullet\}$ *for all* $p(c) \in P^u$,
6. $G^u(t(b), b_\epsilon) = true$ *for all* $t(b) \in T^u$,
7. $W^u((p(c), t(b)), b) = W((p, t), b)(c)'(\bullet)$ *and* $W^u((t(b), p(c)), b) = W((t, p), b)$ $(c)'(\bullet)$ *for all* $p(c) \in P^u$ *and* $t(b) \in T^u$, *and* $W^u((p(\boldsymbol{sum}), t(b)), b) = |W((p, t), b)|'(\bullet)$ *and* $W^u((t(b), p(\boldsymbol{sum})), b) = |W((t, p), b)|'(\bullet)$ *for all* $p(\boldsymbol{sum}) \in P^u$ *and* $t(b) \in T^u$,
8. $W_I^u(p(\boldsymbol{sum}), t(b)) = W_I(p, t)$ *for all* $p(\boldsymbol{sum}) \in P^u$ *and* $t(b) \in T^u$, *and*
9. $M_0^u(p(c)) = M_0(p)(c)'(\bullet)$ *for all* $p(c) \in P^u$ *and* $M_0^u(p(\boldsymbol{sum})) = |M_0(p)|'(\bullet)$ *for all* $p(\boldsymbol{sum}) \in P^u$

where $p(\boldsymbol{sum})$ *denotes the sum of all tokens regardless of color for place* p.

The theorem showing that the unfolded net is bisimilar to the original CPN was proved in [4,17]; we only add a small optimization on the summation places.

Theorem 1. ([4,17]). *Given a CPN* $\mathcal{N} = (P, T, \mathbb{C}, \mathbb{B}, C, G, W, W_I, M_0)$ *and the unfolded CPN* $\mathcal{N}^u = (P^u, T^u, \mathbb{C}^u, \mathbb{B}^u, C^u, G^u, W^u, W_I^u, M_0^u)$ *then* $M_0 \sim M_0^u$ *with labeling function* $\ell(t(b)) = t$ *for all* $t(b) \in T^u$.

3   Color Quotienting

Unfolding a CPN without any further analysis will often lead to many unnecessary places and transitions. We shall now present our first technique that allows to group equivalently behaving colors into equivalence classes in order to reduce the number of colors and hence also to reduce the size of the unfolded net.

As an example consider the CPN in Fig. 2a, the unfolded version of this net adds five places for both p_1 and p_2. However, we see that in p_1 all colors greater than or equal to 3 behave exactly the same throughout the net and can thus be represented by a single color. We can thus *quotient* the CPN by *partitioning* the color domain of each place into a number of *equivalence classes* of colors s.t. the colors behaving equivalently are represented by the same equivalence class. Using this approach we can construct a bisimilar CPN seen in Fig. 2b where the color $([3, 5])$ now represents all colors greater than or equal to 3.

Such a reduction in the number of colors is possible to include already during the design of a CPN model, however, the models may look less intuitive for human modeller or the nets can be auto-generated and hence contain redundant/equivalent colors as observed in the benchmark of CPN models from the annual Model Checking Contest benchmark [18].

We thus introduce *color partition* on places where all colors with similar behaviour in a given place are grouped into an *equivalence class*, denoted by θ. Let us assume a fixed CPN $\mathcal{N} = (P, T, \mathbb{C}, \mathbb{B}, C, G, W, W_I, M_0)$. A partition δ is a function $\delta : P \to 2^{2^C} \setminus \emptyset$ that for a place p returns the equivalence classes of $C(p)$ s.t. $(\bigcup_{\theta \in \delta(p)} \theta) = C(p)$ and $\theta_1 \cap \theta_2 = \emptyset$ for all $\theta_1, \theta_2 \in \delta(p)$ where $\theta_1 \neq \theta_2$.

Definition 3. *Given a partition δ and markings M and M', we write $M(p) \stackrel{\delta}{\equiv} M'(p)$ for a $p \in P$ iff for all $\theta \in \delta(p)$ it holds that $\sum_{c \in \theta} M(p)(c) = \sum_{c \in \theta} M'(p)(c)$. We write $M \stackrel{\delta}{\equiv} M'$ iff $M(p) \stackrel{\delta}{\equiv} M'(p)$ for all $p \in P$. A partition δ is stable if the relation $\stackrel{\delta}{\equiv}$ on markings induced by δ is a bisimulation.*

Consider the CPN in Fig. 2a. The partition shown in the Fig. 2c is not stable as demonstrated by the transition firing from M_1 and M_2 to M_1' and M_2' where $M_1 \stackrel{\delta}{\equiv} M_2$ but $M_1' \stackrel{\delta}{\not\equiv} M_2'$. Figure 2d shows an example of a stable partition (here we describe the partition with ranges in the same manner as in integer CPNs).

We now describe how a CPN may be quotiented using a stable partition. First, we define the notion of binding equivalence under a partition.

Definition 4. *Given a partition δ, a transition $t \in T$ and bindings $b, b' \in B(t)$, we write $b \stackrel{\delta,t}{\equiv} b'$ iff for all $p \in {}^{\bullet}t$ and for all $\theta \in \delta(p)$ it holds that*

$$\sum_{c \in \theta} W((p, t), b)(c) = \sum_{c \in \theta} W((p, t), b')(c)$$

and for all $p \in t^{\bullet}$ and for all $\theta \in \delta(p)$ it holds that

$$\sum_{c \in \theta} W((t, p), b)(c) = \sum_{c \in \theta} W((t, p), b')(c).$$

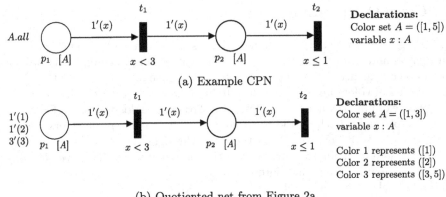

(a) Example CPN

(b) Quotiented net from Figure 2a

$$\delta(p_1) = \{([1,2]),([3,5])\}, \delta(p_2) = \{([1]),([2,5])\}$$

$$M_1 = p_1 : 1'(1) \quad \xrightarrow{t_1} \quad M_1' = p_2 : 1'(1)$$

$$M_1 \overset{\delta}{\equiv} M_2 \qquad\qquad\qquad\qquad M_1' \overset{\delta}{\not\equiv} M_2'$$

$$M_2 = p_1 : 1'(2) \quad \xrightarrow{t_1} \quad M_2' = p_2 : 1'(2)$$

(c) Example of an unstable partition δ and markings showing why it is unstable

$$\delta'(p_1) = \{([1]),([2]),([3,5])\}, \delta'(p_2) = \{([1]),([2,5])\}$$

(d) Example of stable partition δ'

Fig. 2. Quotienting example

We can now define classes of equivalent bindings given a partition δ which are bindings that have the same behaviour for a given transition, formally $B^\delta(t) \overset{\text{def}}{=} \{[b]_t \mid b \in B(t)\}$ where $[b]_t = \{b' \mid b' \overset{\delta,t}{\equiv} b\}$.

For a given stable partition, we now construct a quotiented CPN where the set of colors are the equivalence classes of the stable partition and the set of bindings are the equivalence classes of bindings. As such, we rewrite the arc and guard evaluation functions to instead consider an equivalence class of bindings, which is possible since each binding in the equivalence class behaves equivalently.

Definition 5. *Let* $\mathcal{N} = (P,T,\mathbb{C},\mathbb{B},C,G,W,W_I,M_0)$ *be a CPN and* δ *a stable partition of* $\mathcal{N}$. *The quotiented CPN* $\mathcal{N}^\delta = (P,T,\mathbb{C}^\delta,\mathbb{B}^\delta,C^\delta,G^\delta,W^\delta,W_I^\delta,M_0^\delta)$ *is defined by*

1. $\mathbb{C}^\delta = \bigcup_{p \in P} \delta(p)$
2. $\mathbb{B}^\delta = \biguplus_{t \in T} B^\delta(t)$.
3. $G^\delta(t,[b]_t) = G(t,b)$ *for all* $t \in T$ *and* $[b]_t \in B(t)$,
4. $C^\delta(p) = \delta(p)$ *for all* $p \in P$,

5. $W^\delta((p,t),[b]_t) = S$ where $S(\theta) = \sum_{c\in\theta} W((p,t),b)(c)$ for all $\theta \in \delta(p)$ and
   $W^\delta((t,p),[b]_t) = S$ where $S(\theta) = \sum_{c\in\theta} W((t,p),b)(c)$ for all $\theta \in \delta(p)$
   for all $p \in P$, $t \in T$ and $[b]_t \in \mathbb{B}^\delta$,
6. $W_I^\delta(p,t) = W_I(p,t)$ for all $p \in P$ and $t \in T$, and
7. $M_0^\delta(p) = S$ where $S(\theta) = \sum_{c\in\theta} M_0(p)(c)$ for all $p \in P$ and $\theta \in \delta(p)$.

We can now present our main correctness theorem, stating that the original and quotiented colored nets are bisimilar.

Theorem 2. *Let $\mathcal{N} = (P,T,\mathbb{C},\mathbb{B},C,G,W,W_I,M_0)$ be a CPN, δ a stable partition and $\mathcal{N}^\delta = (P^\delta,T^\delta,\mathbb{C}^\delta,\mathbb{B}^\delta,C^\delta,G^\delta,W^\delta,W_I^\delta,M_0^\delta)$ the quotiented CPN. Then $M_0 \sim M_0^\delta$.*

3.1   Computing Stable Partitions

Our main challenge is how to efficiently compute a stable partition in order to apply the quotienting technique. To do so, we first define a partition refinement.

Definition 6. *Given two partitions δ and δ' we write $\delta \geq \delta'$ iff for all $p \in P$ and all $\theta' \in \delta'(p)$ there exists $\theta \in \delta(p)$ s.t. $\theta' \subseteq \theta$. Additionally, we write $\delta > \delta'$ if $\delta \geq \delta'$ and $\delta' \neq \delta$.*

Note that for any finite CPN as assumed in Remark 1, the refinement relation $>$ is well-founded as for any $\delta > \delta'$ the partition δ' has strictly more equivalence classes for at least one place $p \in P$. We now define also the union of two partitions as the smallest partition that has both of the partitions as refinements.

Definition 7. *Given two partitions δ_1, δ_2 and $p \in P$, let $\leftrightarrow$ be a relation over $\delta_1(p) \cup \delta_2(p)$ s.t. $\theta \leftrightarrow \theta'$ iff $\theta \cap \theta' \neq \emptyset$ where $\theta,\theta' \in \delta_1(p) \cup \delta_2(p)$. Let $\leftrightarrow^*$ be the reflexive, transitive closure of $\leftrightarrow$ and let $[\theta] \stackrel{\text{def}}{=} \bigcup_{\theta'\in\delta_1(p)\cup\delta_2(p),\theta\leftrightarrow^*\theta'} \theta'$ where $\theta \in \delta_1(p) \cup \delta_2(p)$. Finally, we define the partition union operator $\sqcup$ by $(\delta_1 \sqcup \delta_2)(p) = \bigcup_{\theta\in\delta_1(p)\cup\delta_2(p)}\{[\theta]\}$ for all $p \in P$.*

For example, assume some place p s.t. $C(p) = \{([1,5])\}$ and partitions δ_1 and δ_2 s.t. $\delta_1(p) = \{([1,2]),([3,4]),([5])\}$ and $\delta_2(p) = \{([1]),([2,3]),([4]),([5])\}$ then $(\delta_1 \sqcup \delta_2)(p) = \{([1,4]),([5])\}$.

Lemma 1. *Let δ_1 and δ_2 be two partitions. Then (i) $\delta_1 \sqcup \delta_2 \geq \delta_1$ and $\delta_1 \sqcup \delta_2 \geq \delta_2$, and (ii) if δ_1 and δ_2 are stable partitions then so is $\delta_1 \sqcup \delta_2$.*

The lemma above implies the existence of a unique maximum stable partition.

Theorem 3. *There is a unique maximum stable partition δ s.t. $\delta \geq \delta'$ for all stable partitions δ'.*

In order to provide an algorithm for computing a stable partition, we define the maximum arc size for a given CPN $\mathcal{N}$ as the function $max(\mathcal{N}) = \max_{p\in P,t\in T,b\in\mathbb{B}}(|W((p,t),b)|,|W((t,p),b)|)$. The set of all markings smaller than

---

Algorithm 1: *Stabilize($\mathcal{N}$)*

---

1 **Input:** $\mathcal{N} = (P, T, \mathbb{C}, \mathbb{B}, C, G, W, W_I, M_0)$
2 **Output:** Stable partition δ
3 let $\delta(p) := \{C(p)\}$ for all $p \in P$
4 **for** $t \in T$ **do**
5   **while** $\exists M_1, M_2 \in \mathbb{M}^{bounded}(\mathcal{N}). M_1 \stackrel{\delta}{\equiv} M_2 \wedge M_1 \stackrel{t}{\nrightarrow} \wedge M_2 \stackrel{t}{\rightarrow}$ **do**
6   pick $\delta' < \delta$ s.t. $M_1 \stackrel{\delta'}{\not\equiv} M_2$; $\delta := \delta'$
7   **end**
8 **end**
9 let $\mathcal{Q} := P$ //Waiting list of places
10 **while** $\mathcal{Q} \neq \emptyset$ **do**
11   let $p \in \mathcal{Q}$; $\mathcal{Q} := \mathcal{Q} \setminus \{p\}$
12   **for** $t \in {}^{\bullet}p$ **do**
13   **if** $\exists M_1, M_2 \in \mathbb{M}^{bounded}(\mathcal{N}). M_1 \stackrel{\delta}{\equiv} M_2. \exists M_1' \in \mathbb{M}^{bounded}(\mathcal{N}). M_1 \stackrel{t}{\rightarrow}$
         $M_1' \wedge \forall M_2' \in \mathbb{M}^{bounded}(\mathcal{N}). M_2 \stackrel{t}{\rightarrow} M_2' \wedge M_1'(p) \stackrel{\delta}{\not\equiv} M_2'(p)$ **then**
14   pick $\delta' < \delta$ s.t. $M_1 \stackrel{\delta'}{\not\equiv} M_2$ and $\delta'(p') = \delta(p')$ for all $p' \in P \setminus {}^{\bullet}t$
15              $\mathcal{Q} := \mathcal{Q} \cup \{p' \mid \delta'(p') \neq \delta(p')\}$; $\delta := \delta'$
16   **end**
17   **end**
18 **end**
19 **return** δ

---

the *max* arc size over $\mathcal{N}$ is defined by $\mathbb{M}^{bounded}(\mathcal{N}) = \{M \in \mathbb{M}(\mathcal{N}) \mid |M(p)| \leq max(\mathcal{N})$ for all $p \in P\}$. As such, $\mathbb{M}^{bounded}(\mathcal{N})$ is a finite set of all bounded markings of $\mathcal{N}$ with cardinality less than or equal to $max(\mathcal{N})$.

Algorithm 1 now gives a procedure for computing a stable partition over a given CPN. It starts with an initial partition where every color in the color domain is in the same equivalence class for each place. The algorithm is then split into two parts. The first part from line 4 to 8 creates an initial partition applying the guard restrictions to the input places of the transitions. The second part from line 10 to 18 back propagates the guard restrictions throughout the net s.t. only colors that behave the same are quotiented together. Depending on the choices in lines 6 and 14, the algorithm may return the maximum stable partition, however in the practical implementation this is not guaranteed due to an approximation of the guard/arc expression analysis.

Theorem 4. *Given a CPN $\mathcal{N}$, the algorithm Stabilize($\mathcal{N}$) terminates and returns a stable partition of $\mathcal{N}$.*

3.2   Stable Partition Algorithm for Integer CPNs

The *Stabilize* computation presented in Algorithm 1 can be used to find a stable partition for any finite CPN. However, implementation-wise it is inefficient to

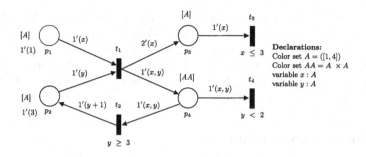

Fig. 3. Example CPN

Table 1. Stages of δ throughout Algorithm 1 for CPN in Fig. 3. The 0th iteration is the state of δ just before the while loop begins. The symbol '-' indicates that the value is the same as in the previous row.

Iteration	p_1	p_2	p_3	p_4	$\mathcal{Q}$
0	$\{([1,4])\}$	$\{([1,4])\}$	$\{([1,3]),([4])\}$	$\{([1,4],[1]),([1,4],[2]),$ $([1,4],[3,4])\}$	$\{p_1,p_2,p_3,p_4\}$
1, $p = p_3$	$\{([1,3]),([4])\}$	-	-	-	$\{p_1,p_2,p_4\}$
2, $p = p_4$	-	$\{([1]),([2]),([3,4])\}$	-	-	$\{p_1,p_2\}$
3, $p = p_2$	-	-	-	$\{([1,4],[1]),([1,4],[2]),$ $([1,4],[3]),([1,4],[4])\}$	$\{p_1,p_4\}$
4, $p = p_4$	-	$\{([1]),([2]),([3]),([4])\}$	-	-	$\{p_1,p_2\}$
5, $p = p_2$	-	-	-	-	$\{p_1\}$
6, $p = p_1$	-	-	-	-	$\{\}$

Table 2. Stages of α when computing the fixed point of E for the CPN in Fig. 3. The symbol '-' indicates that the value is the same as in the previous row.

Iteration	p_1	p_2	p_3	p_4
0, $\alpha = \alpha_0$	$\{([1])\}$	$\{([3])\}$	$\{\}$	$\{\}$
1, $t = t_1$	-	-	$\{([1])\}$	$\{([1],[3])\}$
2, $t = t_2$	-	$\{([3,4])\}$	-	-
3, $t = t_1$	-	-	-	$\{([1],[3,4])\}$
4, $t = t_2$	-	$\{([3,4]),([1])\}$	-	-
5, $t = t_1$	-	-	-	$\{([1],[3,4]),([1],[1])\}$
6, $t = t_2$	-	$\{([1,4])\}$	-	-
7, $t = t_1$	-	-	-	$\{([1],[1,4])\}$

represent every color in a given equivalence class individually. Hence, for integer CPN we represent an equivalence class as a tuple of ranges. As an example of computing stable partitions with Algorithm 1, consider the integer CPN in Fig. 3. Table 1 shows the different stages that δ undergoes in order to become stable. In iteration 0, the guard restrictions from the first for-loop are applied, followed by the iterations of the main while-loop. In our implementation, we do not iterate through every bounded marking and we instead (for efficiency reasons) statically analyze the places, arcs and guards in order to partition the color sets. For example, in iteration number 1, we consider the place p_3 and we can see that the colors in the range $[1, 3]$ must be distinguished from the color 4. This partitioning propagates back to the place p_1 as firing the transition t_1 moves tokens from p_1 to p_3 without changing its color.

4   Color Approximation

We now introduce another technique for safely overapproximating what colors can be present in each place of a CPN. Let $\mathcal{N} = (P, T, \mathbb{C}, \mathbb{B}, C, G, W, W_I, M_0)$ be a fixed CPN for the rest of this section. A *color approximation* is a function $\alpha : P \to 2^{\mathbb{C}}$ where $\alpha(p)$ approximates the possible colors in place $p \in P$ s.t. $\alpha(p) \subseteq C(p)$. Let $\mathbb{A}$ be the set of all color approximations. For a marking M and color approximation α, we write $M \sqsubseteq \alpha$ iff $set(M(p)) \subseteq \alpha(p)$ for all $p \in P$. A *color expansion* is a function $E : \mathbb{A} \to \mathbb{A}$ defined by

$$
E(\alpha)(p) = \begin{cases} \alpha(p) \cup set(W((t,p),b)) & \text{if } \exists t \in T. \exists b \in B(t). \\ & \quad set(W((p,t),b)) \subseteq \alpha(p) \\ \alpha(p) & \text{otherwise.} \end{cases}
$$

A color expansion iteratively expands the possible colors that exist in each place and obviously preserves the following property.

Lemma 2. *Let α be a color approximation then $\alpha(p) \subseteq E(\alpha)(p)$ for all $p \in P$.*

Let α_0 be the initial approximation such that $\alpha_0(p) \stackrel{\text{def}}{=} set(M_0(p))$ for all $p \in P$. Since E is a monotonic function on a complete lattice, we can compute its minimum fixed point and formulate the following key theorem.

Theorem 5. *Let α be a minimum fixed point of E such that $\alpha_0(p) \subseteq \alpha(p)$ for all $p \in P$. If $M_0 \to^* M$ then $M \sqsubseteq \alpha$.*

Given a color approximation α satisfying the preconditions of Theorem 5, we can now construct a reduced CPN $\mathcal{N}^\alpha = (P, T, \mathbb{C}, \mathbb{B}, C^\alpha, G, W, W_I, M_0)$ where $C^\alpha(p) = \alpha(p)$ for all $p \in P$. The net $\mathcal{N}^\alpha$ can hence have possibly smaller set of colors in its color domains and it satisfies the following theorem.

Theorem 6. *The reachable fragments from the initial marking M_0 of the LTSs generated by $\mathcal{N}$ and $\mathcal{N}^\alpha$ are isomorphic.*

4.1   Computing Color Approximation on Integer CPNs

As with color quotienting, representing each color individually becomes inefficient. We thus employ integer ranges to represent color approximations. Consider the approximation α where $\alpha(p) = \{(1, 2), (2, 2), (3, 2), (5, 6), (5, 7)\}$ are possible colors (pairs of integers) in the place p; this can be more compactly represented as a set of tuples of ranges $\{([1, 3], [2, 2]), ([5, 5], [6, 7])\}$.

Table 3. Number of unfolded nets for each unfolder

	Spike	Tapaal	A	ITS	B	MCC	A+B	Total
Unfolded nets	172	174	199	202	204	205	207	208

However, computing the minimum fixed point of E using ranges is not as trivial as using complete color sets. To do so, we need to compute new ranges depending on arcs and guards. We demonstrate this on the CPN in Fig. 3. Table 2 shows the computation of the minimum fixed point of E, starting from the initial approximation α_0. For example, in iteration number 5, we check if firing transition t_1 can produce any additional tokens to the places p_3 and p_4. Clearly, there is no change to the possible token colors in p_3 as $\alpha(p_1)$ did not change, however the addition of the integer range $[1]$ to $\alpha(p_2)$ in the previous iteration now allows us to produce a new token color $(1, 1)$ into p_4 and hence we add the singleton range $([1], [1])$ to $\alpha(p_4)$.

5   Experiments

We implemented the quotienting method from Sect. 3 as well as the color approximation method from Sect. 4 in C++ as an extension to the verification engine *verifypn* [13] from the TAPAAL toolchain [7]. We also implemented the method of variable symmetry identification inspired by its use in ITS-Tools [25]; the effect of this method is marginal as it additionally reduces the size of the unfolded net only on a few instances.

We perform experiments comparing several different approaches; the quotienting approach (method A), the color approximation (method B) and the combination of quotienting, symmetric variables and color approximation (method A+B) against the unfolder MCC [6] (used also by TINA [1] and LoLA [27]), ITSTools unfolder [24] and Spike unfolder [3] (also used by MARCIE [10] and Snoopy [9]) and the previous *verifypn* TAPAAL unfolder (revision 226) referred to as Tapaal. We compare the tools on the complete set of CPN nets and queries from 2020 Model Checking Contest [18]. The experiments are conducted on a compute cluster running Linux version 5.8.0-2, where each experiment is conducted on a AMD Epyc 7551 processor with a 15 GB memory limit and 5 min timeout. A repeatability package is available in [2].

Table 3 shows for each of the unfolders the number of unfolded nets within the memory/time limit. The last column shows the total number of unfolded nets by all tools combined. The single net that we cannot unfold is FamilyReunion3000 which was unfolded by MCC, though we can unfold it given 3 extra minutes. Our method A+B can unfold 3 nets that no other tool can unfold; DrinkVendingMachine48, 72, 96. This is directly attributed to method A.

The comparison of the sizes (total number of transitions and places) of unfolded nets is done by plotting the ratios between the size produced by our A+B method and the competing unfolder. Figure 4a shows the size ratios where

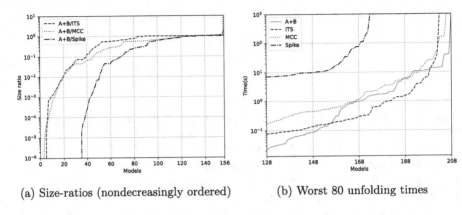

(a) Size-ratios (nondecreasingly ordered)   (b) Worst 80 unfolding times

Fig. 4. Unfolding size and unfolding time comparison

at least one comparison is not equal to 1. We see that our method has a significantly smaller size ratio for 88 colored nets, sometimes reducing the nets by several orders of magnitude. In a few cases ITS-Tools is able to unfold to a smaller net than our method due to their post-reductions. This is most prevalent on VehicularWifi which they unfold to the size of 38429 objects while we create a net of size 85835. The figure also shows one net unfolded by MCC where we timed out.

As our method outperforms the state-of-the-art unfolders w.r.t. the size of the unfolded nets, the question is whether the overhead of the advanced static analysis does not kill the benefits. Fortunately, this is not the case as shown in Fig. 4b where the 80 slowest running times (independently sorted in nondecreasing order) for each tool are depicted. The plots show that ITS, MCC and our unfolder are close in performance, while Spike is slower. ITS-Tools is generally fast on the nets that are unfolded in less than 10 s, however it becomes gradually slower and has problems unfolding the larger nets. The MCC unfolder and our method are similar in performance, except for the largest instances where we are faster.

The overall conclusion is that our advanced analyses adds only a little overhead while significantly decreasing the size of the unfolded nets. This is also confirmed by the number of answered reachability, CTL and LTL queries from the 2020 Model Checking Contest benchmark. The colored nets and queries are unfolded by the different tools and then verified by the TAPAAL engine. Here our unfolding method allows TAPAAL to answer in total 81.7% of all queries whereas the MCC unfolder can answer 76.9% and ITS-Tools unfolder 76.1% of all queries.

6   Conclusion

We presented two complementary methods for reducing the unfolding size of colored Petri nets (CPN). Both methods are proved correct and implemented in an open-source verification engine of the tool TAPAAL. Experimental results show a significant improvement in the size of unfolded nets, compared to state-of-the-art tools, without compromising the unfolding speed. The actual verification on the models and queries from the 2020 Model Checking Contest shows that our unfolding technique allows us to solve 4.8% more queries compared to the second best competing tool. In future work, we plan to combine our approach with structural reduction techniques.

Acknowledgments. We would like to thank Yann Thierry-Mieg for his answers and modifications to the ITS-Tools, Silvano Dal Zilio for his answers/additions concerning the MCC unfolder and Monika Heiner and Christian Rohr for their answers concerning the tools Snoopie, Marcie and Spike.

References

1. Berthomieu, B., Ribet, P.-O., Vernadat, F.: The tool TINA - construction of abstract state spaces for Petri nets and time Petri nets. Int. J. Prod. Res. **42**, 2741–2756 (2004). https://doi.org/10.1080/00207540412331312688
2. Bilgram, A., Jensen, P.G., Pedersen, T., Srba, J., Taankvist, P.H.: Repeatability Package for: Improvements in Unfolding of Colored Petri Nets (2021). https://doi.org/10.5281/zenodo.5255603
3. Chodak, J., Heiner, M.: Spike – reproducible simulation experiments with configuration file branching. In: Bortolussi, L., Sanguinetti, G. (eds.) CMSB 2019. LNCS, vol. 11773, pp. 315–321. Springer, Cham (2019). https://doi.org/10.1007/978-3-030-31304-3_19
4. Christensen, N., Glavind, M., Schmid, S., Srba, J.: Latte: improving the latency of transiently consistent network update schedules. SIGMETRICS Perform. Eval. Rev. **48**(3), 14–26 (2021). https://doi.org/10.1145/3453953.3453957
5. Ciaghi, A., Weldemariam, K., Villafiorita, A., Kessler, F.: Law modeling with ontological support and BPMN: a case study. In: The Second International Conference on Technical and Legal Aspects of the e-Society, CYBERLAWS 2011, pp. 29–34 (2011)
6. Dal Zilio, S.: MCC: a tool for unfolding colored Petri nets in PNML format. In: Janicki, R., Sidorova, N., Chatain, T. (eds.) PETRI NETS 2020. LNCS, vol. 12152, pp. 426–435. Springer, Cham (2020). https://doi.org/10.1007/978-3-030-51831-8_23
7. David, A., Jacobsen, L., Jacobsen, M., Jørgensen, K.Y., Møller, M.H., Srba, J.: TAPAAL 2.0: integrated development environment for timed-arc Petri nets. In: Flanagan, C., König, B. (eds.) TACAS 2012. LNCS, vol. 7214, pp. 492–497. Springer, Heidelberg (2012). https://doi.org/10.1007/978-3-642-28756-5_36
8. Amparore, E.G., Balbo, G., Beccuti, M., Donatelli, S., Franceschinis, G.: 30 years of GreatSPN. In: Fiondella, L., Puliafito, A. (eds.) Principles of Performance and Reliability Modeling and Evaluation. SSRE, pp. 227–254. Springer, Cham (2016). https://doi.org/10.1007/978-3-319-30599-8_9
9. Heiner, M., Herajy, M., Liu, F., Rohr, C., Schwarick, M.: Snoopy – a unifying Petri net tool. In: Haddad, S., Pomello, L. (eds.) PETRI NETS 2012. LNCS, vol. 7347, pp. 398–407. Springer, Heidelberg (2012). https://doi.org/10.1007/978-3-642-31131-4_22

10. Heiner, M., Rohr, C., Schwarick, M.: MARCIE – model checking and reachability analysis done efficiently. In: Colom, J.-M., Desel, J. (eds.) PETRI NETS 2013. LNCS, vol. 7927, pp. 389–399. Springer, Heidelberg (2013). https://doi.org/10.1007/978-3-642-38697-8_21
11. Hillah, L.M.: A hot drink vending machine (2021). https://mcc.lip6.fr/pdf/DrinkVendingMachine-form.pdf
12. Hillah, L.M.: Family Reunion (2021). https://mcc.lip6.fr/pdf/FamilyReunion-form.pdf
13. Jensen, J.F., Nielsen, T., Oestergaard, L.K., Srba, J.: TAPAAL and reachability analysis of P/T nets. In: Koutny, M., Desel, J., Kleijn, J. (eds.) Transactions on Petri Nets and Other Models of Concurrency XI. LNCS, vol. 9930, pp. 307–318. Springer, Heidelberg (2016). https://doi.org/10.1007/978-3-662-53401-4_16
14. Jensen, K.: Coloured Petri nets and the invariant-method. Theor. Comput. Sci. **14**, 317–336 (1981). https://doi.org/10.1016/0304-3975(81)90049-9
15. Jensen, K.: Coloured Petri Nets: Basic Concepts, Analysis Methods and Practical Use, vol. 1, 2nd edn. Springer, Heidelberg (1996). https://www.springer.com/gp/book/9783540609438
16. Jensen, K., Kristensen, L.M.: Coloured Petri Nets, Modelling and Validation of Concurrent Systems, 1st edn. Springer, Heidelberg (2009). https://doi.org/10.1007/b95112
17. Klostergaard, A.H.: Efficient Unfolding and Approximation of Colored Petri Nets with Inhibitor Arcs. Master's thesis, Department of Computer Science, Aalborg University (2018). https://projekter.aau.dk/projekter/files/281079031/main.pdf
18. Kordon, F., et al.: Complete Results for the 2020 Edition of the Model Checking Contest (2020). http://mcc.lip6.fr/2020/results.php
19. Liu, F., Heiner, M., Yang, M.: An efficient method for unfolding colored Petri nets. In: Proceedings of the 2012 Winter Simulation Conference (WSC), pp. 1–12 (2012). https://doi.org/10.1109/WSC.2012.6465203
20. Murata, T.: Petri nets: Properties, analysis and applications. Proc. IEEE **77**(4), 541–580 (1989). https://doi.org/10.1109/5.24143
21. Muschevici, R., Proença, J., Clarke, D.: Modular modelling of software product lines with feature nets. In: Barthe, G., Pardo, A., Schneider, G. (eds.) SEFM 2011. LNCS, vol. 7041, pp. 318–333. Springer, Heidelberg (2011). https://doi.org/10.1007/978-3-642-24690-6_22
22. Petri, C.A.: Kommunikation mit Automaten. Ph.D. thesis, Institut für instrumentelle Mathematik, Bonn (1962)
23. Schwarick, M., Rohr, C., Liu, F., Assaf, G., Chodak, J., Heiner, M.: Efficient unfolding of coloured Petri nets using interval decision diagrams. In: Janicki, R., Sidorova, N., Chatain, T. (eds.) PETRI NETS 2020. LNCS, vol. 12152, pp. 324–344. Springer, Cham (2020). https://doi.org/10.1007/978-3-030-51831-8_16
24. Thierry-Mieg, Y.: Symbolic model-checking using ITS-tools. In: Baier, C., Tinelli, C. (eds.) TACAS 2015. LNCS, vol. 9035, pp. 231–237. Springer, Heidelberg (2015). https://doi.org/10.1007/978-3-662-46681-0_20
25. Thierry-Mieg, Y.: Personal Correspondence with Y. Thierry-Mieg (2021)
26. Thierry-Mieg, Y., Dutheillet, C., Mounier, I.: Automatic symmetry detection in well-formed nets. In: van der Aalst, W.M.P., Best, E. (eds.) ICATPN 2003. LNCS, vol. 2679, pp. 82–101. Springer, Heidelberg (2003). https://doi.org/10.1007/3-540-44919-1_9
27. Wolf, K.: Petri net model checking with LoLA 2. In: Khomenko, V., Roux, O.H. (eds.) PETRI NETS 2018. LNCS, vol. 10877, pp. 351–362. Springer, Cham (2018). https://doi.org/10.1007/978-3-319-91268-4_18

Reachability of Weakly Nonlinear Systems Using Carleman Linearization

Marcelo Forets[1]([⊠]) [iD] and Christian Schilling[2] [iD]

[1] DMA, CURE, Universidad de la República, Montevideo, Uruguay
[2] University of Konstanz, Konstanz, Germany

Abstract. In this article we introduce a solution method for a special class of nonlinear initial-value problems using set-based propagation techniques. The novelty of the approach is that we employ a particular embedding (Carleman linearization) to leverage recent advances of high-dimensional reachability solvers for linear ordinary differential equations based on the support function. Using a global error bound for the Carleman linearization abstraction, we are able to describe the full set of behaviors of the system for sets of initial conditions and in dense time.

Keywords: Carleman linearization · Reachability · Support functions · Epidemic models

1 Introduction

We consider the problem of solving a system of nonlinear ordinary differential equations (ODEs) for a set of initial states. This is better known as *reachability analysis*. While for linear systems there exist very efficient algorithms [1,8,21,29], reachability analysis for nonlinear systems remains a challenging problem.

Traditional approaches [2] include those based on Taylor models [13], simulation [15], or hybridization [30]. In this paper we present a new approach to this problem by transforming the nonlinear system into an infinite-dimensional linear system, which we then truncate. This truncated model approximates the original system.

More specifically, our approach is based on Carleman linearization, which is an established method in mathematical nonlinear control but differs from the above-mentioned approaches. The Taylor-model approach truncates an infinite Taylor polynomial, while we truncate a linear system. Hybridization approaches linearize smalls regions in the state space, while we linearize the whole system.

To achieve good accuracy, the truncation results in a high-dimensional linear system. To solve such systems, we leverage efficient reachability solvers based on the support function that have recently been developed.

The first author is partly supported by Agencia Nacional de Investigación e Innovación (ANII), Uruguay.

P. C. Bell et al. (Eds.): RP 2021, LNCS 13035, pp. 85–99, 2021.
https://doi.org/10.1007/978-3-030-89716-1_6

Our approach can be used to obtain approximate solutions very quickly, but in an unsound way. Alternatively, using an error estimate, one can obtain a sound overapproximation. Under certain conditions (essentially weak nonlinearity), the error estimate converges, resulting in a precise approximation.

Contributions. This paper makes the following contributions:

- We revisit Carleman linearization and explain how it can be used as a fast but unsound way to propagate sets through a nonlinear dynamical system.
- We extend the approach to a sound and practical reachability algorithm for dissipative nonlinear dynamical systems.
- We evaluate the algorithm in two case studies and discuss its strengths.

Related Work. The original idea by Carleman [12, 27] did not receive much attention for several decades. Steeb showed that, while the nonlinear system and its infinite-dimensional embedding share the same analytic solutions, the embedding may admit additional non-analytic solutions [39]. Carleman linearization has since been applied successfully in control theory [14, 19, 33, 36] and physics and chemistry [18, 23].

Several works provide bounds on the approximation error of the truncated linearized system [16, 31]. In this paper we use the error bound derived in [31].

An approach that is related to ours transforms a nonlinear system into a linear or polynomial system via a "change of bases," using polynomials instead of Kronecker powers, and derives conditions under which this transformation preserves invariants [37].

Outline. The next section recalls the mathematical basis used in this paper. Section 3 introduces the classic Carleman linearization. In Sect. 4 we describe how to propagate sets using Carleman linearization. In Sect. 5 we extend this approach to a reachability algorithm for dissipative nonlinear dynamical systems. We evaluate the algorithm in Sect. 6 and conclude in Sect. 7.

2   Preliminaries

In this section we summarize the mathematical prerequisites to make this paper self-contained. For a detailed derivation of the Carleman linearization procedure we refer to [16].

2.1   Vectors, Norms, and Sets

Let $\mathbb{N} = \{1, 2, \ldots\}$ be the set of positive integers and $\mathbb{R}$ the set of real numbers, and for any $N \in \mathbb{N}$ we let $[N] := \{1, 2, \ldots, N\}$. n-dimensional vectors $x \in \mathbb{R}^n$ are understood as column vectors with components $x_i \in \mathbb{R}$, $i \in [n]$. Transposition is written x^T. For any $x \in \mathbb{R}^n$ and $p \in \mathbb{R}_{\geq 1} \cup \{\infty\}$, $\|x\|_p$ denotes the vector p-norm of x, with notable special cases $p = 2$ (Euclidean norm) and $p = \infty$ (supremum norm). If $A = (a_{ij}) \in \mathbb{R}^{m \times n}$ is a matrix, $\|A\|_p$ denotes the matrix norm induced by the vector p-norm, with notable special cases $p = 2$ (spectral norm: the largest singular value) and $p = \infty$ (supremum norm: the maximum absolute row sum). We may abbreviate $\|\cdot\|$ for $\|\cdot\|_\infty$. See [24] for precise definitions of these concepts.

For a compact, i.e. bounded and closed set $\mathcal{X} \subseteq \mathbb{R}^n$, $\|\mathcal{X}\|_p$ denotes the maximum of $\|x\|_p$ over all $x \in \mathcal{X}$. If $\mathcal{X}$ is polytopic (i.e. admits a representation as the finite intersection of half-spaces), its norm can be computed by a finite number of vector p-norm evaluations. Indeed, the map $x \to \|x\|_p$ is convex and the maximum of a convex function over a polytope is attained at one of its vertices. However, computing the vertex representation of a polytope initially given by its half-space representation can be computationally expensive in dimensions higher than two (see [25]). A simpler rule applies if $\mathcal{X}$ is hyperrectangular (i.e., can be represented as an axis-aligned box with center $c \in \mathbb{R}^n$ and radius vector $r \in \mathbb{R}^n$). Then $\|\mathcal{X}\|_p = \|c + Dr\|_p$ where $D = (D_{ij}) \in \mathbb{R}^{n \times n}$ is diagonal with matrix elements $D_{ii} = 1$ if $c_i \geq 0$ and $D_{ii} = -1$ otherwise, $i \in [N]$. We write $\mathcal{B}_r^n$ for the n-dimensional infinity-norm ball with radius r centered in the origin. The projection of a set $\mathcal{X}$ to the first k dimensions is denoted by $\pi_{1:k}(\mathcal{X})$.

2.2 Support Function

A standard approach to operate with compact and convex sets in $\mathbb{R}^n$ is to use the *support function* [28]. The support function of $\mathcal{X} \subseteq \mathbb{R}^n$ along direction $d \in \mathbb{R}^n$, $\rho(d, \mathcal{X})$, is the maximum of $d^T x$ over all $x \in \mathcal{X}$. In particular, if $\mathcal{X}$ is a polytope in half-space representation, its support function can be computed by solving a linear program (LP), and for certain classes of sets analytic formulas exist, which can be numerically evaluated in an efficient way. Such cases include hyperrectangular sets. Since the support function distributes over Minkowski sums, i.e. $\rho(d, \mathcal{X} \oplus \mathcal{Y}) = \rho(d, \mathcal{X}) + \rho(d, \mathcal{Y})$ for any pair of sets $\mathcal{X}$ and $\mathcal{Y}$, and since it holds that $\rho(d, M\mathcal{X}) = \rho(M^T d, \mathcal{X})$ for any matrix $M \in \mathbb{R}^{n \times n}$, the support function has been successfully applied to solve linear set-based recurrences of the form $\mathcal{X}_{k+1} = M\mathcal{X}_k \oplus \mathcal{Y}_k$, either explicitly or implicitly by solving the recurrence only along a predefined number of directions [9,17,29]. It is well-known that such recurrences are prevalent in reachability analysis of linear initial-value problems (IVPs), or nonlinear ones after some form of conservative linearization; see for example [2] and references therein.

2.3 Kronecker Product

For any pair of vectors $x \in \mathbb{R}^n$, $y \in \mathbb{R}^m$, their *Kronecker product* is $w = x \otimes y = (x_1 y_1, \ldots, x_1 y_m, x_2 y_1, \ldots, x_n y_m)^T$, and the dimension is $\dim(w) = mn$. This product is not commutative. For matrices the definition is analogous: if $A \in \mathbb{R}^{m \times n}$ and $B \in \mathbb{R}^{p \times q}$, then $A \otimes B \in \mathbb{R}^{mp \times nq}$ and

$$A \otimes B := \begin{pmatrix} a_{11}B & \cdots & a_{1n}B \\ \vdots & & \vdots \\ a_{m1}B & \cdots & a_{mn}B \end{pmatrix}.$$

The *Kronecker power* $x^{\otimes i}$ of $x \in \mathbb{R}^n$ is a convenient notation to express all possible products of elements of a vector up to a given order:

$$x^{\otimes i} := \underbrace{x \otimes \cdots \otimes x}_{i \text{ times}}, \qquad x \in \mathbb{R}^n.$$

Note that $\dim(x^{\otimes i}) = n^i$, and each component of $x^{\otimes i}$ is of the form $x_1^{\omega_1} x_2^{\omega_2} \cdots x_n^{\omega_n}$ for some multi-index $\omega \in \mathbb{N}^n$, $\|\omega\|_1 = i$. For example, if $n = 2$, the first two Kronecker powers are $x^{\otimes 1} = x = (x_1, x_2)^T$ and $x^{\otimes 2} = x \otimes x = (x_1^2, x_1 x_2, x_2 x_1, x_2^2)^T$. Further properties of Kronecker products can be found in [42] and [40].

3   Carleman Linearization

In this section we recall the classic Carleman linearization approach [12,27].

Polynomial differential equations are an important class of nonlinear systems $x'(t) = f(x(t))$, $f : \mathbb{R}^n \to \mathbb{R}^n$, such that the coordinate functions $f_i : \mathbb{R}^n \to \mathbb{R}$ are multivariate polynomials. Many systems can be rewritten as polynomial vector fields by introducing auxiliary variables, and any polynomial system is formally equivalent to a second-order system, possibly in higher dimensions – for a proof of this statement and an algorithm to compute such transformation see [16]. We can thus focus on quadratic ODEs without loss of generality. Consider the IVP for an n-dimensional quadratic ODE,

$$\frac{dx(t)}{dt} = F_1 x + F_2 x^{\otimes 2}, \tag{1}$$

with initial condition $x(0) \in \mathbb{R}^n$. Each $x_i(t)$, $i \in [n]$, is a function of t over the interval $[0, T]$ where T is the *time horizon*. We assume that the matrices $F_1 \in \mathbb{R}^{n \times n}$ and $F_2 \in \mathbb{R}^{n \times n^2}$ are independent of t. Intuitively, F_1 (resp. F_2) is associated with the linear (resp. nonlinear) behavior of the dynamical system; thus $\|F_2\|_2 / \|F_1\|_2$ being small corresponds to *weak nonlinearity* – a concept we will use in a later section.

The *Carleman linearization* (or *Carleman embedding*) procedure begins by introducing a sequence of auxiliary variables $\hat{y}_j := x^{\otimes j}$, $j \in \mathbb{N}$. Differentiating such variables with respect to time, and repeatedly substituting (1) into the derivatives of each $\hat{y}_j$ gives a formal equivalence with an infinite-dimensional linear system of ODEs [27]. Truncation to order N leads to a *finite* linear IVP in the *lifted* variables $\hat{y} := (\hat{y}_1, \hat{y}_2, \ldots, \hat{y}_N)^T$, namely

$$\frac{d\hat{y}}{dt} = A\hat{y}, \qquad \hat{y}(0) = \hat{y}_0, \tag{2}$$

with initial condition $\hat{y}_0 = (x_0, x_0^{\otimes 2}, \ldots, x_0^{\otimes N})^T$ and coefficients matrix A, which has the bi-diagonal block structure

$$A = \begin{pmatrix} A_1^1 & A_2^1 & 0 & 0 & \cdots & & 0 \\ 0 & A_2^2 & A_3^2 & 0 & \cdots & & 0 \\ 0 & 0 & A_3^3 & A_4^3 & 0 & & \vdots \\ \vdots & \vdots & \vdots & \ddots & \ddots & & 0 \\ 0 & 0 & \cdots & 0 & A_{N-1}^{N-1} & A_N^{N-1} \\ 0 & 0 & \cdots & 0 & 0 & A_N^N \end{pmatrix}, \tag{3}$$

where the A_i^i and A_{i+1}^i, which we call *transfer matrices*, have dimensions $n^i \times n^i$ and $n^i \times n^{i+1}$ respectively, and are defined by the formula

$$A_{i+i'-1}^i = \sum_{\nu=1}^{i} \overbrace{\mathbb{I}_n \otimes \cdots \otimes \underset{\underset{\nu\text{-th position}}{\uparrow}}{F_{i'}} \otimes \cdots \otimes \mathbb{I}_n}^{i \text{ factors}}.$$

for all $i \in [N]$ and where i' is either 1 (A_i^i is placed on the main diagonal) or 2 (A_{i+1}^i is placed on the upper diagonal) and where $\mathbb{I}_n$ is the identity matrix of order n. Note also that $A_1^1 = F_1$ and $A_2^1 = F_2$. The dimension of (2) is $n + n^2 + \cdots + n^N = \frac{n^{N+1}-n}{n-1} = \mathcal{O}(n^N)$.

Running Example. We illustrate the concepts described above in the simplest possible scenario. Consider the logistic equation (a special case of (1) for $n = 1$)

$$\frac{dx(t)}{dt} = rx(1 - x/K). \tag{4}$$

This equation and related generalizations arise naturally in the context of population dynamics, where $r > 0$ controls the initial rate of exponential growth, and $K > 0$ is the asymptotic equilibrium (the other equilibrium being $x = 0$). We transform (4) into the canonical scalar form (1), namely $x'(t) = ax(t) + bx^2(t)$, via $a = r$ and $b = -r/K$. Defining the auxiliary variables $\hat{y}_j = x^j$, $j \in \mathbb{N}$, we see that their first-order derivatives satisfy $\hat{y}_1' = x' = a\hat{y}_1 + b\hat{y}_2$, $\hat{y}_2' = 2x'x = 2a\hat{y}_2 + 2b\hat{y}_3$, etc. Hence the nonlinear ODE (4) is equivalent to the (infinite) linear ODE

$$\hat{y}_j' = ja\hat{y}_j + jb\hat{y}_{j+1}, \qquad j \in \mathbb{N}.$$

If we now fix the truncation order N, say, to $N = 4$, we obtain

$$\frac{d\hat{y}(t)}{dt} = \begin{pmatrix} a & b & 0 & 0 \\ 0 & 2a & 2b & 0 \\ 0 & 0 & 3a & 3b \\ 0 & 0 & 0 & 4a \end{pmatrix} \hat{y}, \qquad \hat{y}(0) = \begin{pmatrix} x_0 \\ x_0^2 \\ x_0^3 \\ x_0^4 \end{pmatrix}.$$

To estimate the quality of the approximation by finite truncation, we plot the solutions of (4) from $x_0 = 0.5$ over a time horizon of 10 and also plot the solution of (2) for several choices of N in Fig. 1(a). The model parameters are

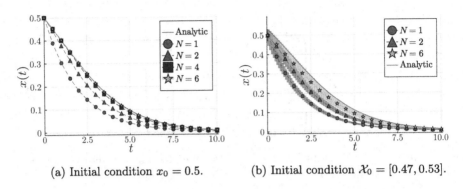

(a) Initial condition $x_0 = 0.5$.   (b) Initial condition $\mathcal{X}_0 = [0.47, 0.53]$.

Fig. 1. Solution of the original and of the truncated linearized IVPs for (4).

$r = -0.5$ and $K = 0.8$. As can be seen, for increasing N the solutions converge to the analytic solution, which in this case is known and given as

$$x(t) = \frac{x_0 a e^{at}}{a + b(1 - e^{at})x_0}.$$

Solving Eq. (2) requires computing the matrix exponential acting on the initial states $\hat{y}(t = k\delta) = e^{Ak\delta}\hat{y}(0)$ at all times, which may be expensive for higher-dimensional systems. In the next section we introduce a method to propagate sets of initial conditions in dense time making use of the particular structure of the matrix (3) using support function techniques. Theoretical estimates of the truncation error are considered in Sect. 5.

4 Set Propagation

In the previous section we saw how to transform a nonlinear IVP into an approximate linear IVP by Carleman linearization and truncation at a chosen order N. In this section we describe how this approach generalizes to IVPs whose initial condition is a set of states $\mathcal{X}_0 \subseteq \mathbb{R}^n$ described by a hyperrectangle. This is a common case, and hyperrectangular approximations can be computed efficiently. We need to discuss two steps: how to transform $\mathcal{X}_0$ to the linear system and how to propagate sets of states for a linear IVP.

For the transformation of $\mathcal{X}_0$ we generalize the Kronecker product to sets with $\mathcal{X}^{\otimes i} := \{x^{\otimes i} \mid x \in \mathcal{X}\}$. For a hyperrectangle $\mathcal{X}$ we approximate $\mathcal{X}^{\otimes i}$ by applying the rules of interval arithmetic to each dimension [32]. We note that one needs to carefully arrange the variables in order to obtain a tight solution. The arrangement consists of grouping the same variables of each monomial; for example, $x_1^2 x_2 x_1$ is evaluated using interval arithmetic as $x_1^3 x_2$ to avoid the dependency problem. To illustrate, consider the extension of the example in Sect. 2.3 to the hyperrectangle $\mathcal{X} = [0.9, 1.1] \times [-0.1, 0.1]$. Then $\mathcal{X}^{\otimes 1} = \mathcal{X} \subseteq \mathbb{R}^2$ and $\mathcal{X}^{\otimes 2} \subseteq [0.81, 1.21] \times [-0.11, 0.11] \times [-0.11, 0.11] \times [0.0, 0.01] \subseteq \mathbb{R}^4$.

There exist many algorithms to propagate a set through an IVP in a conservative way, i.e., the result overapproximates the true solution, in particular for linear IVPs [1–3,8,20–22,26,29]. Most of these approaches first discretize the continuous-time system, for which the error can be made arbitrarily small by choosing a small discretization step δ, and then propagate the sets in discrete time, which in certain cases can be done in an error-free way. We refer the reader to the above works for details about the discretization. Below we explain the second step because it is relevant for the later discussion.

Given a discretized linear IVP with discretized matrix $\Phi = e^{A\delta}$ and discretized initial condition $\hat{\mathcal{X}}_0$,

$$x_{k+1} = \Phi x_k, \quad x_0 \in \hat{\mathcal{X}}_0,$$

the set of reachable states is described by the *flowpipe* $\bigcup_{k \geq 0} \mathcal{R}_k$ where the $\mathcal{R}_k :=$ $\Phi^k \hat{\mathcal{X}}_0$ is the *reach set* for the time span $[k\delta, (k+1)\delta]$. In other words, a flowpipe is a sequence of reach sets given by the matrix powers of Φ applied to $\hat{\mathcal{X}}_0$. This computation scales to systems with hundreds of dimensions.

Example (cont'd). Consider again the logistic system. In Fig. 1(b) we plot the flowpipes obtained for the different truncated approximations with an initial condition $\mathcal{X}_0 = [0.47, 0.53]$.

5   Reachability Algorithm

In this section we discuss an error estimation that allows us to obtain a sound overapproximation of the states reachable by the original nonlinear system.

5.1   Error Bound

We have yet to determine how the solutions of the truncated linear IVP (2) are related to those of the original nonlinear IVP (1). To formulate this relation precisely, we introduce some notation. The error of the j-th block of variables is defined as $\eta_j(t) := x^{\otimes j}(t) - \hat{y}_j(t)$, which is the difference between the Kronecker power of the solution of (1) and the projection of the solution of (2) onto the corresponding block of variables of the lifted $\hat{y}$. We are mostly interested in the first block, i.e., $j = 1$, since $x(t) = x^{\otimes 1}(t)$, and the truncation error corresponds to upper bounding the quantity $\|\eta_1(t)\| \leq \varepsilon(t)$ for some error function $\varepsilon(t)$ to be determined. Ideally, for fixed t the error function should decrease sufficiently fast for increasing order N, so we can use low orders in practice, typically 2 to 6. In [16] the authors derived explicit error bounds for the linearization, i.e., a function $\varepsilon(t)$ that only depends on the initial condition and the norms of the matrices F_1 and F_2. However, that approach is too conservative since $\varepsilon(t)$ diverges in finite time – even in cases when the solution of the linearized system (2) is converging.

Crucial to the present article, the authors in [31] discovered that, by imposing an assumption on the class of quadratic problems considered, an arbitrary-time and exponentially convergent error formula holds. There are two main assumptions: 1) linear terms dominate over nonlinear ones (*weak nonlinearity*) and 2) nonlinear effects play a prominent role during a finite time span, after which only linear terms matter (*linear dissipation*). These definitions are formalized below. In the following we assume that the eigenvalues of F_1 in (1) are sorted (counting multiplicities) such that $\Re(\lambda_n) \leq \cdots \leq \Re(\lambda_1)$, where $\Re(\lambda)$ is the real part of λ.

Definition 1. *System* (1) *is said to be* weakly nonlinear *if the ratio*

$$R := \frac{\|x_0\|\|F_2\|}{|\Re(\lambda_1)|} \tag{5}$$

satisfies $R < 1$.

Definition 2. *System* (1) *is said to be* dissipative *if $\Re(\lambda_1) < 0$ (i.e., the real part of all eigenvalues is negative).*

The conditions $\Re(\lambda_1) < 0$ and $R < 1$ ensure arbitrary-time convergence.

Theorem 1 ([31, **Corollary 1**]). *Assuming that* (1) *is weakly nonlinear and dissipative, the error bound associated with the linearized problem* (2) *truncated at order N satisfies*

$$\|\eta_1(t)\| \leq \varepsilon(t) := \|x_0\|R^N(1 - e^{\Re(\lambda_1)t})^N, \tag{6}$$

with R as defined in (5). *This error bound holds for all $t \geq 0$.*

5.2   Obtaining a Sound Set-Propagation Algorithm

The interesting aspect of (6) is that we can enclose all possible behaviors of a nonlinear problem for a hyperrectangular initial condition $\mathcal{X}_0 \subseteq \mathbb{R}^n$ in two steps: first, propagating the solutions of the high-dimensional linear system (2) forward in time using a suitable linear reachability technique; in a second step, enlarging the solution (a sequence of reach sets $\mathcal{R}_j$ with associated time span $\Delta t = [t, t + \delta]$ for some $\delta > 0$) by taking the Minkowski sum with a ball of radius $r := \max(|a|, |b|)$ where $[a, b]$ is the interval-arithmetic evaluation of $\varepsilon(\Delta t)$. Moreover, the truncation error converges to zero for increasing N and, as we will see in the experiments, typical values of N do not have to be prohibitively large to obtain reasonable approximation bounds.

Theorem 2. *Given a flowpipe, consider any n-dimensional reach set $\mathcal{R}_j$, $j \geq 0$, and its associated time span $\Delta t = [t, t + \delta]$. Let $\overline{\mathcal{R}}_k$ be the true set of reachable states in the time span Δt and r as defined above. Then we have $\overline{\mathcal{R}}_k \subseteq \mathcal{R}_k \oplus \mathcal{B}_r^n$.*

This allows us to present a sound reachability method as shown in Algorithm 1. Crucially, we see that in Line 5 we only require the reach sets $\mathcal{R}_j$ in the first n dimensions. Thus it suffices to compute these sets in a "sparse" way in Line 2. We can use an algorithm based on the support function for *post* to achieve that. In our implementation we use the algorithm from [29], which takes as input a set of direction vectors in which the reach sets are evaluated.

Algorithm 1: Reachability algorithm

Input: $\mathcal{X}_0 \subseteq \mathbb{R}^n$: hyperrectangular initial states; F_1, F_2: system matrices; N: truncation order; T: time horizon; *post*: algorithm to compute a flowpipe for linear systems

Output: flowpipe overapproximating the reachable states until T

1   $A, \hat{\mathcal{X}}_0 \leftarrow linearize(\mathcal{X}_0, F_1, F_2, N)$;   // Carleman linearization
2   $(\mathcal{R}_0, \ldots, \mathcal{R}_m) \leftarrow post(y' = Ay, y(0) \in \hat{\mathcal{X}}_0)$;   // flowpipe for linear system
3   **for** $j \leftarrow 0$ **to** m **do**
4      $\varepsilon \leftarrow error(\mathcal{R}_j, \mathcal{X}_0, F_1, F_2, N)$;   // linearization error
5      $\mathcal{R}_j^\varepsilon \leftarrow \pi_{1:n}(\mathcal{R}_j) \oplus \mathcal{B}_\varepsilon^n$;   // enlarged reach set
6   **end**
7   **return** $(\mathcal{R}_0^\varepsilon, \ldots, \mathcal{R}_m^\varepsilon)$

5.3   Reevaluation of the Error Term

For dissipative systems, while the solution of the linear system may converge to zero, the corrected term including the error estimate may not. This observation leads to the idea of reevaluating the error estimate after some time t^*, since for fixed F_1 and F_2, a decreasing $\|x_0\|$ leads to a smaller value R which, in turn, reduces the error estimate $\varepsilon(t)$. This is, however, nontrivial because by the time one reevaluates, the past error estimate must be taken into account and thus the new state estimate at t^* may already be too pessimistic. In the evaluation we apply such a reevaluation manually.

6   Evaluation

In this section we study two models that have also been used in [31], but we repeat them here to make this article self-contained. In the first model we evaluate all aspects outlined in the present article including the error bounds. In the second model we demonstrate that even if the assumptions for the error bounds do not apply, we can still obtain solutions of useful accuracy.

For comparison we compute an overapproximation of the reachable states for the original nonlinear systems using a Taylor-model (TM) approach implemented in JuliaReach [4,6,7,35], with the default parameters (Taylor polynomials with spatial and temporal expansions of orders 2 and 8 respectively), which generally has high precision. To evaluate the flowpipe for the linear system in Algorithm 1, we use the $2n$ directions $\pm e_i$ for $i \in [n]$, where e_i is the unit vector in dimension i, which corresponds to the outer hyperrectangular approximation of $\pi_{1:n}(\mathcal{R}_j)$. Note that the number of directions, $2n$, is independent of the truncation order N. Interval-arithmetic computations are performed using the Julia library IntervalArithmetic.jl [5], and for set-based computations we use LazySets.jl [38]. The code and scripts to run these problems is available online.[1]

---

[1] github.com/JuliaReach/RP21_RE.

6.1 Epidemic Model (SEIR)

There exist several widely used models of population dynamics that generalize the logistic model from Sect. 3 [10]. We consider the popular *SEIR* epidemic model with data on the early spread of the COVID-19 disease from [34]. A population P is divided into four compartments: susceptible (P_S), exposed (P_E), infectious (P_I), and recovered (P_R). An individual is initially susceptible and becomes exposed/infected with rate r_{tra}. The latent time before an exposed individual becomes infectious themselves is T_{lat}. Finally, an infectious individual recovers after time T_{inf}. New individuals are added to the population with rate Λ. We also consider a vaccination with rate r_{vac} [41]. The system of ODEs is:

$$\frac{\mathrm{d}P_S}{\mathrm{d}t} = -\Lambda\frac{P_S}{P} - r_{\text{vac}}P_S - r_{\text{tra}}P_S\frac{P_I}{P} + \Lambda$$

$$\frac{\mathrm{d}P_E}{\mathrm{d}t} = -\Lambda\frac{P_E}{P} - \frac{P_E}{T_{\text{lat}}} + r_{\text{tra}}P_S\frac{P_I}{P}$$

$$\frac{\mathrm{d}P_I}{\mathrm{d}t} = -\Lambda\frac{P_I}{P} + \frac{P_E}{T_{\text{lat}}} - \frac{P_I}{T_{\text{inf}}}$$

$$\frac{\mathrm{d}P_R}{\mathrm{d}t} = -\Lambda\frac{P_R}{P} + r_{\text{vac}}P_S + \frac{P_I}{T_{\text{inf}}}$$

In this model we assume that $P = P_S + P_E + P_I + P_R$ remains constant, so we need not model P_R. The corresponding F_i matrices thus simplify to

$$F_1 = \begin{pmatrix} -\frac{\Lambda}{P} - r_{\text{vac}} & 0 & 0 \\ 0 & -\frac{\Lambda}{P} - \frac{1}{T_{\text{lat}}} & 0 \\ 0 & \frac{1}{T_{\text{lat}}} & -\frac{\Lambda}{P} - \frac{1}{T_{\text{inf}}} \end{pmatrix}, F_2 = \begin{pmatrix} 0 & 0 & -\frac{r_{\text{tra}}}{P} & 0 & 0 & 0 & 0 & 0 & 0 \\ 0 & 0 & \frac{r_{\text{tra}}}{P} & 0 & 0 & 0 & 0 & 0 & 0 \\ 0 & 0 & 0 & 0 & 0 & 0 & 0 & 0 & 0 \end{pmatrix}.$$

Since F_1 is triangular, $\Re(\lambda_1) = -\frac{\Lambda}{P} - \min\{r_{\text{vac}}, \frac{1}{T_{\text{lat}}}, \frac{1}{T_{\text{inf}}}\}$. We also have $\|F_2\| = \frac{\sqrt{2}r_{\text{tra}}}{P}$ and $\|\mathcal{X}_0\| \leq P$. Thus we can estimate

$$R = \frac{\|\mathcal{X}_0\|\frac{\sqrt{2}r_{\text{tra}}}{P}}{\frac{\Lambda}{P} + \min\{r_{\text{vac}}, \frac{1}{T_{\text{lat}}}, \frac{1}{T_{\text{inf}}}\}} \leq \frac{\sqrt{2}r_{\text{tra}}}{\frac{\Lambda}{P} + \min\{r_{\text{vac}}, \frac{1}{T_{\text{lat}}}, \frac{1}{T_{\text{inf}}}\}}.$$

The time scale is measured in days. We use the same parameters as in [31]: a population of $P = 10^7$, Λ is small (here: $\Lambda = 1$), hence the constant term is disregarded in the analysis, $T_{\text{lat}} = 5.2$, $T_{\text{inf}} = 2.3$, $r_{\text{tra}} = 0.13$ days^{-1}, and $r_{\text{vac}} = 0.19$ days^{-1}. We choose $\mathcal{X}_0 = [6e6, 3e5, 3.7e6] \oplus \mathcal{B}_{1e5}^3$, which results in $R \approx 0.68$ and $\Re(\lambda_1) \approx -0.19$ and thus Theorem 1 is applicable.

The analysis results without and with conservative error estimate are plotted in Fig. 2, where we used the discretization step $\delta = 0.1$. We can see that the non-conservative Carleman approximation is precise even for the small value $N = 2$. However, the error estimate is too conservative for such small value of N thus it is not plotted. However, using $N = 5$ the error estimate improves significantly, but only until around time $t = 4$; this is due to the large values in $\mathcal{X}_0$. At $t = 4$

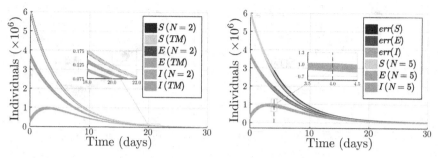

(a) Reach sets $\mathcal{R}_j$ without error estimate. (b) Reach sets $\mathcal{R}_j^\varepsilon$ including error estimate with a reevaluation at $t = 4$ (cf. zoom).

Fig. 2. Results for the SEIR model.

Table 1. Run times for the SEIR model and the Burgers model obtained for the Taylor-model (TM) approach and the Carleman linearization with different truncation orders N.

	SEIR model		Burgers model	
	No error bound	Incl. error bound	Initial point	Initial set
TM	6.14 s		0.88 s	0.91 s
Carleman	$N = 2$: 0.006 s	$N = 5$: 0.185 s	$N = 2$: 0.0065 s	$N = 2$: 0.0067 s
			$N = 3$: 0.24 s	$N = 3$: 0.29 s

we reevaluate the estimate. Since the state and with it the norm has changed, the new error estimate is more optimistic and converges quickly. The run times are given in Table 1.

6.2 Burgers Partial Differential Equation

We study a model arising from the discretization of a partial differential equation (PDE). Consider the viscous Burgers equation to model convective flow [11]

$$\partial_t u + x \partial_x u = \nu \partial_x^2 u.$$

We use the following model parameters: viscosity $\nu = 0.05$, domain length $L_0 = 1$, and $U_0 = 1$. We consider the initial condition $u(x,0) = -U_0 \sin(2\pi x/L_0)$ on the domain $x \in \pm L_0/2$ and Dirichlet conditions $u(x,0) = 0$ at the boundaries. We distribute this initial condition to a set by keeping the end points fixed and enlarging the initial point to some width $w = 0.06$. For the PDE discretization we use central differences obtaining the coupled differential equations

$$\partial_t u_i = \nu \frac{u_{i+1} - 2u_i + u_{i-1}}{\Delta x^2} - \frac{u_{i+1}^2 - u_{i-1}^2}{4\Delta x}. \tag{7}$$

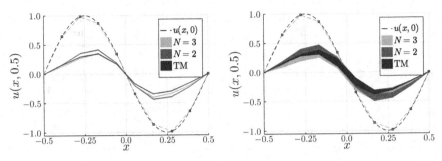

(a) Point initial condition ($w = 0$).   (b) Distributed initial condition ($w = 0.06$).

Fig. 3. Results for the Burgers model at $t = 0.5$ with initial condition width w.

We use $n_x = 10$ points and $\Delta x = L_0/(n_x - 1)$. Equation (7) has the form of (1) that we need to apply Carleman linearization. We obtain $\Re(\lambda_1) \approx -0.488 < 0$ but $R \approx 18.58$, i.e., R as defined in Eq. 5 is not smaller than one. Although the theoretical error bounds from Theorem 1 are not applicable here, it is interesting to observe that the set-based solution is reasonably accurate with respect to the solution obtained for the original nonlinear system. In Fig. 3 we plot the results at $t = 0.5$. For the linear reachability algorithm we used the step size $\delta = 0.01$. We can see that we still obtain good approximations that decrease exponentially by incrementing the truncation N. The run times are given in Table 1.

7   Conclusions

In this paper we have presented a reachability method that abstracts nonlinear terms into a higher-dimensional space such that the evolution is approximately linear. The main advantage of the method is that we can leverage recent set propagation techniques that are specialized to high-dimensional linear ODEs. However, the method does not apply to general nonlinear systems but requires weak nonlinearity, i.e., the relative norm of the nonlinear term should be smaller than that of the linear term. Under such limitations, the presented method outperforms other reachability methods because linear reachability in high dimension can be solved efficiently.

This work can be extended in several ways. First, we can consider time-dependent terms; an error bound is derived in [31]. Second, in our experimental evaluation we observed that manually reevaluating the error bound can improve the precision if the norm of the states shrinks (which should generally happen for dissipative systems). It would be interesting to automate this process. Third, the reachability analysis can be accelerated, e.g., using Krylov methods to work more efficiently in high dimensions. A more challenging direction is to devise a new reachability algorithm that exploits the structure of the linearized system.

Acknowledgments. The first author acknowledges fruitful discussions with Amaury Pouly and Goran Frehse. We are grateful to the anonymous reviewers for helpful comments.

References

1. Althoff, M., Frehse, G.: Combining zonotopes and support functions for efficient reachability analysis of linear systems. In: CDC, pp. 7439–7446. IEEE (2016). https://doi.org/10.1109/CDC.2016.7799418
2. Althoff, M., Frehse, G., Girard, A.: Set propagation techniques for reachability analysis. Ann. Rev. Control Robot. Auton. Syst. **4**, 369–395 (2020)
3. Bak, S., Duggirala, P.S.: Simulation-equivalent reachability of large linear systems with inputs. In: Majumdar, R., Kunčak, V. (eds.) CAV 2017. LNCS, vol. 10426, pp. 401–420. Springer, Cham (2017). https://doi.org/10.1007/978-3-319-63387-9_20
4. Benet, L., Sanders, D.P.: TaylorSeries.jl: Taylor expansions in one and several variables in Julia. J. Open Sour. Softw. **4**(36), 1043 (2019). https://doi.org/10.21105/joss.01043
5. Benet, L., Sanders, D.P.: JuliaIntervals/IntervalArithmetic.jl, May 2021. https://github.com/JuliaIntervals/IntervalArithmetic.jl. https://doi.org/10.5281/zenodo.3336308
6. Benet, L., Sanders, D.P.: JuliaIntervals/TaylorModels.jl, June 2021. https://github.com/JuliaIntervals/TaylorModels.jl. https://doi.org/10.5281/zenodo.2613102
7. Bogomolov, S., Forets, M., Frehse, G., Potomkin, K., Schilling, C.: JuliaReach: a toolbox for set-based reachability. In: HSCC, pp. 39–44. ACM (2019). https://doi.org/10.1145/3302504.3311804
8. Bogomolov, S., Forets, M., Frehse, G., Viry, F., Podelski, A., Schilling, C.: Reach set approximation through decomposition with low-dimensional sets and high-dimensional matrices. In: HSCC, pp. 41–50. ACM (2018). https://doi.org/10.1145/3178126.3178128
9. Bogomolov, S., Forets, M., Frehse, G., Viry, F., Podelski, A., Schilling, C.: Reach set approximation through decomposition with low-dimensional sets and high-dimensional matrices. In: Proceedings of the 21st International Conference on Hybrid Systems: Computation and Control (part of CPS Week), pp. 41–50 (2018)
10. Brauer, F., Castillo-Chavez, C., Castillo-Chavez, C.: Mathematical Models in Population Biology and Epidemiology, vol. 2. Springer, Heidelberg (2012). https://doi.org/10.1007/978-1-4614-1686-9
11. Burgers, J.: A mathematical model illustrating the theory of turbulence. In: Advances in Applied Mechanics, vol. 1, pp. 171–199. Elsevier (1948). https://doi.org/https://doi.org/10.1016/S0065-2156(08)70100-5
12. Carleman, T.: Application de la théorie des équations intégrales linéaires aux systèmes d'équations différentielles non linéaires. Acta Math. **59**(1), 63–87 (1932)
13. Chen, X., Ábrahám, E., Sankaranarayanan, S.: Flow*: an analyzer for non-linear hybrid systems. In: Sharygina, N., Veith, H. (eds.) CAV 2013. LNCS, vol. 8044, pp. 258–263. Springer, Heidelberg (2013). https://doi.org/10.1007/978-3-642-39799-8_18
14. Collado, J., Sánchez, I.: Modified Carleman linearization and its use in oscillators. In: 2008 5th International Conference on Electrical Engineering, Computing Science and Automatic Control, CCE 2008, pp. 13–19. IEEE (2008)

15. Donzé, A.: Breach, a toolbox for verification and parameter synthesis of hybrid systems. In: Touili, T., Cook, B., Jackson, P. (eds.) CAV 2010. LNCS, vol. 6174, pp. 167–170. Springer, Heidelberg (2010). https://doi.org/10.1007/978-3-642-14295-6_17

16. Forets, M., Pouly, A.: Explicit error bounds for carleman linearization. arXiv preprint arXiv:1711.02552 (2017)

17. Frehse, G., et al.: SpaceEx: scalable verification of hybrid systems. In: Gopalakrishnan, G., Qadeer, S. (eds.) CAV 2011. LNCS, vol. 6806, pp. 379–395. Springer, Heidelberg (2011). https://doi.org/10.1007/978-3-642-22110-1_30

18. Gaude, B.W.: Solving nonlinear aeronautical problems using the Carleman linearization method (2001)

19. Germani, A., Manes, C., Palumbo, P.: Filtering of differential nonlinear systems via a Carleman approximation approach. In: 44th IEEE Conference on Decision and Control, 2005 and 2005 European Control Conference, CDC-ECC 2005, pp. 5917–5922. IEEE (2005)

20. Girard, A.: Reachability of uncertain linear systems using zonotopes. In: Morari, M., Thiele, L. (eds.) HSCC 2005. LNCS, vol. 3414, pp. 291–305. Springer, Heidelberg (2005). https://doi.org/10.1007/978-3-540-31954-2_19

21. Girard, A., Le Guernic, C., Maler, O.: Efficient computation of reachable sets of linear time-invariant systems with inputs. In: Hespanha, J.P., Tiwari, A. (eds.) HSCC 2006. LNCS, vol. 3927, pp. 257–271. Springer, Heidelberg (2006). https://doi.org/10.1007/11730637_21

22. Han, Z., Krogh, B.H.: Reachability analysis of large-scale affine systems using low-dimensional polytopes. In: Hespanha, J.P., Tiwari, A. (eds.) HSCC 2006. LNCS, vol. 3927, pp. 287–301. Springer, Heidelberg (2006). https://doi.org/10.1007/11730637_23

23. Hashemian, N., Armaou, A.: Fast moving horizon estimation of nonlinear processes via Carleman linearization. In: American Control Conference, ACC 2015, Chicago, IL, USA, 1–3 July 2015, pp. 3379–3385. IEEE (2015). https://doi.org/10.1109/ACC.2015.7171854. https://doi.org/10.1109/ACC.2015.7171854

24. Horn, R.A., Johnson, C.R.: Matrix Analysis. Cambridge University Press, Cambridge (2012)

25. Kaibel, V., Pfetsch, M.E.: Some algorithmic problems in polytope theory. In: Joswig, M., Takayama, N. (eds.) Algebra, Geometry and Software Systems, pp. 23–47. Springer, Heidelberg (2003). https://doi.org/10.1007/978-3-662-05148-1_2

26. Kaynama, S., Oishi, M.: Complexity reduction through a Schur-based decomposition for reachability analysis of linear time-invariant systems. Int. J. Control $84(1)$, 165–179 (2011). https://doi.org/10.1080/00207179.2010.543703

27. Kowalski, K., Steeb, W.H.: Nonlinear Dynamical Systems and Carleman Linearization. World Scientific (1991)

28. Le Guernic, C.: Reachability analysis of hybrid systems with linear continuous dynamics. Ph.D. thesis, Université Grenoble 1 - Joseph Fourier (2009)

29. Le Guernic, C., Girard, A.: Reachability analysis of linear systems using support functions. Nonlinear Anal.: Hybrid Syst. $4(2)$, 250–262 (2010). https://doi.org/10.1016/j.nahs.2009.03.002

30. Li, D., Bak, S., Bogomolov, S.: Reachability analysis of nonlinear systems using hybridization and dynamics scaling. In: Bertrand, N., Jansen, N. (eds.) FORMATS 2020. LNCS, vol. 12288, pp. 265–282. Springer, Cham (2020). https://doi.org/10.1007/978-3-030-57628-8_16

31. Liu, J.P., Kolden, H.Ø., Krovi, H.K., Loureiro, N.F., Trivisa, K., Childs, A.M.: Efficient quantum algorithm for dissipative nonlinear differential equations. Proc. Natl. Acad. Sci. **118**(35) (2021)

32. Moore, R.E., Kearfott, R.B., Cloud, M.J.: Introduction to Interval Analysis. SIAM (2009)

33. Mozyrska, D., Bartosiewicz, Z.: Carleman linearization of linearly observable polynomial systems. In: Sarychev, A., Shiryaev, A., Guerra, M., Grossinho, M.R. (eds.) Mathematical Control Theory and Finance, pp. 311–323. Springer, Berlin (2008). https://doi.org/10.1007/978-3-540-69532-5_17

34. Pan, A., et al.: Association of public health interventions with the epidemiology of the COVID-19 outbreak in Wuhan. China. JAMA **323**(19), 1915–1923 (2020). https://doi.org/10.1001/jama.2020.6130

35. Pérez-Hernández, J.A., Benet, L.: PerezHz/TaylorIntegration.jl, May 2021. https://github.com/PerezHz/TaylorIntegration.jl.   https://doi.org/10.5281/zenodo.2562352

36. Rauh, A., Minisini, J., Aschemann, H.: Carleman linearization for control and for state and disturbance estimation of nonlinear dynamical processes. IFAC Proc. Vol. **42**(13), 455–460 (2009)

37. Sankaranarayanan, S.: Change-of-bases abstractions for non-linear hybrid systems. Nonlinear Anal.: Hybrid Syst. **19**, 107–133 (2016). https://doi.org/10.1016/j.nahs.2015.08.006

38. Schilling, C., Forets, M.: JuliaReach/LazySets.jl: v1.45.1, June 2021. https://github.com/JuliaReach/LazySets.jl.   https://doi.org/10.5281/zenodo.4896008. Accessed 31 May 2021

39. Steeb, W.H.: A note on Carleman linearization. Phys. Lett. A **140**(6), 336–338 (1989). https://doi.org/10.1016/0375-9601(89)90631-2

40. Steeb, W.H., Hardy, Y.: Matrix Calculus and Kronecker Product: A Practical Approach to Linear and Multilinear Algebra. World Scientific (2011)

41. Zaman, G., Han Kang, Y., Jung, I.H.: Stability analysis and optimal vaccination of an sir epidemic model. Biosystems **93**(3), 240–249 (2008). https://doi.org/10.1016/j.biosystems.2008.05.004

42. Zhang, F.: Matrix Theory: Basic Results and Techniques. Springer, Heidelberg (2011). https://doi.org/10.1007/978-1-4614-1099-7

Continued Fraction Approach to Gauss Reduction Theory

Oleg Karpenkov[(✉)] [iD]

University of Liverpool, Liverpool L69 7ZL, UK
karpenk@liverpool.ac.uk

Abstract. Jordan Normal Forms serve as excellent representatives of conjugacy classes of matrices over algebraically closed fields. Once we know normal forms, we can compute functions of matrices, their main invariants, etc. The situation is more complicated if we search for normal forms for conjugacy classes over fields that are not closed and especially over rings.

In this paper we study $\mathrm{PGL}(2,\mathbb{Z})$-conjugacy classes of $\mathrm{GL}(2,\mathbb{Z})$ matrices. For the ring of integers the Jordan approach has various limitations and in fact it is not effective. The normal forms of conjugacy classes of $\mathrm{GL}(2,\mathbb{Z})$ matrices are provided by an alternative theory, which is known as Gauss Reduction Theory. We introduce new techniques to compute reduced forms in Gauss Reduction Theory in terms of the elements of certain continued fractions. The current approach is based on recent progress in the field of the geometry of numbers. The proposed technique provides an explicit computation of periods of continued fractions for the slopes of eigenvectors.

Keywords: Integer matrices · Gauss reduction theory · Continued fractions · Geometry of numbers

Introduction

In this paper we study the structure of the conjugacy classes of $\mathrm{GL}(2,\mathbb{Z})$. Recall that $\mathrm{GL}(2,\mathbb{Z})$ is the group of all invertible matrices with integer coefficients. As a consequence the determinants of such matrices are ± 1. We say that the matrices A and B from $\mathrm{GL}(2,\mathbb{Z})$ are $\mathrm{PGL}(2,\mathbb{Z})$-*conjugate* if there exists a $\mathrm{GL}(2,\mathbb{Z})$ matrix C such that $B = \pm CAC^{-1}$. In the integer case projectivity simply means that all matrices are considered up to the multiplication by ± 1.

Recall that for algebraically closed fields every matrix is conjugate to its Jordan Normal Form. The situation with $\mathrm{GL}(n,\mathbb{Z})$ is not so simple as the set of integer numbers does not have a field structure. A description of $\mathrm{PGL}(2,\mathbb{Z})$-conjugacy classes in the two-dimensional case is the subject of Gauss Reduction Theory. The conjugacy classes are classified by periods of certain periodic continued fractions (for additional information we refer to [13,17,18]; for the algorithms of the conjugacy test in $\mathrm{GL}(2,\mathbb{Z})$ see [4,6]). The first geometric invariants

© Springer Nature Switzerland AG 2021
P. C. Bell et al. (Eds.): RP 2021, LNCS 13035, pp. 100–114, 2021.
https://doi.org/10.1007/978-3-030-89716-1_7

of GL(2, ℤ) matrices in the spirit of continued fractions were studied in [9]. The question of the classification of conjugacy classes is closely related to the study of homogeneous forms (see e.g. in [2]) and the theory of Markov and Lagrange spectra (see e.g. in [5]).

Our aim is to study a natural class of reduced matrices that represent every conjugacy class, which are good candidates for normal forms in integer settings. Note that the number of reduced matrices in any PGL(2, ℤ)-conjugacy class of matrices is finite (see, e.g., in Chapter 7 of [11]). In this paper we approach the following problem.

Problem 1. Find explicit expressions for normal forms PGL(2, ℤ)-conjugate to a given matrix.

We solve this problem by introducing a new surprising explicit formula to generate all reduced matrices PGL(2, ℤ)-conjugate to a given one via certain long continued fractions that are built using the elements of the matrices. We show how write all the reduced matrices in Sect. 3. The formula is justified by Theorem 3 which is supplemented by technical statements of Theorem 2, Theorem 4 and Proposition 2. The new method is based on lattice trigonometry introduced in [7,8] (see also in [11]).

We expect that the computational complexity of the new method is comparable to the algorithm of Chapter 7 in [11]. One of the advantages of the proposed new approach is that it constructs all reduced matrices while the classical algorithms result in a single reduced matrix. In addition all the reduced operators of the proposed approach are explicitly described via geometric invariants, which is potentially useful for the multidimensional case. Recall that the studies of the conjugacy classes of GL(n, ℤ) for $n > 2$ were motivated by V. Arnold (see, e.g., in [1]) who revived the notion of multidimensional continued fractions in the sense of Klein ([15, 16]). The first results in higher dimensional cases were obtained in [10] (see also [11], Chapter 21), however the theory is far from its final form even for the case of $n = 3$. We hope that the approach of the current paper will give some hints for numerous open problems in the multidimensional case.

This paper is organized as follows. In Sect. 1 we start with necessary notions and definitions of geometry of numbers. In particular we introduce the notion of the semigroup of reduced matrices. We discuss three different cases of GL(2, ℤ) matrices in general in Sect. 2. In Sect. 3 we bring together all the stages of finding all reduced matrices PGL(2, ℤ)-conjugate to a given one. Finally in Sect. 4 we discuss some technical details used in the construction of reduced matrices.

1   Background

In this section we briefly discuss basic notions used in the computation of reduced matrices. We start in Subsect. 1.1 with elementary notions and definitions of lattice geometry. In Subsect. 1.2 we define sails of integer angles; and introduce LLS sequences for broken lines. Further we define LLS sequences for integer angles.

Sails and LLS sequences are important invariants related to conjugacy classes of GL(2, $\mathbb{Z}$) matrices. We continue in Subsect. 1.3 with the notion of periods of LLS sequences related to matrices. In Subsect. 1.4 we introduce reduced matrices and give a continuant representation for them. We conclude this section with a general definition of difference of sequences in Subsect. 1.5.

1.1 Basics of Integer Geometry in the Plane

We say that a point is *integer* if its coordinates are integers. A segment is integer if its endpoints are integer. An angle is called *integer* if its vertex is an integer point. We also say that an integer angle is *rational* if its edges contain integer points distinct to the vertex.

An affine transformation is said to be integer if it is a one-to-one mapping of the lattice $\mathbb{Z}^2$ to itself. Note that the set of integer transformations is a semidirect product of the group of translations by an integer vector and the group GL(2, $\mathbb{Z}$). Two sets are *integer congruent* if there exists an integer affine transformation providing a bijection between these two sets.

Definition 1. *The integer length of an integer segment AB is the number of integer points inside its interior plus one. Denote it by* $l\ell(AB)$.

The integer sine of a rational angle $\angle ABC$ is the following integer: $\frac{|\det(AB,BC)|}{l\ell(AB)\cdot l\ell(BC)}$, *where* $|\det(AB,BC)|$ *is the absolute value of the determinant of the matrix of the pair of vectors* (AB,BC). *Denote it by* $l\sin\angle ABC$.

The integer lengths and sines are invariants of integer affine transformations.

1.2 Sail and LLS Sequences

Let us now study an important invariant of angles and broken lines. It will be employed in the proofs, however from computational perspectives one can use the statement of Theorem 4 as the explicit definition of LLS sequences for angles (without appealing to integer geometry).

Let $\angle ABC$ be an integer angle. The boundary of the convex hull of all integer points in the convex closure of $\angle ABC$ except B is called the *sail* of $\angle ABC$.

Note that the sail of a rational angle is a finite broken line, while the sail of an integer angle that is not rational is a broken line infinite on one or both sides.

Definition 2. *Let $A_1,\ldots,A_n$ be a broken line (here we can consider finite or infinite broken lines) such that A_i, A_{i+1}, and O are not in one line for all admissible parameters of i. Define*

$$a_{2k} = \det(OA_k, OA_{k+1}) \quad and \quad a_{2k-1} = \frac{\det(A_kA_{k-1}, A_kA_{k+1})}{a_{2k-2}a_k}.$$

for all admissible k. The sequence $(a_0,\ldots,a_{2n})$ (or an infinite one respectively) is called the LLS sequence of the broken line $A_0\ldots A_n$.

Definition 3. *Consider an integer angle* $\angle ABC$. *Let* $\ldots A_{i-1}, A_i A_{i+1}, \ldots$ *be the sail of* $\angle ABC$. *Here we consider the broken line directed from the edge AB to the edge BC. Let the LLS sequence for the broken line* $\ldots A_{i-1}, A_i A_{i+1}, \ldots$ *be* $(\ldots a_{2k-1}, a_{2k}, a_{2k+1}, \ldots)$ *(finite or infinite). Then the sequence*

$$(\ldots |a_{2k-1}|, |a_{2k}|, |a_{2k+1}|, \ldots)$$

is called the Lattice Length Sine sequence (or simply LLS sequence, for short) of the angle $\angle ABC$ *and is denoted by* $LLS(\angle ABC)$.

Remark 1. Note that the LLS sequence can be defined for any lattice (not necessarily for the integer lattice).

Remark 2. Consider a rational angle $\angle ABC$ with a positive $\det(AO, BC)$. Then its LLS sequence $(a_0, \ldots, a_{2n})$ consists of an odd number of elements and

$$a_{2k} = \mathrm{l\ell} A_k A_{k+1} \quad \text{and} \quad a_{2k-1} = \mathrm{lsin} \angle A_{k-1} A_k A_{k+1} \quad \text{for all admissible } k.$$

Now let us recall the definition of a continuant.

Definition 4. *Let n be a positive integer. A continuant K_n is a polynomial with integer coefficients defined recursively by*

$$K_{-1}() = 0; \quad K_0() = 1; \quad K_1(a_1) = a_1;$$
$$K_n(a_1, a_2, \ldots, a_n) = a_n K_{n-1}(a_1, a_2, \ldots, a_{n-1}) + K_{n-2}(a_1, a_2, \ldots, a_{n-2}).$$

Remark 3. Note that we have the following general expression relating continued fractions and continuants. For any real numbers $a_1, \ldots, a_n$ it holds that

$$[a_1; a_2 : \cdots : a_n] = \frac{K_n(a_1, a_2, \ldots, a_n)}{K_{n-1}(a_2, \ldots, a_n)}.$$

We use the following important geometric property of LLS sequences.

Theorem 1 ([7] **2008**). *Consider a finite broken line $A_1, \ldots, A_n$ with LLS sequence $(a_0, \ldots, a_{2n})$. Let also $A_0 = (1, 0)$ and $A_1 = (1, a_0)$. Then*

$$A_n = \big(K_{2n+1}(a_0, \ldots, a_{2n}), K_{2n}(a_1, \ldots, a_{2n})\big).$$

For further additional information on the geometry of continued fractions see [11].

1.3   LLS Periods of GL(2, $\mathbb{Z}$) Matrices

Let M be a (2×2)-matrix with two distinct real eigenvalues. In this case M has two eigenlines. The complement to these eigenlines is a union of four cones. We say that the sails of these cones are the *sails associated to M*.

Definition 5. *We say that a sequence of positive integers is an LLS sequence of M if this sequence is the LLS sequence of one of the sails associated to M.*

Remark 4. It turns out that in the case of $\mathrm{GL}(2,\mathbb{Z})$ matrices with real irrational eigenvalues the LLS sequences of all associated sails coincide up to a possible index shift and reversal (see Section 7 of [11]). So the LLS sequence is uniquely defined by the matrix in this case.

We conclude this subsection with the following fundamental definition.

Definition 6. *Let M be a $\mathrm{GL}(2,\mathbb{Z})$ matrix with real irrational eigenvalues. Then its LLS sequence is periodic. In addition M^2 acts as a periodic shift on every one of the sails. Assume that M^2 shifts the sail by n vertices. Then any period of length n is called an LLS period of M. (Here we write the elements of the period in order from a vertex v on the sail to the vertex $M^2(v)$ on the sail.)*

Remark 5. Note that matrices inverse to each other have reversed periods.

1.4   Reduced Matrices and Continuants

In this section we introduce reduced matrices. Their elements have a nice representation in terms of continuants. Let us fix the following notation.

Definition 7. *Let a be a real number, denote $M_a = \begin{pmatrix} 0 & 1 \\ 1 & a \end{pmatrix}$.*

Now let $(a_1, \ldots, a_n)$ be any sequence of real numbers, we set

$$M_{a_1,\ldots,a_n} = \prod_{k=1}^{n} \begin{pmatrix} 0 & 1 \\ 1 & a_k \end{pmatrix}.$$

Definition 8. *Consider a sequence of positive integers $(a_1, \ldots, a_n)$. Then the matrix $M_{a_1,\ldots,a_n}$ is said to be reduced.*

There are two main benefits for the proposed choice of reduced matrices. Firstly, they form a semigroup with respect to matrix multiplication. Secondly, there is the following explicit description of such matrices.

Proposition 1. *Let $n \geq 0$ and let $(a_1, \ldots, a_n) \in \mathbb{R}^n$. Then we have*

$$M_{a_1,\ldots,a_n} = \begin{pmatrix} K_{n-2}(a_2,\ldots,a_{n-1}) & K_{n-1}(a_2,\ldots,a_n) \\ K_{n-1}(a_1,a_2,\ldots,a_{n-1}) & K_n(a_1,a_2,\ldots,a_n) \end{pmatrix}.$$

In addition, we have $\det M_{a_1,\ldots,a_n} = (-1)^n$.

Example 1. Consider

$$M_{3,-3,-2,5} = M_3 \cdot M_{-3} \cdot M_{-2} \cdot M_5.$$

Hence M is represented by the following sequence: $(3, -3, -2, 5)$. By Proposition 1 we immediately have

$$M_{3,-3,-2,5} = \begin{pmatrix} K_2(-3,-2) & K_3(-3,-2,5) \\ K_3(3,-3,-2) & K_4(3,-3,-2,5) \end{pmatrix}.$$

Therefore,

$$M_{3,-3,-2,5} = \begin{pmatrix} 7 & 32 \\ 19 & 87 \end{pmatrix}.$$

Here we actually have

$$\frac{19}{7} = [3:-3:-2] \quad \text{and} \quad \frac{87}{19} = [3:-3:-2:5].$$

Note also that

$$\det M = (-1)^4 = 1.$$

Proof of Proposition 1. The proof is done by induction in n.

Base of Induction. For $n = 1, 2$ we have respectively

$$M_{a_1} = \begin{pmatrix} 0 & 1 \\ 1 & a_1 \end{pmatrix} = \begin{pmatrix} K_{-1}() & K_0() \\ K_0() & K_1(a_1) \end{pmatrix}.$$

$$M_{a_1,a_2} = M_{a_1} M_{a_2} = \begin{pmatrix} 1 & a_2 \\ a_1 & 1 + a_1 a_2 \end{pmatrix} = \begin{pmatrix} K_0() & K_1(a_2) \\ K_1(a_1) & K_2(a_1, a_2) \end{pmatrix}.$$

Step of Induction. We have

$$M_{a_1,\ldots,a_{n+1}} = M_{a_1,\ldots,a_n} \cdot M_{a_{n+1}} =$$
$$\begin{pmatrix} K_{n-2}(a_2,\ldots,a_{n-1}) & K_{n-1}(a_2,\ldots,a_n) \\ K_{n-1}(a_1,\ldots,a_{n-1}) & K_n(a_1,\ldots,a_n) \end{pmatrix} \cdot \begin{pmatrix} 0 & 1 \\ 1 & a_{n+1} \end{pmatrix} =$$
$$\begin{pmatrix} K_{n-1}(a_2,\ldots,a_n) & K_{n-2}(a_2,\ldots,a_{n-1}) + a_{n+1}K_{n-1}(a_2,\ldots,a_n) \\ K_n(a_1,\ldots,a_n) & K_{n-1}(a_1,\ldots,a_{n-1}) + a_{n+1}K_n(a_1,\ldots,a_n) \end{pmatrix} =$$
$$\begin{pmatrix} K_{n-1}(a_2,\ldots,a_n) & K_n(a_2,\ldots,a_{n+1}) \\ K_n(a_1,\ldots,a_n) & K_{n+1}(a_1,\ldots,a_{n+1}) \end{pmatrix}.$$

The last equality is a classical relation for the numerators and denominators of continued fractions (see, e.g., in [14] or in [11]). This concludes the proof for the induction step.

Finally, since $\det M_a = -1$ we have $\det M = (-1)^n$. ☐

1.5 Difference of Sequences

Finally let us give the following general combinatorial definition.

Definition 9. *Let $m > n$ be two non-negative integers and consider two sequences of real numbers $S_a = (a_1,\ldots,a_m)$ and $S_b = (b_1,\ldots,b_n)$. We say that there exists a difference of S_a and S_b if there exists $k \leq m+1$ such that the following conditions are fulfilled: (i) $b_i = a_i$ for $1 \leq i < k$; (ii) either $k = m+1$ or $b_k \neq a_k$; (iii) $b_{k+i} = a_{k+i+m-n}$ for $0 \leq i \leq n-k$. In this case we denote $S_a - S_b = (a_k, a_{k+1},\ldots,a_{k+n-m-1})$.*

Example 2. (i) We have $(1,2,3,4,5,6,7,8) - (1,2,3,6,7,8) = (4,5)$.
(ii) The expression $(1,2,3,4,5,6,7,8) - (1,5,8)$ is not defined.

2   Three Cases of GL(2, ℤ) Matrices

It is natural to split the matrices of GL(2, ℤ) into three cases with respect to their spectra (set of eigenvalues). We distinguish the cases of complex, rational, and real irrational spectra. The cases of complex and rational cases are rather straightforward, they are not included in Gauss Reduction Theory. The case of real irrational spectra is more complicated, it is central for this paper. Let us now briefly discuss these three cases in this section.

Case of Complex Spectra: We start with GL(2, ℤ) matrices whose characteristic polynomials have a pair of complex conjugate roots. There are exactly three PGL(2, ℤ)-conjugacy classes of such matrices (these classes are perfectly distinguished by traces of matrices). They are represented by

$$\begin{pmatrix} 1 & 1 \\ -1 & 0 \end{pmatrix}, \quad \begin{pmatrix} 0 & 1 \\ -1 & 0 \end{pmatrix}, \quad \text{and} \quad \begin{pmatrix} 0 & 1 \\ -1 & -1 \end{pmatrix}.$$

The author does not have a link to the proof of the classification in the complex case, however it is a classical result. The complete proof will be shortly available in the second edition of [11].

Case of Rational Spectra: It turns out that such matrices have eigenvalues equal to ±1, any of rational spectra matrices are PGL(2, ℤ)-conjugate to exactly one of the following matrices

$$\begin{pmatrix} 1 & m \\ 0 & 1 \end{pmatrix} \quad \text{for} \quad m \geq 0, \quad \begin{pmatrix} 1 & 0 \\ 0 & -1 \end{pmatrix}, \quad \text{or} \quad \begin{pmatrix} 1 & 1 \\ 0 & -1 \end{pmatrix}.$$

(Note that the rational spectra case contains the degenerate case of coinciding roots.) For the proofs in the rational spectra case see [3].

Case of Real Irrational Spectra: This case is the most complicated. It is described by a so-called Gauss Reduction Theory, which is based on Euclidean type algorithms providing a descent to reduced matrices (see Chapter 7 of [11]). It is interesting to note that the number of reduced matrices integer congruent to a given one is finite and equal to the number of elements in the minimal period of the regular continued fraction for the tangent of the slope of any eigenvector of the matrix. In the next section we introduce an alternative algorithm based on explicit expressions for reduced matrices that originated in geometry of numbers.

3   Techniques to Find Reduced Matrices PGL(2, ℤ)-Conjugate to a Given One

Let us outline the main stages of the reduced matrices construction. All the statements involved in it are proven in the next section. The construction is based on general Theorem 3 and several supplementary technical statements.

Remark 6. The proposed algorithm provides an answer to Problem 1.

Goal of the Algorithm. List all reduced matrices $PGL(2,\mathbb{Z})$-conjugate to M.

Input Data. We are given a $GL(2,\mathbb{Z})$ matrix. Namely we have $M = \begin{pmatrix} p & r \\ q & s \end{pmatrix}$.

Step 1. Starting with any point P_0 we set $P_1 = M^4(P_0)$ and $P_2 = M^6(P_0)$ and compute $LLS(\angle P_0OP_1)$ and $LLS(\angle P_0OP_2)$ using Theorem 4.

Step 2. By Proposition 2 one of the periods of the LLS sequence for M is a half of $LLS(\angle P_0OP_2) - LLS(\angle P_0OP_1)$. We take the first half of this sequence, so let the period be $(a_1, \ldots, a_n)$ and let the lengths of the minimal possible periods be m.

Step 3. Now we can write down the reduced matrices in accordance with Theorem 2 and Proposition 1.

Output. All the reduced matrices $PGL(2,\mathbb{Z})$-conjugate to M will be of the form

$$\begin{pmatrix} K_{n-2}(a_{k+2}, \ldots, a_{k+n-1}) & K_{n-1}(a_{k+2}, \ldots, a_{k+n}) \\ K_{n-1}(a_{k+1}, a_{k+2}, \ldots, a_{k+n-1}) & K_n(a_{k+1}, a_{k+2}, \ldots, a_{k+n}) \end{pmatrix}, k = 0, \ldots, m-1.$$

Example 3. **Input:** Find all reduced matrices for the matrix $M = \begin{pmatrix} 7 & -30 \\ -10 & 43 \end{pmatrix}$.

Step 1. Starting with any point $P_0 = (1,1)$ set

$$P_1 = M^4(P_0) = (-2875199, 4119201) \quad \text{and}$$
$$P_2 = M^6(P_0) = (-7182245951, 10289762449).$$

Let us first compute $LLS(\angle P_0OP_1)$. First of all note that

$$\varepsilon = -\text{sign}\frac{1}{1} = -1, \ \delta = \text{sign}\frac{-2875199}{4119201} = -1 \quad \text{and} \quad \det(OP_1, OP_2) \cdot (-1) > 0.$$

Hence we take the following odd regular continued fractions: $\frac{1}{1} = [1]$ and

$$\left|\frac{-2875199}{4119201}\right| = \frac{2875199}{4119201} = [0; 1:2:3:4:1:2:3:4:1:2:3:4:1:2:3:3].$$

Now we combine these two continued fractions in accordance with Theorem 4:

$$[-1; 0:0:-1:-2:-3:-4:-1:-2:-3:-4:-1:-2:-3:-4:$$
$$-1:-2:-3:-3] = \frac{-6994400}{4119201}.$$

We have

$$\left|\frac{-6994400}{4119201}\right| = \frac{6994400}{4119201} = [1; 1:2:3:4:1:2:3:4:1:2:3:4:1:2:3:3].$$

Therefore, $LLS(\angle P_0OP_1) = (1,1,2,3,4,1,2,3,4,1,2,3,4,1,2,3,\overline{3})$.
   Similarly we get

$$LLS(\angle P_0OP_2) = (\underline{1,1,2,3,4,1,2,3,4,1,2,3,4,1,2,3,}\boxed{4,1,2,3,4,1,2,3},\overline{3}).$$

(Here we show the difference of the sequences in the box).

Step 2. By Proposition 2 one of the periods of the LLS sequence for M is a half of the sequence $LLS(\angle P_0 O P_2) - LLS(\angle P_0 O P_1) = (4,1,2,3,4,1,2,3)$, which is $(4,1,2,3)$. The minimal possible period is of length 4 (so $m = 4$).

Step 3. We can write down the reduced matrices in accordance with Theorem 2 and Proposition 1 for all distinct periods of length 4, i.e. for

$$(4,1,2,3), \quad (1,2,3,4), \quad (2,3,4,1), \quad \text{and} \quad (3,4,1,2).$$

Output. Finally applying Proposition 1 to these four sequences we have the list of all reduced matrices $PGL(2, \mathbb{Z})$-conjugate to M:

$$\begin{pmatrix} K_2(1,2) & K_3(1,2,3) \\ K_3(4,1,2) & K_4(4,1,2,3) \end{pmatrix} = \begin{pmatrix} 3 & 10 \\ 14 & 47 \end{pmatrix}, \quad \begin{pmatrix} 7 & 30 \\ 10 & 43 \end{pmatrix}, \quad \begin{pmatrix} 13 & 16 \\ 30 & 37 \end{pmatrix}, \quad \begin{pmatrix} 5 & 14 \\ 16 & 45 \end{pmatrix}.$$

(We show continuants only for the first matrix and omit them for the others.)

4   Technical Aspects of Reduced Matrices Computation

In this section we show some technical statements involved in the justification of the above algorithm. We start in Subsect. 4.1 with writing periods of LLS sequences for reduced matrices. In Subsect. 4.2 we explain how to list all reduced matrices $PGL(2, \mathbb{Z})$-conjugate to the given one (the reduced matrices are given in terms of LLS periods of original matrices). Then we show in general how to compute LLS sequences of angles in Subsect. 4.3. Finally in Subsect. 4.4 we state how to compute the periods of LLS sequences.

4.1   Continued Fraction Enumeration of Reduced Matrices

Let us find a period of the LLS sequence for matrices $M_{a_1, a_2, \ldots, a_n}$.

Theorem 2. *Let n, $a_1, \ldots, a_n$ be positive integers. Then one of the periods of the LLS sequence for $M_{a_1, a_2, \ldots, a_n}$ is $(a_1, a_2, \ldots, a_n)$.*

Proof. Consider the sequence of integer points $(x_k, y_k) = M_{a_1, a_2, \ldots, a_n}^k (1, 0)$ for positive integer values of k. By Proposition 1 and Definition 7 for every k we know the coordinates x_k and y_k via continuants. So from the general theory of continued fractions they are relatively prime and further by Remark 3 they satisfy

$$\frac{y_k}{x_k} = [(a_1; a_2 : \cdots : a_n)^k].$$

Therefore, all the points (x_k, y_k) are vertices of the sail of the periodic continued fraction $\alpha = [(a_1; a_2 : \cdots : a_n)]$. (This is a classical statement of geometry of numbers (Theorem 3.1 of [11]).) This immediately implies that the direction of the vector $(1, \alpha)$ is the limiting direction for the sequence of directions for the vectors (x_k, y_k), and in particular that $\lim_{k \to \infty} (y_k/x_k) = \alpha$. Hence $(1, \alpha)$ is one of the eigenvectors corresponding to the maximal eigenvalue (and thus the eigenvalues are both real and distinct). By construction the LLS sequence for α is periodic with period $(a_1, a_2, \ldots, a_n)$.

Finally the sail for α from some element coincides with the sail for M. Since the sail for M is periodic, the period is the same as for α, i.e. $(a_1, a_2, \ldots, a_n)$. $\square$

4.2   Matrices $\mathbf{PGL(2, \mathbb{Z})}$-Conjugate to a Given One

The following theorem produces the list of all reduced matrices $\mathrm{PGL}(2, \mathbb{Z})$-conjugate to a given one.

Theorem 3. *Let M be a $\mathrm{GL}(2, \mathbb{Z})$ matrix and let $(a_1, \ldots, a_n)$ be a period of the LLS sequence corresponding to M. Finally let m be the minimal length of the period of the LLS sequence. Then the list of all reduced matrices $\mathrm{PGL}(2, \mathbb{Z})$-conjugate to M consists of the following m matrices:*

$$M_{a_{1+k}, \ldots, a_{n+k}}, \qquad k = 1, \ldots, m.$$

Let us first prove the following lemma.

Lemma 1. *Two operators have the same LLS sequences if and only if their unions of eigenlines are integer congruent to each other.*

Proof. The LLS sequence is an invariant of arrangements of two lines with respect to integer congruences, hence they are the same if the unions of eigenlines for the operators are integer congruent to each other.

Now let the unions of eigenlines have the same LLS sequences. Pick any of the four angles for the first unions of the eigenlines. Now we pick another angle for the second union of the eigenlines in such a way that their subsequences of integer lengths and integer sines coincide respectively. This is always possible as the adjacent angles have the same LLS sequence with subsequence of integer angles equal to the subsequence of integer sines and vice versa. This is a consequence of a classical duality of sails for adjacent angles ([11], Proposition 8.5).

Such angles are integer congruent. This follows from the fact that the sail is uniquely reconstructed by the LLS sequence, one of its vertices, and the direction of one of the adjacent edges to this vertex. Once LLS sequence is reconstructed, the integer angle is reconstructed itself (here we assume that we consider the angles with vertex at the origin). For further details we refer to [11], Theorem 4.11. Since the angles are integer congruent, the unions of eigenlines are integer congruent as well. $\square$

Proof of Theorem 3. By Lemma 1 we know that two operators have the same LLS sequences if and only if their unions of eigenlines are integer congruent to each other. In Theorem 2 we showed that the LLS sequence of $M_{b_1,b_2,\ldots,b_r}$ has a period

$$(b_1, b_2, \ldots, b_r).$$

Therefore, by Lemma 1, M could be congruent only to reduced matrices whose units of eigenlines are integer congruent to the units of eigenlines

$$\pm M_{a_{1+k},\ldots,a_{n+k}}$$

for $k = 1, \ldots, m$ (these are the only matrices with LLS sequences of length n that have such LLS sequences). By the structure of the sails of reduced operators (as the first segment of the sail in the positive octant containing $(1, 0)$ is orthogonal to the x-axis) reduced matrices with congruent units of eigenlines have coinciding eigenlines. By a general statement in geometry of numbers, the operators with coinciding eigenlines are the elements of the same Dirichlet group and in the two-dimensional case they are some rational powers of each other (see Section 8.1 of [11]).

The LLS sequence of M^2 shifts the LLS sequence by n, and hence the reduced matrices integer conjugate to $\pm M$ should be defined by sequences of length n (or, equivalently, that they have periods of length n). Note that the powers of matrices $M_{a_{1+k},\ldots,a_{n+k}}$ are defined by a sequence of length n if and only if the exponents are either 1 or -1.

In the case of the exponent equal to 1 we have matrices $M_{a_{1+k},\ldots,a_{n+k}}$ for $k = 1, \ldots, m$ themselves. In case of the exponent equal to -1 the LLS sequences are reversed, so this case is possible only for palindromic sequences, and hence we arrive to the same matrices $M_{a_{1+k},\ldots,a_{n+k}}$ for $k = 1, \ldots, m$. Therefore, the list of all reduced matrices $\mathrm{PGL}(2, \mathbb{Z})$-conjugate to M consists of m matrices of the form $M_{a_{1+k},\ldots,a_{n+k}}$ for $k = 1, \ldots, m$. This concludes the proof. □

4.3 Computation of LLS Sequences for Rational Angles

In this subsection we formulate a theorem that provides an explicit formula for the LLS sequence of a given matrix. This formula is very much in the spirit of generalized Perron Identity introduced in our recent paper [12].

Theorem 4. *Consider two linearly independent integer vectors $A = (p, q)$ and $B = (r, s)$. We assume that none of them are proportional either to $(1, 0)$ or to $(0, 1)$. Let two sequences of integers $(a_0, a_1, \ldots, a_{2m})$ and $(b_0, b_1, \ldots, b_{2n})$ be defined as the sequences of elements of the odd regular continued fractions of*

- $|q/p|$ *and* $|s/r|$ *in case of* $\det(OA, OB) \cdot \mathrm{sign}\frac{p}{q} < 0$;
- $|p/q|$ *and* $|r/s|$ *in case of* $\det(OA, OB) \cdot \mathrm{sign}\frac{p}{q} > 0$.

Further we set $\varepsilon = -\mathrm{sign}\frac{p}{q}$ and $\delta = \mathrm{sign}\frac{r}{s}$. Denote also

$$\alpha = [\varepsilon a_{2m} : \varepsilon a_{2m-1} : \cdots : \varepsilon a_1 : \varepsilon a_0 : 0 : \delta b_0 : \delta b_1 : \cdots : \delta b_{2n}].$$

Let $|\alpha| = [c_0; c_1 : \cdots : c_{2k}]$ be the regular odd continued fraction for $|\alpha|$. Set

- $S = (c_0, c_1, \ldots, c_{2k})$ in the case $c_0 \neq 0$;
- $S = (c_2, \ldots, c_{2k})$ in the case $c_0 = 0$.

Then S is the LLS sequence for the angle $\angle AOB$.

Remark 7. In fact it is possible to simplify the computation of the continued fraction for α. Namely we take

$$\alpha = [\varepsilon a_{2m} : \varepsilon a_{2m-1} : \cdots : \varepsilon a_1 : \varepsilon a_0 : 0 : \delta w];$$

where $w = s/r$ if $\det(OA, OB) \cdot \text{sign}\frac{p}{q} < 0$ and $w = r/s$ otherwise.

We continue with the following remark.

Remark 8. Recall one technical statement for angles represented by slopes with tangents less than 1: the angles represented by the continued fractions

$$[0; a_1 : a_2 : \cdots : a_{2n}] \quad \text{and} \quad [a_2; \cdots : a_{2n}]$$

are integer congruent. In particular, they have the same LLS sequences.

Proof of Theorem 4. First we set $E = (1, 0)$. Consider the broken line that is a concatenation of the sail of the angle $\angle AOE$ (in case the last edge of this sail is not vertical we add the infinitesimal edge EE of zero integer length with vertical direction and 0 integer length) and the sail for the angle $\angle EOB$ (again we add another infinitesimal edge EE in case the first edge of the sail of the angle is not vertical).

Note that this broken line L has the following properties:

- it starts at the ray OA and ends at the ray OB;
- the direction of the first edge is towards the interior of the angle $\angle AOB$.

Then the angle is integer congruent to the angle $\angle EOC$ with $C = (1, \alpha)$ where $|\alpha|$ is defined by the LLS sequence of the above broken line as

$$\alpha = [\varepsilon a_{2m} : \varepsilon a_{2m-1} : \cdots : \varepsilon a_1 : \varepsilon a_0 : 0 : \delta b_0 : \delta b_1 : \cdots : \delta b_{2n}].$$

The proof for this formula is given by the study of numerous straightforward cases of various signs for p, q, r, s and $\det(OA, OB)$.

Let us study the case $p, q, r, s > 0, \det(OA, OB) < 0$. In this case, the first part of the broken line L will be the sail of $\angle AOE$ passed clockwise. Hence the elements of the LLS sequence will be reversed and negative to the values of the LLS sequence for $\angle AOE$. Note that in the case of $q/p < 1$ we end up with an infinitesimal (zero integer length) vertical vector which additionally brings two elements: the element $\lfloor p/q \rfloor$ for the angle with the vertical line passing through E, and the element 0 indicating that we stay at E. Then we switch to the second sail. Both sails are starting vertically (or asymptotically vertical in the case of a_1 or b_1 are zeroes), hence the angle between the edges corresponding to a_0 and b_0 is zero. So we add a zero element to the LLS sequence for L here. Finally we continue back following the sail of the angle $\angle EOB$, which is described by the continued fraction $[b_0 : b_1 : \cdots : b_{2n}]$ (here again we have $b_0 = 0$ and $b_1 = \lfloor s/r \rfloor$ for the case of $r/s < 1$). Hence the LLS sequence of the broken line L is

$$(-a_{2m}, -a_{2m-1}, \ldots, -a_1, -a_0, 0, b_0, b_1, \ldots, b_{2n}).$$

Finally we get $\alpha = [-a_{2m} : -a_{2m-1} : \cdots : -a_1 : -a_0 : 0 : b_0 : b_1 : \cdots : b_{2n}]$.

The cases for the rest choices of signs for p, q, r, s and $\det(OA, OB)$ are considered similarly, so we omit them here.

Now let $|\alpha| = [c_0; c_1 : \cdots : c_{2k}]$. Therefore (c.f. Remark 8) the LLS sequence for $\angle EOC$ is either $(c_0, c_1, c_2, \ldots, c_{2k})$ if $c_0 \neq 0$, or $(c_2, \ldots, c_{2k})$ otherwise.   □

4.4   Periods of the LLS Sequences Corresponding to Matrices

In this subsection we show how to extract periods of the LLS sequence for a given matrix.

Proposition 2. *Let a $GL(2, \mathbb{Z})$ matrix M have distinct irrational eigenvalues (not necessarily positive). Let also P_0 be any non-zero integer point. Denote $P_1 = M^4(P_0)$ and $P_2 = M^6(P_0)$. Then there exists a difference $LLS(\angle P_0OP_2) - LLS(\angle P_0OP_1)$, which is a period of the LLS sequence for M repeated twice.*

Remark 9. The obtained period of the LLS sequence is not necessarily minimal.

We start the proof with the following lemma.

Lemma 2. *Let a $GL(2, \mathbb{Z})$ matrix M have distinct irrational positive eigenvalues. Let also P_0 be any non-zero integer point. Denote $P_1 = M^2(P_0)$ and $P_2 = M^3(P_0)$. Then there exists a difference $LLS(\angle P_0OP_2) - LLS(\angle P_0OP_1)$, which is a period of the LLS sequence for M.*

Remark 10. It is not enough to consider the difference of the LLS sequences for the angles $\angle P_0OP_1$ and $\angle P_0OQ$ (where $Q = M(P_0)$), as it is not possible to determine the last integer sine of the period then. Let us illustrate this with the following example.

Consider a matrix $M = \begin{pmatrix} 1 & 2 \\ 1 & 3 \end{pmatrix}$ and the point $P = (4, -1)$. Then

$$Q = M(P_0) = (2, 1), \quad P_1 = M^2(P_0) = (4, 5), \quad \text{and} \quad P_2 = M^3(P_0) = (14, 19).$$

The LLS sequences for the angles $\angle P_0OQ$, $\angle P_0OP_1$ and $\angle P_0OP_2$ are respectively

$$(1, 4, 1); \quad (1, 3, 1, 3, 1); \quad \text{and} \quad (1, 3, 1, 2, 1, 3, 1).$$

We have

$$(1, 3, 1, 2, 1, 3, 1) - (1, 3, 1, 3, 1) = (2, 1)$$

which is the correct period for the LLS sequence of M, while the difference $(1, 3, 1, 3, 1) - (1, 4, 1)$ is not even defined.

Proof of Lemma 2. Set $Q = M(P_0)$. First of all note that $\angle P_0OQ$ is a fundamental domain of one of the angles C whose edges are eigenvectors of M up to
the action of the group of (integer) powers of M. Hence it contains at least one
vertex of the sail. Denote this vertex by v. Then the angle $\angle P_0OP_2$ contains
vertices $v_0 = v$, $v_1 = M(v)$, and $v_2 = M^2(v)$. Thus by convexity reasons, the
sail for the angle $\angle P_0OP_2$ contains the part of the sail of C between v_0 and v_2.
Namely there will be four parts of the sail:

- S_1: a part of the sail contained in P_0Ov_0;
- S_2: a part of the sail contained in v_0Ov_1;
- S_3: a part of the sail contained in v_1Ov_2;
- S_4: a part of the sail contained in v_2OP_2.

Here S_2 and S_3 are periods of the sail for the angle $\angle P_0OP_2$.

Now by the same reason we have v_0 and v_1 in the sail for angle $\angle P_0OP_1$. We
have the following parts:

- S_1': a part of the sail contained in P_0Ov_0;
- S_2': a part of the sail contained in v_0Ov_1;
- S_3': a part of the sail contained in v_1OP_1.

Note that

$$S_1' = S_1, \quad S_2' = S_2 \cong S_3, \quad \text{and} \quad S_3' \cong S_4.$$

Therefore, the difference of the LLS sequences for the angle $\angle P_0OP_2$ and the
angle $\angle P_0OP_1$ is precisely the period of the LLS sequence between the points
v_1 and v_2. This period corresponds to M as $M(v_1) = v_2$. This concludes the
proof.   □

Proof of Proposition 2. First of all let us study the LLS sequences of reduced
operators. Let $M = M_{a_1,\ldots,a_n}$ be a reduced operator for the sequence of positive
integers $(a_1, \ldots, a_n)$. Then from Definition 7 we have

$$M^2 = M_{a_1,\ldots,a_n}^2 = M_{a_1,\ldots,a_n,a_1,\ldots,a_n}.$$

Hence the period of the LLS sequence of M^2 is twice the period of M.
For an arbitrary M we know that

$$M^2 \cong M_{a_1,\ldots,a_n,a_1,\ldots,a_n} = M_{a_1,\ldots,a_n}^2.$$

Hence M itself is PGL$(2,\mathbb{Z})$-congruent to $M_{a_1,\ldots,a_n}$ Therefore, the period of the
LLS sequence corresponding to M^2 will be twice the period of the LLS sequence
for M. By Lemma 2 the difference $LLS(\angle P_0OP_3) - LLS(\angle P_0OP_2)$ exists and
it is a period for M^2. Finally by the above the resulting sequence is a period of
the LLS sequence for M repeated twice.   □

References

1. Arnold, V.I.: Continued fractions (in Russian). Moscow Center of Continuous Mathematical Education, Moscow (2002)
2. Arnold, V.I.: Arithmetics of binary quadratic forms, symmetry of their continued fractions and geometry of their de Sitter world (dedicated to the 50th anniversary of IMPA). Bull. Braz. Math. Soc. (N.S.) **34**(1), 1–42 (2003)
3. Baake, M., Roberts, J.A.G.: Reversing symmetry group of GL(2, $\mathbb{Z}$) and PGL(2, $\mathbb{Z}$) matrices with connections to cat maps and trace maps. J. Phys. A **30**(5), 1549–1573 (1997)
4. Campbell, J.T., Trouy, E.C.: When are two elements of GL(2, $\mathbb{Z}$) similar? Linear Algebra Appl. **157**, 175–184 (1991)
5. Cusick, T.W., Flahive, M.E.: The Markoff and Lagrange spectra. Mathematical Surveys and Monographs, vol. 30. American Mathematical Society, Providence (1989)
6. Henniger, J.P.: Factorization and similarity in GL(2, $\mathbb{Z}$). Linear Algebra Appl. **251**, 223–237 (1997)
7. Karpenkov, O.: Elementary notions of lattice trigonometry. Math. Scand. **102**(2), 161–205 (2008)
8. Karpenkov, O.: On irrational lattice angles. Funct. Anal. Other Math. **2**(2–4), 221–239 (2009)
9. Karpenkov, O.: On determination of periods of geometric continued fractions for twodimensional algebraic hyperbolic operators. Math. Notes **88**(1–2), 28–38 (2010). Russ. Version: Mat. Zametki **88**(1), 30–42 (2010)
10. Karpenkov, O.: Multidimensional gauss reduction theory for conjugacy classes of SL(n, $\mathbb{Z}$). J. Théor. Nombres Bordeaux **25**(1), 99–109 (2013)
11. Karpenkov, O.: Geometry of continued fractions. Algorithms and Computation in Mathematics, vol. 26. Springer, Berlin (2013). https://doi.org/10.1007/978-3-642-39368-6
12. Karpenkov, O., Van-Son, M.: Perron identity for arbitrary broken lines. J. Théor. Nombres Bordeaux **31**(1), 131–144 (2019)
13. Katok S.: Continued fractions, hyperbolic geometry and quadratic forms. In: MASS selecta, pp. 121–160. American Mathematical Society, Providence (2003)
14. Khinchin, A.Ya.: Continued fractions. FISMATGIS, Moscow (1961)
15. Klein, F.: Ueber eine geometrische Auffassung der gewöhnliche Kettenbruchentwicklung. Nachr. Ges. Wiss. Göttingen Math.-Phys. Kl **3**, 352–357 (1895)
16. Klein, F.: Sur une représentation géométrique de développement en fraction continue ordinaire. Nouv. Ann. Math. **15**(3), 327–331 (1896)
17. Lewis, J., Zagier, D.: Period functions and the Selberg zeta function for the modular group. In the mathematical beauty of physics (Saclay, 1996). Adv. Ser. Math. Phys. **24**, 83–97 (1997)
18. Manin, Y.I., Marcolli, M.: Continued fractions, modular symbols, and noncommutative geometry. Selecta Math. (N.S.) **8**(3), 475–521 (2002)

Absent Subsequences in Words

Maria Kosche$^{(\boxtimes)}$, Tore Koß , Florin Manea , and Stefan Siemer

Göttingen University, Göttingen, Germany
{maria.kosche,tore.koss,florin.manea,stefan.siemer}@cs.uni-goettingen.de

Abstract. An absent factor of a string w is a string u which does not occur as a contiguous substring (a.k.a. factor) inside w. We extend this well-studied notion and define absent subsequences: a string u is an absent subsequence of a string w if u does not occur as subsequence (a.k.a. scattered factor) inside w. Of particular interest to us are minimal absent subsequences, i.e., absent subsequences whose every subsequence is not absent, and shortest absent subsequences, i.e., absent subsequences of minimal length. We show a series of combinatorial and algorithmic results regarding these two notions. For instance: we give combinatorial characterisations of the sets of minimal and, respectively, shortest absent subsequences in a word, as well as compact representations of these sets; we show how we can test efficiently if a string is a shortest or minimal absent subsequence in a word, and we give efficient algorithms computing the lexicographically smallest absent subsequence of each kind; also, we show how a data structure for answering shortest absent subsequence-queries for the factors of a given string can be efficiently computed.

Keywords: Absent subsequence · Arch-factorization · Stringology · Subsequence · Subsequence-Universality

1 Introduction

A word u is a subsequence (also called scattered factor or subword) of a string w if there exist (possibly empty) strings $v_1, \ldots, v_{\ell+1}$ and $u_1, \ldots, u_\ell$ such that $u = u_1 \ldots u_\ell$ and $w = v_1 u_1 \ldots v_\ell u_\ell v_{\ell+1}$. In other words, u can be obtained from w by removing some of its letters.

The study of the relationship between words and their subsequences has been a central topic in combinatorics on words and string algorithms, as well as in language and automata theory (see, e.g., the chapter *Subwords* in [47, Chapter 6] for an overview of the fundamental aspects of this topic). Subsequences appear in many areas of theoretical computer science, such as logic of automata theory [28, 30–32, 35, 36, 52, 53, 57], combinatorics on words [24, 37, 38, 40, 46, 48, 50], as well as algorithms [3, 10, 11, 39, 56]. From a practical point of view, subsequences are generally used to model corrupted or lossy representations of an original string, and appear, for instance, in applications related to formal verification, see [28, 57] and the references therein, or in bioinformatics-related problems, see [49].

© Springer Nature Switzerland AG 2021
P. C. Bell et al. (Eds.): RP 2021, LNCS 13035, pp. 115–131, 2021.
https://doi.org/10.1007/978-3-030-89716-1_8

In most investigations related to subsequences, comparing the sets of subsequences of two different strings is usually a central task. In particular, Imre Simon defined and studied (see [47,52,53]) the relation $\sim_k$ (now called the Simon's Congruence) between strings having exactly the same set of subsequences of length at most k (see, e.g., [32] as well as the surveys [43,44] and the references therein for the theory developed around $\sim_k$ and its applications). In particular, $\sim_k$ is a well-studied relation in the area of string algorithms. The problems of deciding whether two given strings are $\sim_k$-equivalent, for a given k, and to find the largest k such that two given strings are $\sim_k$-equivalent (and their applications) were heavily investigated in the literature, see, e.g., [16,23,26,29,54,55] and the references therein. Last year, optimal solutions were given for both these problems [4,27]. Two concepts seemed to play an important role in all these investigations: on the one hand, the notion of distinguishing word, i.e., the shortest subsequence present in one string and *absent* from the other. On the other hand, the notion of universality index of a string [4,19], i.e., the largest k such that the string contains as subsequences all possible strings of length at most k; that is, the length of the shortest subsequence *absent* from that string, minus 1.

Motivated by these two concepts and the role they play, we study in this paper the set of *absent subsequences* of a string w, i.e., the set of strings which *are not* subsequences of w. As such, our investigation is also strongly related to the study of *missing factors* (or missing words, MAWs) in strings, where the focus is on the set of strings which are not substrings (or factors) of w. The literature on the respective topic ranges from many very practical applications of this concept [5,12,13,18,45,51] to deep theoretical results of combinatorial [9,17,20–22,41,42] or algorithmic nature [1,2,5,6,14,15,25]. Absent subsequences are also related to the well-studied notion of patterns avoided by permutations, see for instance [33], with the main difference being that a permutation is essentially a word whose letters are pairwise distinct.

Moreover, absent subsequences of a string (denoted by w in the following) seem to naturally occur in many practical scenarios, potentially relevant in the context of reachability and avoidability problems.

On the one hand, assume that w is some string (or stream) we observe, which may represent e.g. the trace of some computation or, in a totally different framework, the DNA-sequence describing some gene. In this framework, absent subsequences correspond to sequences of letters avoided by the string w. As such, they can be an avoided sequence of events in the observed trace or an avoided scattered sequence of nucleotides in the given gene. Understanding the set of absent subsequences of the respective string, and in particular its extremal elements with respect to some ordering, as well as being able to quickly retrieve its elements and process them efficiently seems useful to us.

On the other hand, when considering problems whose input is a set of strings, one could be interested in the case when the respective input can be compactly represented as the set of absent subsequences (potentially with some additional combinatorial properties, which make this set finite) of a given string. Clearly, one would then be interested in processing the given string and representing its set of absent subsequences by some compact data structure which further would allow querying it efficiently.

In this context, our paper is focused on two particular classes of absent subsequences: *minimal absent subsequences* (MAS for short), i.e., absent subsequences whose every subsequence is not absent, and *shortest absent subsequences* (SAS for short), i.e., absent subsequences of minimal length. In Sect. 3, we show a series of novel combinatorial results: we give precise characterizations of the set of minimal absent subsequences and shortest absent subsequences occurring in a word, as well as examples of words w having an exponential number (w.r.t. the length of w) of minimal absent subsequences and shortest absent subsequences, respectively. We also identify, for a given number k, a class of words having a maximal number of SAS, among all words whose SAS have length k.

We continue with a series of algorithmic results in Sect. 4. We first show a series of simple algorithms, useful to test efficiently if a string is a shortest or minimal absent subsequence in a word. Motivated by the existence of words with exponentially large sets of minimal absent subsequences and shortest absent subsequences, our main contributions show, in Sects. 4.1 and 4.2, how to construct compact representations of these sets. These representations are fundamental to obtaining efficient algorithms querying the set of SAS and MAS of a word, and searching for such absent subsequences with certain properties or efficiently enumerating them. These results are based on the combinatorial characterizations of the respective sets combined with an involved machinery of data structures, which we introduce gradually for the sake of readability. In Sect. 4.1, we show another main result of our paper, where, for a given word w, we construct in linear time a data structure for efficiently answering queries asking for the shortest absent subsequences in the factors of w (note that the same problem was recently approached in the case of missing factors [2]).

The techniques used to obtain these results are a combination of combinatorics on words results with efficient data structures and algorithmic techniques. For space reasons, the detailed proofs and algorithms for our results are given in the full version of this paper available on arXiv [34].

2   Basic Definitions

Let $\mathbb{N}$ be the set of natural numbers, including 0. For $m, n \in \mathbb{N}$, we let $[m : n] = \{m, m + 1, \ldots, n\}$. An alphabet Σ is a nonempty finite set of symbols called *letters*. A *string (also called word)* is a finite sequence of letters from Σ, thus an element of the free monoid Σ^*. For the rest of the paper, we assume that the strings we work with are over an alphabet $\Sigma = \{1, 2, \ldots, \sigma\}$.

Let $\Sigma^+ = \Sigma^* \setminus \{\varepsilon\}$, where ε is the empty string. The *length* of a string $w \in \Sigma^*$ is denoted by $|w|$. The ith letter of $w \in \Sigma^*$ is denoted by $w[i]$, for $i \in [1 : |w|]$. For $m, n \in \mathbb{N}$, we let $w[m : n] = w[m]w[m + 1] \ldots w[n]$, $|w|_a = |\{i \in [1 : |w|] \mid w[i] = a\}|$. A string $u = w[m : n]$ is a *factor* of w, and we have $w = xuy$ for some $x, y \in \Sigma^*$. If $x = \varepsilon$ (resp. $y = \varepsilon$), u is called a *prefix* (resp. *suffix*) of w. Let $\text{alph}(w) = \{x \in \Sigma \mid |w|_x > 0\}$ be the smallest subset $S \subset \Sigma$ such that $w \in S^*$. We can now introduce the notion of subsequence.

Definition 1. *We call u a subsequence of length k of w, where $|w| = n$, if there exist positions $1 \leq i_1 < i_2 < \ldots < i_k \leq n$, such that $u = w[i_1]w[i_2] \cdots w[i_k]$.*

We recall the notion of k-universality of a string as presented in [4].

Definition 2. *We call a word w k-universal if any string v of length $|v| \leq k$ over alph(w) appears as a subsequence of w. For a word w, we define its universality index $\iota(w)$ to be the largest integer k such that w is k-universal.*

If $\iota(w) = k$, then w is ℓ-universal for all $\ell \leq k$. Note that the universality index of a word w is always defined w.r.t. the alphabet of the word w. For instance, $w = 01210$ is 1-universal (as it contains all words of length 1 over $\{0, 1, 2\}$ but would not be 1-universal if we consider an extended alphabet $\{0, 1, 2, 3\}$. The fact that the universality index is computed w.r.t. the alphabet of w also means that every word is at least 1-universal. Note that in our results we either investigate the properties of a given word w or we show algorithms working on some input word w. In this context, the universality of the factors of w and other words we construct is defined w.r.t. alph(w). See [4,19] for a detailed discussion on this.

We recall the arch factorisation, introduced by Hebrard [29].

Definition 3. *For $w \in \Sigma^*$, with $\Sigma = $ alph(w), the arch factorisation of w is defined as $w = \mathrm{ar}_w(1) \cdots \mathrm{ar}_w(\iota(w))\mathrm{r}(w)$ where for all $i \in [1 : \iota(w)]$ the last letter of $\mathrm{ar}_w(i)$ occurs exactly once in $\mathrm{ar}_w(i)$, each arch $\mathrm{ar}_w(i)$ is 1-universal, and alph$(\mathrm{r}(w)) \subsetneq \Sigma$. The words $\mathrm{ar}_w(i)$ are called arches of w, $\mathrm{r}(w)$ is called the rest.*

Let $m(w) = \mathrm{ar}_w(1)[|\mathrm{ar}_w(1)|] \cdots \mathrm{ar}_w(k)[|\mathrm{ar}_w(k)|]$ be the word containing the unique last letters of each arch.

Note that by definition each arch $\mathrm{ar}_w(i)$ from a word w is 1-universal. By an abuse of notation, we can write $i \in \mathrm{ar}_w(\ell)$ if i is a natural number such that $|\mathrm{ar}_w(1) \cdots \mathrm{ar}_w(\ell - 1)| < i \leq |\mathrm{ar}_w(1) \cdots \mathrm{ar}_w(\ell)|$, i.e., i is a position of w contained in the ℓth arch of w.

The main concepts discussed in this paper are the following.

Definition 4. *A word v is an absent subsequence of w if v is not a subsequence of w. An absent subsequence v of w is a minimal absent subsequence (for short, MAS) of w if every proper subsequence of v is a subsequence of w. We will denote the set of all MAS of w by MAS(w). An absent subsequence v of w is a shortest absent subsequence (for short, SAS) of w if $|v| \leq |v'|$ for any other absent subsequence v' of w. We will denote the set of all SAS of w by SAS(w).*

Note that any SAS of w has length $\iota(w) + 1$ and v is an MAS of w if and only if v is absent and every subsequence of v of length $|v| - 1$ is a subsequence of w.

3   Combinatorial Properties of SAS and MAS

We begin with a presentation of several combinatorial properties of the MAS and SAS. Let us first take a closer look at MAS.

If $v = v[1] \cdots v[m + 1]$ is an MAS of w then $v[1] \cdots v[m]$ is a subsequence of w. Hence, we can go left-to-right through w and greedily choose positions $1 \le i_1 < \ldots < i_m \le n = |w|$ such that $v[1] \cdots v[m] = w[i_1] \cdots w[i_m]$ and i_ℓ is the leftmost occurrence of $w[i_\ell]$ in $w[i_{\ell-1} + 1 : n]$ (as described in Algorithm 1 in Sect. 4). Because v itself is absent, $v[m+1]$ cannot occur in the suffix of w starting at $i_m + 1$. Furthermore, we know that $v[1] \cdots v[m-1]v[m+1]$ is a subsequence of w. Hence, $v[m+1]$ occurs in the suffix of w starting at $i_{m-1} + 1$. We deduce $v[m+1] \in \mathrm{alph}(w[i_{m-1}+1 : i_m]) \backslash \mathrm{alph}(w[i_m+1 : n])$. This argument is illustrated in Fig. 1 and can be applied inductively to deduce $v[k] \in \mathrm{alph}(w[i_{k-2} + 1 : i_{k-1}]) \setminus \mathrm{alph}(w[i_{k-1} + 1 : i_k - 1])$ for all $k \ne 1$. The choice of $v[1] \in \mathrm{alph}(w)$ is arbitrary. More details are given in the proof to the following theorem which is in the full version of this paper available on arXiv [34]. For notational reasons we introduce $i_0 = 0$ and $i_{m+1} = n + 1$.

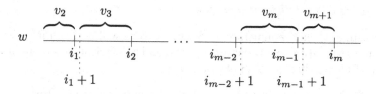

Fig. 1. Illustration of positions and intervals inside word w

Theorem 1. *Let $v, w \in \Sigma^*$, $|v| = m + 1$ and $|w| = n$, then v is an MAS of w if and only if there are positions $0 = i_0 < i_1 < \ldots < i_m < i_{m+1} = n + 1$ such that all of the following conditions are satisfied.*

(i) $v = w[i_1] \cdots w[i_m]v[m + 1]$
(ii) $v[1] \notin \mathrm{alph}(w[1 : i_1 - 1])$
(iii) $v[k] \notin \mathrm{alph}(w[i_{k-1} + 1 : i_k - 1])$ for all $k \in [2 : m + 1]$
(iv) $v[k] \in \mathrm{alph}(w[i_{k-2} + 1 : i_{k-1}])$ for all $k \in [2 : m + 1]$

Properties (i) to (iii) (the latter for $k \le m$ only) are satisfied if we choose the positions $i_1, \ldots, i_m$ greedily, as described in the beginning of this section.

By Theorem 1, we have no restriction on the first letter of an MAS and indeed we can find an MAS starting with an arbitrary letter.

Remark 1. For every $x \in \mathrm{alph}(w)$, $x^{|w|_x+1}$ is an MAS of w, hence, for every choice of $x \in \mathrm{alph}(w)$, we can find an MAS v starting with x.

Using Theorem 1 we can now determine the whole set of MAS of a word w. This will be formalized later in Theorem 8. For now, we just give an example.

Example 1. Let $w = 0011 \in \{0, 1\}^*$ and we want to construct v, an MAS of w. We start by choosing $v[1] = 0$. Then $i_1 = 1$ and by item (iv). $v[2] \in \mathrm{alph}(w[1 : 1]) = \{0\}$, so $i_2 = 2$ (by item (iii)). Again by item (iv), we have $v[3] \in \mathrm{alph}(w[2 : 2]) = \{0\}$. The letter $v[3]$ does not occur in $w[i_2 + 1 : n]$, hence, $i_3 = n + 1$, and

$v = 0^3$ is an MAS of w. If we let $v[1] = 1$, we have $i_1 = 3$. By item (iv), we have $v[2] \in \text{alph}(w[1:3]) = \{0,1\}$. If we choose $v[2] = 1$, we obtain $v = 1^3$ with an argument analogous to the first case. So let us choose $v[2] = 0$. Then $i_2 = n+1$, and $v = 10$ is an MAS of w. Theorem 1 claims $\text{MAS}(w) = \{0^3, 10, 1^3\}$ and indeed 10 is the only absent sequence of length 2, and every word of length ≥ 3 is either not absent (001, 011 and 0011) or contains 10, 0^3 or 1^3 as a subsequence.

From this example also follows that not every MAS is an SAS. The converse is necessarily true. So, for any SAS v of w we have $|v| = \iota(w) + 1$, and we can find positions $1 \leq i_1 < i_2 \leq \ldots < i_{\iota(w)} \leq n$ satisfying Theorem 1. The following theorem claims that every arch of w (see Definition 3) contains exactly one of these positions. A proof is given in the paper's full version [34].

Theorem 2. *Let $w = \text{ar}_w(1) \cdots \text{ar}_w(\iota(w))\text{r}(w)$ as in Definition 2. Then, v is an SAS of w if and only if there are positions $i_0 = 0$, $i_\ell \in \text{ar}_w(\ell)$ for all $1 \leq \ell \leq \iota(w)$, and $i_{\iota(w)+1} = n+1$ satisfying Theorem 1.*

A way to efficiently enumerate all SAS in a word will be given later in Theorem 7. Here, we only give an example based on a less efficient, but more intuitive, strategy of identifying the SAS of a word.

Example 2. Let $w = 012121012$ with $\iota(w) = 2$, and the arch factorisation of w is $w = 012 \cdot 1210 \cdot 12$. We construct v, an SAS of w. By Theorem 2, we have $|v| = \iota(w) + 1 = 3$ and by item (iv) of Theorem 1 the letter $v[3]$ does not occur in $\text{alph}(w[i_2 : n]) \supset \text{alph}(\text{r}(w))$, so $v[3]$ is not contained in $\text{alph}(\text{r}(w))$. Hence, $v[3] = 0$ and its rightmost position in $\text{ar}_w(2)$ is on position 7. Therefore, $v[2]$ should not appear before position 7 in $\text{ar}_w(2)$ (as $v[1]$ appears in $\text{ar}_w(1)$ for sure). So, $v[2] \notin \text{alph}(w[4:6]) = \{1,2\}$ and $v[2] = 0$. Ultimately, the rightmost occurrence of $v[2]$ in $\text{ar}_w(1)$ is on position 1, and we can arbitrarily choose $v[1] \in \text{alph}(\text{ar}_w(1)) = \{0,1,2\}$. We conclude that $\text{SAS}(w) = \{000, 100, 200\}$.

To better understand the properties of SAS and MAS, we analyse some particular words. For simplicity, assume for the rest of this section that σ is a large even constant, and $k = (2\sigma + 2)m$ where m is a natural number. For $k \geq 1$, we define the words $A_{2k-1} = ((1 \cdot 2 \cdots \cdot \sigma)(\sigma \cdot (\sigma - 1) \cdots \cdot 1))^{k-1}(1 \cdot 2 \cdots \cdot \sigma)$, $A_{2k} = A_{2k-1}(\sigma \cdot (\sigma - 1) \cdots \cdot 1)$, and $B_k = (1 \cdot 2 \cdots \cdot \sigma)^k$. We can show the following results.

Proposition 1. *The word B_k has a polynomial number of SAS and exponentially (in the length of the word) more MAS than SAS.*

Based on Theorems 1 and 2, it follows that the SAS of B_k correspond to decreasing sequences of length $k+1$ of numbers from $\{1, \ldots, \sigma\}$. A family of words included in $\text{MAS}(B_k)$, which is disjoint from $\text{SAS}(B_k)$, consists of the words $v = (\Pi_{t=1,m}(\sigma \cdot u_i \cdot 1 \cdot \sigma))\sigma$, where u_i is a decreasing sequence of length 2σ of numbers from $\{1, \ldots, \sigma\}$, for all i. By counting arguments, we obtain the result stated above. However, there are words whose sets of MAS and SAS coincide.

Proposition 2. $\mathrm{MAS}(A_k) = \mathrm{SAS}(A_k)$.

In particular, one can show that the number of SAS in the words A_k is exponential in the length of the word. The main idea is to observe that an SAS in A_k is a sequence $i_1, \ldots, i_{k+1}$ of numbers from $\{1, \ldots, \sigma\}$, such that $i_{2\ell-1} \geq i_{2\ell}$ for all $\ell \in [1 : \lceil k/2 \rceil]$ and $i_{2\ell} \leq i_{2\ell+1}$ for all $\ell \in [1 : \lfloor k/2 \rfloor]$. We then can estimate the number of such sequences of numbers and obtain the following result.

Proposition 3. *The word A_k has an exponential (in $|A_k|$) number of* SAS.

The following proposition formalises an additional insightful observation.

Proposition 4. $|\mathrm{SAS}(A_k)| \geq |\mathrm{SAS}(w)|$ *holds for all $w \in \Sigma^*$ with $\iota(w) = k$.*

A proof is sketched in the full version of this paper [34].

Propositions 1 and 3 motivate our investigation for compact representations of the sets of SAS and MAS of words. These sets can be exponentially large, and we would still like to have efficient (i.e., polynomial) ways of representing them, allowing us to explore and efficiently search these sets.

4   Algorithms

The results we present from now on are of algorithmic nature. The computational model we use to describe our results is the standard unit-cost RAM with logarithmic word size: for an input of size n, each memory word can hold $\log n$ bits. In all the problems, we assume that we are given a word w of length n over an *integer alphabet* $\Sigma = \{1, 2, \ldots, \sigma\}$, with $|\Sigma| = \sigma \leq n$. As the problems considered here are trivial for unary alphabets, we also assume $\sigma \geq 2$. For a more detailed general discussion on this model see the full version of this paper [34].

We start with some preliminaries and simple initial results. The decomposition of word w into its arches can be done with a greedy approach. A detailed description of how to do so can be seen in the full version of this paper available on arXiv [34]. The following theorem is well known and a proof can be seen for example in [4]. It shows that the universality index and the decomposition into arches can be obtained in linear time.

Theorem 3. *Given a word w, of length n, we can compute in linear time $O(n)$ $\iota(w)$ and the arch factorisation $\mathrm{ar}_w(1) \cdots \mathrm{ar}_w(\iota(w))\mathrm{r}(w)$ of w.*

For a word w with length n, further helpful notations are $\mathrm{next}_w(a, i)$, which denotes the next occurrence of letter a in the word $w[i : n]$, and $\mathrm{last}_w(a, i)$, which denotes the last occurrence of letter a in the word $w[1 : i]$. Both these values can be computed by traversing w from position i to the right or left, respectively (see full version on arXiv [34]). While doing so, the runtime of computing $\mathrm{next}_w(a, i)$ is proportional to the length of the shortest factor $w[i : j]$ of w such that $w[j] = a$, and the runtime of $\mathrm{last}_w(a, i)$ is proportional to the length of the shortest factor $w[j : i]$ of w such that $w[j] = a$.

Based on these notations, we can define the function isSubseq(w, u) which checks if a word u is a subsequence of a word w. This can be done by utilizing a greedy approach as discussed in Sect. 3 and depicted in Algorithm 1. While this approach is standard and relatively straightforward, it is important to note it before proceeding with our algorithms. The idea is the following. We consider the letters of u one by one, and try to identify the shortest prefix $w[1 : i_j]$ of w which contains $u[1 : j]$ as a subsequence. To compute the shortest prefix $w[1 : i_{j+1}]$ of w which contains $u[1 : j+1]$, we simply search for the first occurrence of $u[j+1]$ in w after position i_j. The runtime of the algorithm isSubseq is clearly linear in the worst case. When u is a subsequence of w, then $w[1 : pos]$ is the shortest prefix of w which contains u, and the runtime of the algorithm is $O(pos)$.

Algorithm 1: isSubseq(w,u)

Input: Word w with $|w| = n$, word u with $|u| = m$ to be tested
1 pos $\leftarrow$ 1;
2 **for** $i = 1$ **to** m **do**
3 | pos $\leftarrow$ next$_w$($u[i], pos$);
4 **return** pos $== \infty$? false : true;

A further helpful notation is llo(w) = min$\{$last$_w$(a, n) $\mid a \in \Sigma\}$, the position of the leftmost of the last occurrences of the letters of Σ in w. The following lemma is not hard to show.

Lemma 1. *Given a word w of length n, we can compute* llo(w) *in $O(n)$ time.*

Based on these notions, we can already present our first results, regarding the basic algorithmic properties of SAS and MAS. Firstly, we can easily compute an SAS (and, therefore, an MAS) in a given word.

Lemma 2. *Given a word w of length n with $\iota(w) = k$ and its arch decomposition, we can retrieve in $O(k)$ time an SAS (and, therefore, an MAS) of w.*

The following theorem shows that we can efficiently test if a given word u is an SAS or MAS of a given word w.

Theorem 4. *Given a word w of length n and a word u of length m, we can test in $O(n)$ time whether u is an SAS or MAS of w.*

4.1   A Compact Representation of the SAS of a Word

We now introduce a series of data structures which are fundamental for the efficient implementation of the main algorithms presented in this paper.

For a word w of length n with arch factorization $w = \mathrm{ar}_w(1) \cdots \mathrm{ar}_w(k)\mathrm{r}(w)$, we define two $k \times \sigma$ arrays firstInArch$[\cdot][\cdot]$ and lastInArch$[\cdot][\cdot]$ by the following relations. For $\ell \in [1 : k]$ and $a \in \Sigma$, firstInArch$[\ell][a]$ is the leftmost position of

$\mathrm{ar}_w(\ell)$ where a occurs and lastInArch$[\ell][a]$ is the rightmost position of $\mathrm{ar}_w(\ell)$ where a occurs. These two arrays are very intuitive: they simply store for each letter of the alphabet its first and last occurrence inside the arch.

Example 3. For $w = 12213.113312.21$, with arches $\mathrm{ar}_w(1) = 12213$ and $\mathrm{ar}_w(2) = 113312$ and rest $r(w) = 21$, we have the following.

	firstInArch$[\cdot][1]$	firstInArch$[\cdot][2]$	firstInArch$[\cdot][3]$
firstInArch$[1][\cdot]$	1	2	5
firstInArch$[2][\cdot]$	6	11	8
	lastInArch$[\cdot][1]$	lastInArch$[\cdot][2]$	lastInArch$[\cdot][3]$
lastInArch$[1][\cdot]$	4	3	5
lastInArch$[2][\cdot]$	10	11	9

Lemma 3. *For a word w of length n, we can compute* firstInArch$[\cdot][\cdot]$ *and* lastInArch$[\cdot][\cdot]$ *in $O(n)$ time.*

We continue with the array minArch$[\cdot]$ with n-elements, where, for $i \in [1 : n]$, minArch$[i] = j$ if and only if $j = \min\{g \mid \mathrm{alph}(w[i : g]) = \Sigma\}$. If $\{g \mid \mathrm{alph}(w[i : g]) = \Sigma\} = \emptyset$, then minArch$[i] = \infty$. Intuitively, minArch$[i]$ is the end point of the shortest 1-universal factor (i.e., arch) of w starting at i.

Example 4. Consider the word $w = 12213.113312.21$ with the arches $\mathrm{ar}_w(1) = 12213$ and $\mathrm{ar}_w(2) = 113312$ and the rest $r(w) = 21$. We have minArch$[j] = 5$ for $j \in [1 : 3]$, minArch$[j] = 11$ for $j \in [4 : 9]$, and minArch$[j] = \infty$ for $j \in [10 : 13]$.

The array minArch$[\cdot]$ can be computed efficiently.

Lemma 4. *For a word w of length n, we can compute* minArch$[\cdot]$ *in $O(n)$ time.*

A very important consequence of Lemma 4 is that we can define a tree-structure of the arches (i.e., the 1-universal factors occurring in a word).

Definition 5. *Let w be a word of length n over Σ. The arch-tree of w, denoted by $\mathcal{A}_w$, is a rooted labelled tree defined as follows:*

- *The set of nodes of the tree is $\{i \mid 0 \leq i \leq n+1\}$, where the node $n+1$ is the root of the tree $\mathcal{A}_w$. The root node $n+1$ is labelled with the letter $w[\mathrm{llo}(w)]$, the node i is labelled with the letter $w[i]$, for all $i \in [1 : n]$, and the node 0 is labelled with $\uparrow$.*
- *For $i \in [1 : n-1]$, we have two cases:*
  - *if* minArch$[i+1] = j$ *then node i is a child of node j.*
  - *if* minArch$[i+1] = \infty$ *then node i is a child of the root $n+1$.*
- *Node n is a child of node $n+1$.*

Example 5. For the word $w = 12213.113312.21$, the root 14 of $\mathcal{A}$ has the children $9, 10, 11, 12, 13$ and is labelled with 3, the node 11 has the children $3, 4, 5, 6, 7, 8$, and the node 5 has the children $0, 1, 2$. So, the root 14 and the nodes 11 and 5 are internal nodes, while all other nodes are leaves.

Theorem 5. *For a word w of length n, we can construct $\mathcal{A}_w$ in $O(n)$ time.*

Constructed in a straightforward way based on Lemma 4, the arch-tree $\mathcal{A}_w$ encodes all the arches occurring in w. Now, we can identify an SAS in $w[i : n]$ by simply listing (in the order from $i - 1$ upwards to $n + 1$) the labels of the nodes met on the path from $i - 1$ to $n + 1$, without that of node $i - 1$.

For a word w and each $i \in [0 : n]$, we define depth(i) as the number of edges on the shortest path from i to the root of $\mathcal{A}_w$. In this case, for $i \in [0 : n]$, we have that $w[i + 1 : n]$ has universality index depth$(i) - 1$.

Example 6. For the word $w = 12213.113312.21$, an SAS in $w[5 : 13]$ contains the letters $w[11] = 2$ and the label 3 of 14, so 23 (corresponding to the path $4 \rightarrow 11 \rightarrow 14$). An SAS in $w[2 : 13]$ contains, in order, the letters $w[5] = 3, w[11] = 2$ and the label 3 of 14, so 323 (corresponding to the path $1 \rightarrow 5 \rightarrow 11 \rightarrow 14$). We also have depth$(4) = 2$, so $\iota(w[5 : 13]) = 1$, while depth$(1) = 3$ and $\iota(w[2 : 13]) = 2$.

Enhancing the construction of $\mathcal{A}_w$ from Theorem 5 with level ancestor data structures [8] for this tree, we can now efficiently process *internal* SAS *queries* for a given word w, i.e., we can efficiently retrieve a compact representation of an SAS for each factor of w.

Theorem 6. *For a word w of length n we can construct in $O(n)$ time data structures allowing us to answer in $O(1)$ time queries* sasRange(i, j): *"return a representation of an SAS of $w[i : j]$".*

Proof. We start with the preprocessing phase, in which we construct the data structures allowing us to answer the queries efficiently.

We first construct the tree $\mathcal{A}_w$ for the word w. For each node i of $\mathcal{A}_w$, we compute depth(i). This can be done in linear time in a standard way.

Then we construct a solution for the *Level Ancestor Problem* for the rooted tree $\mathcal{A}_w$. This is defined as follows (see [8]). For a rooted tree T, LA$_T(u, d) = v$ where v is an ancestor of u and depth$(v) = d$, if such a node exists, or $\uparrow$ otherwise. The *Level Ancestor Problem* can now be formulated.

- Preprocessing: A rooted tree T with N vertices. ($T = \mathcal{A}_w$ in our case and $N = n + 1$)
- Querying: For a node u in the rooted tree T, query levelAncestor$_T(u, d)$ returns LA$_T(u, d)$, if it exists, and false otherwise.

A simple and elegant solution for this problem which has $O(N)$ preprocessing time and $O(1)$ time for query-answering can be found in, e.g., [8] (see also [7] for a more involved discussion). So, for the tree $\mathcal{A}_w$ we can compute in $O(n)$ time data structures allowing us to answer levelAncestor$_{\mathcal{A}_w}$ queries in $O(1)$ time.

This is the entire preprocessing we need in order to be able to answer sasRange-queries in constant time.

We will now explain how an sasRange-query is answered.

Let us assume we have to answer sasRange(i, j), i.e., to return a representation of an SAS of $w[i : j]$. The compact representation of an SAS of $w[i : j]$ will consist in two nodes of the tree A_w and in the following we explain both how to compute these two nodes, and what is their semantics (i.e., how an SAS can be retrieved from them).

Assume that depth$(i-1) = x$ and depth$(j-1) = y$. We retrieve the ancestor t of the node $i-1$ which is at distance $x-y$ from this node. So t is the ancestor of depth $y+1$ of node $i-1$, and can be retrieved as levelAncestor$_{A_w}(i-1, y+1)$. We check whether $t > j$ (i.e., $w[i : j]$ is a prefix of $w[i : t]$). If $t > j$, then we set t' to be the successor of t on the path to $i-1$. If $t \leq j$, we set $t = t'$.

The answer to sasRange(i, j) is the pair of nodes $(i-1, t')$. This answer can be clearly computed in constant time after the preprocessing we performed.

We claim that this pair of nodes is a compact representation of an SAS of $w[i : j]$, and such an SAS can be obtained as follows: we go in the tree A_w from the node $i-1$ on the path towards node t' and output, in order, the labels of the nodes we meet (except the label of node $i-1$). Then we output the label of the parent node of t'. This is an SAS of $w[i : j]$.

Let us now explain why the above claim holds.

Firstly, from the fact that depth$(i-1) = x$ and depth$(j-1) = y$ we get that $\iota(w[i : n]) = x - 1$ and $\iota(w[j : n]) = y - 1$. Therefore, $(x - 1) - (y - 1) - 1 = x - y - 1 \leq \iota(w[i : j]) \leq (x - 1) - (y - 1) = x - y$. Thus, we compute $w[i : t]$, the shortest factor of w starting on position i which is $x - y$ universal; clearly, $t = $ levelAncestor$_{A_w}(i - 1, y + 1)$. Now, there are two possibilities. In the first case, $\iota(w[i : j]) = x - y - 1$ and $j < t$. Then, for t' the successor of t on the path to $i-1$, we have that $w[i : t']$ is the shortest $(x-y-1)$-universal prefix of $w[i : j]$ and $w[t]$ is not contained in $w[t' + 1 : j]$. In the second case, $\iota(w[i : j]) = x - y$ and $j \geq t$. Then, for $t' = t$, we have that $w[i : t']$ is the shortest $(x-y)$-universal prefix of $w[i : j]$ and $w[t'']$ is not contained in $w[t+1 : j]$, where t'' is the parent of t. Note that, in this case, since $\iota(w[i : j]) \leq x - y$ and $\iota(w[i : t'']) = x - y + 1$, we have that $j < t''$.

In both cases, the label of the nodes found on the path from node $i - 1$ towards node t', without the label of $i - 1$, form the subsequence $m(w[i : j])$, from Definition 3. To this subsequence we add either $w[t]$ (if $t \neq t'$) or $w[t'']$ (otherwise), and obtain an absent subsequence of length $\iota(w[i : j]) + 1$ of $w[i : j]$. This concludes our proof. □

In order to obtain compact representations of all the SAS and MAS of a word w, we need to define a series of additional arrays.

For a word w of length n, we define the array dist$[\cdot]$ with n-elements, where, for $i \in [1 : n]$, dist$[i] = \min\{|u| \mid u$ is an absent subsequence of minimal length of $w[i : n]$, starting with $w[i]\}$. The intuition behind the array dist$[\cdot]$, and the way we will use it, is the following. Assume that w has k arches ar$_w(1), \ldots,$ ar$_w(k)$, and $i \in$ ar$_w(\ell)$. Then there exists an SAS of w, denoted by $w[i_1] \ldots w[i_{k+1}]$, which contains position i only if $\text{dist}[i] = k + 1 - (\ell - 1) = k - \ell + 2$. Indeed, an SAS contains one position of every arch, so if i is in that SAS, then it should be its ℓth position, and there should be a word u starting on position i, with $|u| = k - \ell + 2$, such that u is not a subsequence of $w[i : n]$. Nevertheless, for all positions j of $\text{ar}_w(\ell)$ it holds that $\text{dist}[j] \geq k - \ell + 2$.

Example 7. For the word $w = 12213.113312.21$, we have $\text{dist}[i] = 2$ for $i \in [9 : 13]$ (as exemplified by the word $w[i]3$), $\text{dist}[i] = 3$ for $i \in [3 : 8]$ (as exemplified by the word $w[i]23$), and $\text{dist}[i] = 4$ for $i \in [1 : 2]$ (as exemplified by the word $w[i]323$). Note that the single shortest absent sequence in this word is 323.

Lemma 5. *For a word w of length n, we can construct $\text{dist}[\cdot]$ in $O(n)$ time.*

Next, we introduce two additional arrays $\text{sortedLast}[\cdot][\cdot]$ and $\text{Leq}[\cdot][\cdot]$ which are crucial in our representation of the shortest absent subsequences of a word. Let w be a word of length n, with arch factorization $w = \text{ar}_w(1) \cdots \text{ar}_w(k)\text{r}(w)$. For each $\ell \in [1 : k - 1]$, we define L_ℓ to be the set $\{\text{lastInArch}[\ell][a] \mid a \in \Sigma\}$. We define the set $L'_\ell = L_\ell \setminus \{\text{lastInArch}[\ell][a] \mid \text{dist}(\text{firstInArch}[\ell+1][a]) > k - \ell + 1\}$. Finally, we define the array $\text{sortedLast}[\ell][\cdot]$, with $|L'_\ell|$ elements, which contains the elements of L'_ℓ sorted in ascending order. For $\ell = k$, we proceed in a similar way. We define L_k to be the set $\{\text{lastInArch}[k][a] \mid a \in \Sigma\}$. However, we define $L'_k = L_k \setminus \{\text{lastInArch}[k][a] \mid a \in \text{alph}(\text{r}(w))\}$. Then, once more, we define the array $\text{sortedLast}[k][\cdot]$, with $|L'_k|$ elements, which contains the elements of L'_k sorted in ascending order.

Moreover, we define for each ℓ an array with $|\text{ar}_w(\ell)|$ elements $\text{Leq}[\ell][\cdot]$ where we have $\text{Leq}[\ell][i] = \max\{t \mid \text{sortedLast}[\ell][t] \leq i\} \cup \{-\infty\}$ for $i \in \text{ar}_w(\ell)$. For simplicity, we assume that $\text{Leq}[\ell][\cdot]$ is indexed by the positions of $\text{ar}_w(\ell)$.

The intuition behind these arrays is the following. Assume that i is a position in $\text{ar}_w(\ell)$. Then, by Theorems 1 and 2, it is clear that i can be contained in an SAS only if $i = \text{firstInArch}[\ell][w[i]]$. Moreover, we need to have that $\text{dist}[i] = k - \ell + 2$, as explained when the intuition behind the array $\text{dist}[\cdot]$ was described. That is, i needs to be in $L'_{\ell-1}$. Finally, an SAS going through i can only continue with a letter a of the arch $\ell + 1$ such that $\text{dist}[\text{firstInArch}[\ell + 1][a]] = k - \ell + 1$, which, moreover, occurs last time in the arch ℓ on a position $\leq i$ (otherwise, the SAS would have two letters in arch ℓ, a contradiction). So, a is exactly one of the letters on the positions given by the elements of $\text{sortedLast}[\ell][1 : \text{Leq}[\ell][i]]$.

Example 8. For $w = 12213.113312.21$ we have $\text{ar}_w(1) = 12213$, $\text{ar}_w(2) = 113312$, and $L_1 = \{3, 4, 5\}$. From this set, we eliminate positions $\text{lastInArch}[1][1] = 4$ and $\text{lastInArch}[1][2] = 3$, since $\text{dist}[\text{firstInArch}[2][1]] = \text{dist}[6] = 3 > 2 - 1 + 1$ and $\text{dist}[\text{firstInArch}[2][2]] = \text{dist}[7] = 3 > 2 - 1 + 1$. So $L'_1 = \{5\}$. Thus, $\text{sortedLast}[1][\cdot]$ has only one element, namely 5. Accordingly, $\text{Leq}[1][i] = -\infty$ for $i \in [1 : 4]$ and $\text{Leq}[1][5] = 1$. We have $L_2 = \{9, 10, 11\}$. From this set, we once more eliminate two positions $\text{lastInArch}[1][1] = 10$ and $\text{lastInArch}[1][2] = 11$, because $1, 2 \in \text{alph}(\text{r}(w))$. So $L'_2 = \{10\}$. Thus, $\text{sortedLast}[2][\cdot]$ has only one element, namely 10. Accordingly, $\text{Leq}[2][i] = -\infty$ for $i \in [6 : 9]$ and $\text{Leq}[2][10] = \text{Leq}[2][11] = 10$.

Based on the arrays sortedLast$[\ell][\cdot]$, for $\ell \leq k$, we define the corresponding arrays lexSmall$[\ell][\cdot]$ with, respectively, $|L'_\ell|$ elements, where lexSmall$[\ell][i] = t$ if and only if $w[t] = \min\{w[j] \mid j \in$ sortedLast$[\ell][1 : i]\}$. In other words, $w[\,$lexSmall$[\ell][i]\,]$ is the lexicographically smallest letter occurring on the positions of w corresponding to the first i elements of sortedLast$[\ell][\cdot]$. Let init also be an element of startSAS such that $w[$init$]$ is lexicographically smaller than $w[j]$, for all $j \in$ startSAS $\setminus \{$init$\}$. Finally, we collect in a list startSAS the elements firstInArch$[1][a]$, for $a \in \Sigma$, such that dist$[$firstInArch$[1][a]] = k + 1$.

Lemma 6. *For a word w of length n, we can construct* sortedLast$[\cdot][\cdot]$, Leq$[\cdot][\cdot]$, lexSmall$[\cdot][\cdot]$, *and the list* startSAS *in* $O(n)$ *time.*

We now formalize the intuition that firstInArch$[1][\cdot]$, sortedLast$[\cdot][\cdot]$, and Leq$[\cdot][\cdot]$ are a compact representation of all the SAS of a given word w.

Theorem 7. *Given a word w of length n with k arches* $\mathrm{ar}_w(1), \ldots, \mathrm{ar}_w(k)$, *as well as the arrays* firstInArch$[\cdot][\cdot]$, sortedLast$[\cdot][\cdot]$, Leq$[\cdot][\cdot]$, lexSmall$[\cdot][\cdot]$, *the set* startSAS, *and the position* init *of w, which can all be computed in linear time, we can perform the following tasks:*

1. *We can check in $O(k)$ time if a word u of length $k + 1$ is an SAS of w.*
2. *We can compute in $O(k)$ time the lexicographically smallest SAS of w.*
3. *We can efficiently enumerate (i.e., with polynomial delay) all the SAS of w.*

Proof. We just give here the intuition behind this representation. As in Definition 3, let $w = \mathrm{ar}_w(1) \cdots \mathrm{ar}_w(k)\mathrm{r}(w)$. We observe that the arrays firstInArch$[\cdot][\cdot]$, sortedLast$[\cdot][\cdot]$, Leq$[\cdot][\cdot]$, and the set startSAS induce a tree structure $\mathcal{T}_w$ for w, called the SAS-tree of w, which is defined inductively as follows.

- The root of $\mathcal{T}_w$ is $\bullet$ while all the nodes of $\mathcal{T}_w$ of depth 1 to k are positions of w. The nodes of depth $k + 1$ of $\mathcal{T}_w$ are letters of Σ.
- The children of $\bullet$ are the positions of the set startSAS. These are the only nodes of depth 1.
- For $\ell \in [1 : k - 1]$, we define the nodes of depth $\ell + 1$ as follows. The children of a node i of depth ℓ are the nodes firstInArch$[\ell + 1][w[j]]$ where $j \in$ Leq$[\ell][i]$.
- For $\ell = k$, we define the nodes of depth $k + 1$ (the leaves) as follows. The children of a node i from level k are the letters of $\{w[j] \mid j \in$ Leq$[k][i]\}$.
- $\mathcal{T}_w$ contains no other nodes than the one defined above.

We claim that the paths in the tree from $\bullet$ to the leaves correspond exactly to the set of SAS of w. Moreover, we do not need to construct this (potentially very large) tree: it is compactly represented by the data structures enumerated in the statement. However, based on this claim and the intuitive tree representation of SAS(w), the statement of the theorem can be shown. In particular, the array lexSmall$[\cdot][\cdot]$ and position init of w are important in showing (2): they allow us to identify the path corresponding to the lexicographically smallest SAS of w. $\square$

4.2   A Compact Representation of the MAS of a Word

Finally, we move our attention to computing a compact representation of the MAS of a word. Our main result is the following.

Theorem 8. *For a word w, we can construct in $O(n^2\sigma)$ time data structures allowing us to efficiently perform the following tasks:*

1. *We can check in $O(m)$ time if a word u of length m is an MAS of w.*
2. *We can compute in polynomial time the longest MAS of w.*
3. *We can check in polynomial time for a given length ℓ if there exists an MAS of length ℓ of w.*
4. *We can efficiently enumerate (with polynomial delay) all the MAS of w.*

Proof. The compact representation of $\mathrm{MAS}(w)$ is based on Theorem 1. We define a directed acyclic graph $\mathcal{D}_w$ with the nodes $\{(i,j) \mid 0 \le j < i \le n\} \cup \{(0,0), f\}$. The edges (represented as arrows $A \to B$ between nodes A and B) are defined as follows:

- We have an edge $(0,0) \to (i,0)$ if there exists a letter $a \in \Sigma$ such that $i = \mathrm{firstInArch}[1][a]$. This edge is labelled with a.
- We have an edge $(i,j) \to (k,i)$ if there exists a letter $a \in \Sigma$ such that $k = \mathrm{next}_w(a, i+1)$ and $a \in \mathrm{alph}(w[j+1:i])$. This edge is labelled with a.
- We have an edge $(i,j) \to f$ if there exists $b \in \mathrm{alph}(w[j+1:i])$ and $b \notin \mathrm{alph}(w[i+1:n])$. This edge is labelled with b.

We claim that the words of $\mathrm{MAS}(w)$ correspond one-to-one to the paths in the graph $\mathcal{D}_w$ from $(0,0)$ to f. Based on this claim, the statement of the theorem can be shown (see full version on arXiv [34]). $\square$

It is worth noting that the lexicographically smallest MAS of a word w is $a^{|w|_a+1}$ where a is the lexicographically smallest letter of Σ which occurs in w.

Based on Theorem 1, we can also show the following result.

Corollary 1. *For a word w of length n, we can construct in $O(n\sigma)$ time data structures allowing us to answer $\mathrm{masExt}(u)$ queries: for a subsequence u of w, decide whether there exists an MAS uv of w, and, if yes, construct such an MAS uv of minimal length. The time needed to answer a query is $O(|v| + |u|)$.*

References

1. Ayad, L.A., Badkobeh, G., Fici, G., Héliou, A., Pissis, S.P.: Constructing antidictionaries in output-sensitive space. In: 2019 Data Compression Conference (DCC), pp. 538–547. IEEE (2019)
2. Badkobeh, G., Charalampopoulos, P., Pissis, S.: Internal shortest absent word queries. In: Proceeding of the CPM 2021 (2021)
3. Baeza-Yates, R.A.: Searching subsequences. Theor. Comput. Sci. **78**(2), 363–376 (1991)

4. Barker, L., Fleischmann, P., Harwardt, K., Manea, F., Nowotka, D.: Scattered factor-universality of words. In: Jonoska, N., Savchuk, D. (eds.) DLT 2020. LNCS, vol. 12086, pp. 14–28. Springer, Cham (2020). https://doi.org/10.1007/978-3-030-48516-0_2

5. Barton, C., Heliou, A., Mouchard, L., Pissis, S.P.: Linear-time computation of minimal absent words using suffix array. BMC Bioinformatics **15**(1), 1–10 (2014). https://doi.org/10.1186/s12859-014-0388-9

6. Barton, C., Heliou, A., Mouchard, L., Pissis, S.P.: Parallelising the computation of minimal absent words. In: Wyrzykowski, R., Deelman, E., Dongarra, J., Karczewski, K., Kitowski, J., Wiatr, K. (eds.) PPAM 2015. LNCS, vol. 9574, pp. 243–253. Springer, Cham (2016). https://doi.org/10.1007/978-3-319-32152-3_23

7. Ben-Amram, A.M.: The Euler path to static level-ancestors. CoRR abs/0909.1030 (2009). http://arxiv.org/abs/0909.1030

8. Bender, M.A., Farach-Colton, M.: The level ancestor problem simplified. Theor. Comput. Sci. **321**(1), 5–12 (2004). https://doi.org/10.1016/j.tcs.2003.05.002

9. Bernardini, G., Marchetti-Spaccamela, A., Pissis, S., Stougie, L., Sweering, M.: Constructing strings avoiding forbidden substrings. In: Proceeding of the CPM 2021 (2021)

10. Bringmann, K., Chaudhury, B.R.: Sketching, streaming, and fine-grained complexity of (weighted) LCS. In: Proceedings FSTTCS 2018. LIPIcs, vol. 122, pp. 40:1–40:16 (2018)

11. Bringmann, K., Künnemann, M.: Multivariate fine-grained complexity of longest common subsequence. In: Proceedings of the SODA 2018, pp. 1216–1235 (2018)

12. Chairungsee, S., Crochemore, M.: Using minimal absent words to build phylogeny. Theoret. Comput. Sci. **450**, 109–116 (2012)

13. Charalampopoulos, P., Crochemore, M., Fici, G., Mercaş, R., Pissis, S.P.: Alignment-free sequence comparison using absent words. Inf. Comput. **262**, 57–68 (2018)

14. Charalampopoulos, P., Crochemore, M., Pissis, S.P.: On extended special factors of a word. In: Gagie, T., Moffat, A., Navarro, G., Cuadros-Vargas, E. (eds.) SPIRE 2018. LNCS, vol. 11147, pp. 131–138. Springer, Cham (2018). https://doi.org/10.1007/978-3-030-00479-8_11

15. Crochemore, M., Héliou, A., Kucherov, G., Mouchard, L., Pissis, S.P., Ramusat, Y.: Absent words in a sliding window with applications. Inf. Comput. **270**, 104461 (2020)

16. Crochemore, M., Melichar, B., Tronícek, Z.: Directed acyclic subsequence graph - overview. J. Discrete Algorithms **1**(3–4), 255–280 (2003)

17. Crochemore, M., Mignosi, F., Restivo, A.: Automata and forbidden words. Inf. Process. Lett. **67**(3), 111–117 (1998)

18. Crochemore, M., Mignosi, F., Restivo, A., Salemi, S.: Data compression using antidictionaries. Proc. IEEE **88**(11), 1756–1768 (2000)

19. Day, J.D., Fleischmann, P., Kosche, M., Koß, T., Manea, F., Siemer, S.: The edit distance to k-subsequence universality. In: Bläser, M., Monmege, B. (eds.) 38th International Symposium on Theoretical Aspects of Computer Science, STACS 2021, 16–19 March, 2021, Saarbrücken, Germany (Virtual Conference). LIPIcs, vol. 187, pp. 25:1–25:19. Schloss Dagstuhl - Leibniz-Zentrum für Informatik (2021). https://doi.org/10.4230/LIPIcs.STACS.2021.25

20. Fici, G., Gawrychowski, P.: Minimal absent words in rooted and unrooted trees. In: Brisaboa, N.R., Puglisi, S.J. (eds.) SPIRE 2019. LNCS, vol. 11811, pp. 152–161. Springer, Cham (2019). https://doi.org/10.1007/978-3-030-32686-9_11

21. Fici, G., Mignosi, F., Restivo, A., Sciortino, M.: Word assembly through minimal forbidden words. Theoret. Comput. Sci. **359**(1–3), 214–230 (2006)
22. Fici, G., Restivo, A., Rizzo, L.: Minimal forbidden factors of circular words. Theoret. Comput. Sci. **792**, 144–153 (2019)
23. Fleischer, L., Kufleitner, M.: Testing Simon's congruence. In: Proceedings of the MFCS 2018. LIPIcs, vol. 117, pp. 62:1–62:13 (2018)
24. Freydenberger, D.D., Gawrychowski, P., Karhumäki, J., Manea, F., Rytter, W.: Testing k-binomial equivalence. In: Multidisciplinary Creativity, a Collection of Papers Dedicated to G. Păun 65th Birthday, pp. 239–248 (2015). CoRR abs/1509.00622
25. Fujishige, Y., Tsujimaru, Y., Inenaga, S., Bannai, H., Takeda, M.: Computing dawgs and minimal absent words in linear time for integer alphabets. In: 41st International Symposium on Mathematical Foundations of Computer Science (MFCS 2016). Schloss Dagstuhl-Leibniz-Zentrum fuer Informatik (2016)
26. Garel, E.: Minimal separators of two words. In: Apostolico, A., Crochemore, M., Galil, Z., Manber, U. (eds.) CPM 1993. LNCS, vol. 684, pp. 35–53. Springer, Heidelberg (1993). https://doi.org/10.1007/BFb0029795
27. Gawrychowski, P., Kosche, M., Koß, T., Manea, F., Siemer, S.: Efficiently testing simon's congruence. In: Bläser, M., Monmege, B. (eds.) 38th International Symposium on Theoretical Aspects of Computer Science, STACS 2021, March 16–19, 2021, Saarbrücken, Germany (Virtual Conference). LIPIcs, vol. 187, pp. 34:1–34:18. Schloss Dagstuhl - Leibniz-Zentrum für Informatik (2021). https://doi.org/10.4230/LIPIcs.STACS.2021.34
28. Halfon, S., Schnoebelen, P., Zetzsche, G.: Decidability, complexity, and expressiveness of first-order logic over the subword ordering. In: Proceeding of the LICS 2017, pp. 1–12 (2017)
29. Hebrard, J.J.: An algorithm for distinguishing efficiently bit-strings by their subsequences. Theoret. Comput. Sci. **82**(1), 35–49 (1991)
30. Karandikar, P., Kufleitner, M., Schnoebelen, P.: On the index of Simon's congruence for piecewise testability. Inf. Process. Lett. **115**(4), 515–519 (2015)
31. Karandikar, P., Schnoebelen, P.: The height of piecewise-testable languages with applications in logical complexity. In: Proceedings of the CSL 2016. LIPIcs, vol. 62, pp. 37:1–37:22 (2016)
32. Karandikar, P., Schnoebelen, P.: The height of piecewise-testable languages and the complexity of the logic of subwords. Log. Methods Comput. Sci. **15**(2) (2019)
33. Kitaev, S.: Patterns in Permutations and Words. Monographs in Theoretical Computer Science. An EATCS Series, Springer (2011). https://doi.org/10.1007/978-3-642-17333-2
34. Kosche, M., Koß, T., Manea, F., Siemer, S.: Absent subsequences in words. CoRR to appear (2021)
35. Kuske, D.: The subtrace order and counting first-order logic. In: Fernau, H. (ed.) CSR 2020. LNCS, vol. 12159, pp. 289–302. Springer, Cham (2020). https://doi.org/10.1007/978-3-030-50026-9_21
36. Kuske, D., Zetzsche, G.: Languages ordered by the subword order. In: Proceedings of the FOSSACS 2019. Lecture Notes in Computer Science, vol. 11425, pp. 348–364 (2019)
37. Lejeune, M., Leroy, J., Rigo, M.: Computing the k-binomial complexity of the Thue-Morse word. In: Proceedings of the DLT 2019. Lecture Notes in Computer Science, vol. 11647, pp. 278–291 (2019)
38. Leroy, J., Rigo, M., Stipulanti, M.: Generalized Pascal triangle for binomial coefficients of words. Electron. J. Combin. **24**(1.44), 36 (2017)

39. Maier, D.: The complexity of some problems on subsequences and supersequences. J. ACM **25**(2), 322–336 (1978)
40. Mateescu, A., Salomaa, A., Yu, S.: Subword histories and Parikh matrices. J. Comput. Syst. Sci. **68**(1), 1–21 (2004)
41. Mignosi, F., Restivo, A., Sciortino, M.: Words and forbidden factors. Theoret. Comput. Sci. **273**(1–2), 99–117 (2002)
42. Mieno, T., et al.: Minimal unique substrings and minimal absent words in a sliding window. In: Chatzigeorgiou, A., et al. (eds.) SOFSEM 2020. LNCS, vol. 12011, pp. 148–160. Springer, Cham (2020). https://doi.org/10.1007/978-3-030-38919-2_13
43. Pin, Jean-Eric.: The consequences of IMRE Simon's work in the theory of automata, languages, and semigroups. In: Farach-Colton, Martín (ed.) LATIN 2004. LNCS, vol. 2976, p. 5. Springer, Heidelberg (2004). https://doi.org/10.1007/978-3-540-24698-5_4
44. Pin, Jean-Éric: The influence of IMRE Simon's work in the theory of automata, languages and semigroups. Semigroup Forum **98**(1), 1–8 (2019). https://doi.org/10.1007/s00233-019-09999-8
45. Pratas, D., Silva, J.M.: Persistent minimal sequences of SARS-CoV-2. Bioinformatics (2020)
46. Rigo, M., Salimov, P.: Another generalization of abelian equivalence: binomial complexity of infinite words. Theor. Comput. Sci. **601**, 47–57 (2015)
47. Sakarovitch, J., Simon, I.: Subwords. In: Lothaire, M. (ed.) Combinatorics on Words, chap. 6, pp. 105–142. Cambridge University Press (1997)
48. Salomaa, A.: Connections between subwords and certain matrix mappings. Theoret. Comput. Sci. **340**(2), 188–203 (2005)
49. Sankoff, D., Kruskal, J.: Time Warps, String Edits, and Macromolecules The Theory and Practice of Sequence Comparison. Cambridge University Press, Cambridge (2000), Originally Published in 1983
50. Seki, S.: Absoluteness of subword inequality is undecidable. Theor. Comput. Sci. **418**, 116–120 (2012)
51. Silva, R.M., Pratas, D., Castro, L., Pinho, A.J., Ferreira, P.J.: Three minimal sequences found in Ebola virus genomes and absent from human DNA. Bioinformatics **31**(15), 2421–2425 (2015)
52. Simon, I.: Hierarchies of events with dot-depth one - Ph.D. Thesis. University of Waterloo (1972)
53. Simon, I.: Piecewise testable events. In: Automata Theory and Formal Languages, 2nd GI Conference LNCS, vol. 33, pp. 214-222 (1975)
54. Simon, I.: Words distinguished by their subwords (extended abstract). In: Proceedings of the WORDS 2003. TUCS General Publication, vol. 27, pp. 6–13 (2003)
55. Troniĉek, Z.: Common subsequence automaton. In: Champarnaud, J.-M., Maurel, D. (eds.) CIAA 2002. LNCS, vol. 2608, pp. 270–275. Springer, Heidelberg (2003). https://doi.org/10.1007/3-540-44977-9_28
56. Wagner, R.A., Fischer, M.J.: The string-to-string correction problem. J. ACM **21**(1), 168–173 (1974)
57. Zetzsche, G.: The complexity of downward closure comparisons. In: Proceedings of the ICALP 2016. LIPIcs, vol. 55, pp. 123:1–123:14 (2016)

Minimal Number of Calls
in Propositional Protocols

Joseph Livesey$^{(\boxtimes)}$ and Dominik Wojtczak$^{(\boxtimes)}$ (ID)

University of Liverpool, Liverpool, UK
{joseph.livesey,d.wojtczak}@liverpool.ac.uk

Abstract. Gossip protocols are programs that can be used by a group of agents to synchronise what information they have. Namely, assuming each agent holds a secret, the goal of a protocol is to reach a situation in which all agents are experts, i.e., know all secrets. Distributed epistemic gossip protocols use epistemic formulas in the component programs for the agents. In this paper, we investigate in-depth one of the simplest classes of such gossip protocols: propositional gossip protocols, in which whether an agent wants to initiate a call depends only the set of secrets that the agent currently knows. We establish important properties about the order of calls possible in a correct propositional gossip protocol, i.e., a one that terminates in the desired all-expert state. This allows us to solve the following open problem: all correct propositional gossip protocols for $n \geq 4$ agents require at least $2n - 2$ calls in the worst case.

1 Introduction

1.1 Background and Motivation

Gossip protocols have the goal of spreading information through a network via point-to-point communications (which we refer to as calls). Each agent holds initially a secret and the aim is to arrive at a situation in which all agents know each other secrets. During each call the caller and callee exchange all secrets that they know at that point. Such protocols were successfully used in a number of domains, for instance communication networks [17], computation of aggregate information [21], and data replication [23]. For a more recent account see [20] and [22]. One of the early results established by a number of authors in the seventies, e.g., [25], is that for n agents $2n - 4$ calls are necessary and sufficient when every agent can communicate with any other agent. When such a communication graph is not complete, $2n - 3$ calls may be needed [11] but are sufficient for any connected communication graph [16]. However, all such protocols considered in these papers were centralised.

In [10] a dynamic epistemic logic was introduced in which gossip protocols could be expressed as formulas. These protocols rely on agents' knowledge and are distributed, so they are *distributed epistemic gossip protocols*. This also means that they can be seen as special cases of knowledge-based programs introduced in [14].

© Springer Nature Switzerland AG 2021
P. C. Bell et al. (Eds.): RP 2021, LNCS 13035, pp. 132–148, 2021.
https://doi.org/10.1007/978-3-030-89716-1_9

In [2] a simpler modal logic was introduced that is sufficient to define these protocols and to reason about their correctness. This logic is interesting in its own rights and was subsequently studied in a number of papers. In this paper, we are going to focus on its simplest propositional fragment.

Propositional gossip protocols are a particular type of epistemic gossip protocols in which all guards are propositional. This means that calls being made by each agent are dependent only on the secrets that the agent have had access to. Clearly, this can lead to states where multiple calls are possible at the same time. Then a scheduler would decide which call takes priority. Throughout this paper, we assume that the scheduler is demonic and it picks the order of calls in a way such that the protocol fails or to maximise the number of calls made before termination. In other words, we study these gossip protocols in their worst-case scenario.

In [9], many challenging open problems about general as well as propositional gossip protocols were listed. In this paper, we solve its Problem 7, which ask to show that no correct propositional gossip exists that always terminates within $2n - 2$ steps for $n \geq 4$ agents. Note that we prove this lower bound holds even if the communication graph is a complete graph.

1.2   Related Work

Much work has been done on general epistemic gossip protocols. The various types of calls used in [10] and [2] were presented in a uniform framework in [3], where in total 18 types of communication were considered and compared w.r.t. their epistemic strength. In [5], and its full version [8], the decidability of the semantics of the gossiping logic and truth was established for its limited fragment (namely, without nesting of modalities). Building upon these results it was proved in [5] that the distributed gossip protocols, the guards of which are defined in this logic, are implementable, that their partial correctness is decidable, and in [7] that termination and two forms of fair termination of these protocols are decidable, as well. Building on that, [29] showed decidability of the full logic for various variants of the gossiping model. Further, in [4] the computational complexity of this fragment was studied and in [6] an extension with the common knowledge operator was considered and analogous decidability results were established there.

Despite how simple this modal logic seems to be, there remain natural open problems about it and the gossip protocols defined using it. These problems were discussed at length in [9], where partial results were presented. Open problems listed there regarding axiomatisations for knowledge in gossiping logic were subsequently solved in [29]. In [24] we addressed several of its open problems regarding propositional gossip protocols. In particular, we showed that no correct propositional gossip protocol exists when, ignoring calls' direction, any two agents cannot directly call each other and that checking the correctness of a given protocol is co-NP-complete. However, its Problem 7 that conjectures any such protocol to need at least $2n - 2$ calls in the worst case was left open. We were only able to show $2n - 3$ lower bound in [24] for this problem, but improving this to $2n - 2$ in this paper requires many new ideas and a detailed case analysis.

Centralised gossip protocols were studied in [18] and [19]. These had the goal to achieve higher-order shared knowledge. This was investigated further in [12], where optimal protocols for various versions of such a generalised gossip problem were given. These protocols depend on various parameters, such as the type of the underlying graph or communication. Additionally, different gossip problems which contained some negative goals, for example that certain agents must not know certain secrets, were studied. Such problems were further studied in [13] with temporal constraints, i.e., a given call has to (or can only) be made within a given time interval.

The number of calls needed to reach the desired all expert situation in the distributed but synchronous setting was studied in [26]. In the synchronous setting, agents are notified if a call was made, but may not necessary know which agents were involved. In this paper we study the more complex fully distributed asynchronous setting, where agents are not aware of the calls they do not participate in. In [27,28] the expected time of termination of several gossip protocols for complete graphs was studied.

Dynamic distributed gossip protocols were studied in [30], in which the calls allow the agents to transmit the links as well as share secrets. These protocols were characterised in terms of the class of graphs for which they terminate. Various dynamic gossip protocols were proposed and analysed in [31]. In [15] these protocols were analysed by embedding them in a network programming language NetKAT [1].

1.3   Plan of the Paper

We will firstly go through the logic, originally defined in [2]. We will show a couple of examples of propositional gossip protocols and prove their correctness. We will then perform a thorough case analysis of possible call scenarios of a correct propositional gossip protocol, and show that in each of them at least $2n - 2$ calls are needed in the worst-case to terminate in the all-expert situation, where $n > 3$ is the number agents.

2   Gossiping Logic

We recall here the framework of [2], which we restrict to the propositional setting. We assume a fixed set A of $n \geq 3$ *agents* and stipulate that each agent holds exactly one *secret*, and that there exists a bijection between the set of agents and the set of secrets. We use it implicitly by denoting the secret of agent a by A, of agent b by B, etc. We denote by Sec the set of all secrets.

The propositional language $\mathcal{L}_p$ is defined by the following grammar:

$$\phi ::= F_a S \mid \neg \phi \mid \phi \wedge \phi,$$

where $S \in$ Sec and $a \in$ A. We will distinguish the following sublanguage $\mathcal{L}_p^a$, where $a \in$ A is a fixed agent, which disallow all F_b operators for $b \neq a$.

So $F_a S$ is an atomic formula, which we read as 'agent a is familiar with the secret S'. Note that in [2], a compound formula $K_a \phi$, i.e., 'agent a knows the formula ϕ is true', was used. Dropping $K_a \phi$ from the logic simplifies greatly its semantics and the execution of a gossip protocol, while it is still capable of describing a rich class of protocols. Below we shall freely use other Boolean connectives that can be defined using $\neg$ and $\wedge$ in a standard way. We shall use the following formula

$$Exp_i \equiv \bigwedge_{S \in \text{Sec}} F_i S,$$

that denotes the fact that agent i is an *expert*, i.e., he is familiar with all the secrets.

Each *call*, written as ab or a, b, concerns two different agents, the *caller*, a, and the *callee*, b. After the call the caller and the callee learn each others secrets. Calls are denoted by c, d. Abusing notation we write $a \in$ c to denote that agent a is one of the two agents involved in the call c.

In what follows we focus on call sequences. Unless explicitly stated each call sequence is assumed to be finite. The empty sequence is denoted by ϵ. We use c to denote a call sequence and **C** to denote the set of all finite call sequences. Given call sequences **c** and **d** and a call c we denote by **c**.c the outcome of adding c at the end of the sequence **c** and by **c**.**d** the outcome of appending the sequences **c** and **d**. We say that **c**′ is an *extension* of a call sequence **c** if for some call sequence **d** we have **c**′ = **c**.**d**.

The agents and possible calls of a given protocol can be thought of as nodes (agents) and edges (calls) of its *communication graph*. The *graph of calls made* during a given call sequence is a pruned communication graph where edges between agents that did not call each other in this call sequence were removed. Unless explicitly stated, all these graphs are undirected, i.e., we ignore the direction of calls here.

To describe what secrets the agents are familiar with, we use the concept of a *gossip situation*. It is a sequence s $= (Q_a)_{a \in \text{A}}$, where $\{A\} \subseteq Q_a \subseteq$ Sec for each agent a. Intuitively, Q_a is the set of secrets a is familiar with in the gossip situation s. The *initial gossip situation* is the one in which each Q_a equals $\{A\}$ and is denoted by root. It reflects the fact that initially each agent is familiar only with his own secret. Note that an agent a is an expert in a gossip situation s iff $Q_a =$ Sec.

Each call transforms the current gossip situation by modifying the sets of secrets the agents involved in the call are familiar with as follows. Consider a gossip situation s$:=(Q_d)_{d \in \text{A}}$ and a call ab.
Then

$$ab(\text{s}) := (Q_d')_{d \in \text{A}},$$

where $Q_a' = Q_b' = Q_a \cup Q_b$, and for $c \notin \{a, b\}$, $Q_c' = Q_c$.

So the effect of a call is that the caller and the callee share the secrets they are familiar with.

The result of applying a call sequence to a gossip situation s is defined inductively as follows:

$$\epsilon(\mathsf{s}) := \mathsf{s}, \quad (\mathsf{c}.\mathsf{c})(\mathsf{s}) := \mathsf{c}(\mathsf{c}(\mathsf{s})).$$

Example 1. We will use the following concise notation for gossip situations. Sets of secrets will be written down as lists. e.g., the set $\{A, B, C\}$ will be written as ABC. Gossip situations will be written down as lists of lists of secrets separated by a comma. e.g., if there are three agents, a, b and c, then root $= A, B, C$ and the gossip situation $(\{A, B\}, \{A, B\}, \{C\})$ will be written as AB, AB, C.

Let $\mathsf{A} = \{a, b, c\}$. Consider the call sequence $ac.cb.ac$. It generates the following successive gossip situations starting from root:

$$A, B, C \xrightarrow{ac} AC, B, AC \xrightarrow{cb} AC, ABC, ABC \xrightarrow{ac} ABC, ABC, ABC.$$

Hence $(ac.cb.ac)(\mathsf{root}) = (ABC, ABC, ABC)$.   □

Definition 2. *Consider a call sequence $\mathsf{c} \in \mathsf{C}$. We define the satisfaction relation $\models$ inductively as follows:*

$$\mathsf{c} \models F_a S \text{ iff } S \in \mathsf{c}(\mathsf{root})_a,$$
$$\mathsf{c} \models \neg\phi \text{ iff } \mathsf{c} \not\models \phi,$$
$$\mathsf{c} \models \phi_1 \wedge \phi_2 \text{ iff } \mathsf{c} \models \phi_1 \text{ and } \mathsf{c} \models \phi_2.$$

So a formula $F_a S$ is true after the call sequence c whenever secret S belongs to the set of secrets agent a is familiar with in the situation generated by the call sequence c applied to the initial situation root. Hence $\mathsf{c} \models Exp_a$ iff agent a is an expert in $\mathsf{c}(\mathsf{root})$.

By a **propositional component program**, in short a **program**, for an agent a we mean a statement of the form

$$*[[]_{j=1}^{m} \psi_j \to \mathsf{c}_j],$$

where $m \geq 0$ and each $\psi_j \to \mathsf{c}_j$ is such that

– agent a is the caller in the call c_j,
– $\psi_j \in \mathcal{L}_p^a$.

We call each such construct $\psi \to \mathsf{c}$ a **rule** and refer in this context to ψ as a **guard**. If the guard of a rule is true then the corresponding agent and call is called to be **active**.

Intuitively, $*$ denotes a repeated execution of the rules, one at a time, where each time non-deterministically an active rule is selected.

Consider a **propositional gossip protocol**, P, that is a parallel composition of the propositional component programs $*[[]_{j=1}^{m_a} \psi_j^a \to \mathsf{c}_j^a]$, one for each agent $a \in \mathsf{A}$.

The **computation tree** of P is a directed tree defined inductively as follows. Its nodes are call sequences and its root is the empty call sequence ϵ. Further, if $\mathbf{c}$ is a node and for some rule $\psi_j^a \to c_j^a$ we have $\mathbf{c} \models \psi_j^a$, then $\mathbf{c}.c_j^a$ is a node that is a direct descendant of $\mathbf{c}$. Intuitively, the arc from $\mathbf{c}$ to $\mathbf{c}.c_j^a$ records the effect of the execution of the rule $\psi_j^a \to c_j^a$ performed after the call sequence $\mathbf{c}$ took place.

By a **computation** of a gossip protocol P we mean a maximal rooted path in its computation tree. In what follows we identify each computation with the unique call sequence it generates. Any prefix of such a call sequence is called a **prefix of** P. We say that the gossip protocol P is **partially correct** if for all leaves $\mathbf{c}$ of the computation tree of P, and all agents a, we have $\mathbf{c} \models Exp_a$, i.e., if each agent is an expert in the gossip situation $\mathbf{c}(\text{root})$.

We say furthermore that P **terminates** if all its computations are finite and say that P **is correct** if it is partially correct and terminates.

In [10] the following correct propositional gossip protocol, called *Learn New Secrets* (LNS in short), for complete digraphs was proposed.

Example 3 (LNS protocol). The following program is used by agent i:

$$*[[]_{j\in A}\neg F_i J \to ij].$$

Informally, agent i calls agent j if agent i is not familiar with j's secret.

In [24] a propositional protocol *Learn Next Secret (LXS)* was proposed. First of all, agents were only able to call agents with a higher "index", which for instance can be their phone number or name, with the corresponding total order ($>$) on A. Second, just like in the LNS protocol, agents were only able to call another agent if they did not know their secret. Finally, it was required that an agent can make a call to another agent only if he already knows all the secrets of agents with the index value lower than the agent to be called.

Example 4 (LXS protocol). The following program is used by agent i:

$$*[[]_{\{j\in A|j>i\}}\neg F_i J \wedge \bigwedge_{\{k\in A|k<j\}} F_i K \to ij].$$

Note that although the communication graph of LXS protocol is not complete, a call between any two agents is possible if its direction is ignored. We now prove that this LXS protocol is correct.

Theorem 5. *The Learn Next Secret (LXS) protocol proposed in [24] is a correct propositional gossip protocol.*

Proof. Note that as all calls are determined only by the secrets currently known by the agent, so the protocol is indeed propositional.

Termination can be seen as each call made ensures the caller learns at least one secret, hence the protocol terminates, as we have a finite number of secrets to be learned, and a finite number of agents learning them.

It remains to be shown that when the protocol terminates, all agents are experts.

Assume the protocol is not correct. As we know the protocol terminates, this must mean that when we terminate at least one agent is not an expert. Let a be the agent with the lowest index which is not an expert. Now, consider the agent with the lowest index whose secret agent a does not know.

If that agent b has higher index than a, then by definition of the LXS protocol, ab would be available; a contradiction. So the index of b has to be lower than the index of a. Therefore, by definition of the LXS protocol, a could not make any calls before termination.

Now, all agents with lower index than a, including b, must be experts, and hence know secret A. This means that a was called by an agent say c. But for ca to be available, c must know all secrets corresponding to agents of index lower than a, including B. Hence when a was first called by c, a learned B; a contradiction. □

Finally, we now define a new protocol, *Learn New Secrets with a special one (LNSwS1)*, where one agent whose secret acts as guard that all the other agents wait for before making their calls. Formally, we define it as follows where the special agent and its secret is denoted by x and X, respectively.

Example 6 (LNSwS1 protocol). The following program is used by the special agent x:

$$*[[]_{\{j \in A\}} \neg F_x J \to xj].$$

The following program is used by agents $i \in A \setminus \{x\}$:

$$*[[]_{\{j \in A \setminus \{x\}\}} F_i X \wedge \neg F_i J \to ij].$$

Again, we now show this protocol's correctness.

Theorem 7. *The LNSwS1 protocol is a correct propositional gossip protocol.*

Proof. Note that as all calls are determined only by the secrets currently known by the agent, the protocol is indeed propositional.

Termination can be seen as each call made ensures the caller learns at least one secret, hence the protocol terminates, as we have a finite number of secrets to be learned, and a finite number of agents learning them.

It remains to be shown that when the protocol terminates, all agents are experts.

Assume the protocol is not correct. As we know the protocol terminates, this must mean that when we terminate at least one agent, say y, is not an expert. As x is always happy to initiate a call with any agent it does not know the secret of, as does any agent which knows X, any agent which is not an expert when the protocol terminates must not know X.

However, by definition of the LNSwS1 protocol, every agent which initiates a call must know X, and hence every agent which has been involved in any call must know X. Yet, x is an expert, and so must know Y. This means that y must have been involved in a call, and hence must know X; a contradiction. □

3   Minimal Number of Calls

In the rest of the paper, we improve the lower bound on the minimal number of calls required in the worst-case by a correct propositional gossip protocol to terminate in the all-expert situation, thus solving Problem 7 as stated in [9].

Theorem 8. *Every correct propositional protocol on $n > 3$ agents uses at least $2n - 2$ calls in the worst case.*

In other words, Theorem 8 says that the height of the computation tree of every correct propositional protocol is at least $2n - 2$. In order to prove this theorem, we first need to establish many intermediate partial results and analyse different call scenarios. We will also make use of the following results from [24].

Lemma 9. *No correct proposition protocol for 4 agents exists with fewer than 6 calls.*

Due to Lemma 9, in the rest of the paper will assume that $n > 4$. We will also use the following observations from [24].

Lemma 10 (Call Removal). *Consider a propositional gossip protocol P. Let $\mathbf{c.d}$ be a prefix of P such that $\mathbf{c.d} \not\models F_a B$. Let $\mathbf{d'}$ be $\mathbf{d}$ where all calls that involve an agent familiar with B are removed, then $\mathbf{c.d'}$ is also a prefix of P and, moreover, $(\mathbf{c.d})(\text{root})_a = (\mathbf{c.d'})(\text{root})_a$.*

Lemma 11 (Initiation). *Consider any call sequence $\mathbf{c}$ which is a prefix of a computation of a correct propositional gossip protocol P such that $\mathbf{c} \models F_a B$. There does not exist a call sequence $\mathbf{d}$ such that $\mathbf{c.d}.ab$ is a prefix of P. (In other words, agent a will never call agent b if agent a already knows B.)*

Lemma 12 (Conversation). *For a protocol on n agents to correctly terminate in m calls, every agent must be involved in a call after at most $m - n + 2$ calls. Furthermore, after $m - n + p$ calls, each secret must be known by at least p agents.*

3.1   Basic Call Structure of a Correct Propositional Protocol

We will now show a necessary possible structure of a correct propositional protocol.

Lemma 13. *Every correct propositional protocol admits a scenario where an agent, say a, is initially involved in a call with an agent b, which is then involved in a call with an agent c.*
*From here, every correct propositional protocol admits a scenario where ac is the next call involving either b or c. We will refer to this structure as **CC** (cycle component).*

Proof. In Lemma 5 in [9] it was shown that every gossip protocol has a computation that starts with the same agent being involved in its first two calls. By relabeling the names of the agents, we can assume that the first call is between

a and b, followed by a call between b and c, hence we get the situation where a is initially involved in a call with an agent b, which is then involved in a call with an agent c.

Now, every agent which knows C also knows A. Hence by Lemma 11, no agent with C will ever initiate a call with a, and so a must learn C in a call initiated by a himself. Also by Lemma 11, a will never have a further call with b. Now, assume ac is never available. Agent a must learn C from initiating a call with an agent, say d.

Let us pick a computation where a knows the greatest number of secrets before learning C. In other words, if $\mathbf{c}.ad$ is a prefix of a computation which starts with a call between a and b, followed by a call between b and c, and where a learns C during the call ad, we require the size of $\mathbf{c}(\text{root})_a$ to be the largest possible. This is well-defined as this value is an integer between 1 and $|A|$.

We know that $\mathbf{c} \models \neg F_a D$, because otherwise ad would not be possible due to Lemma 11. We can then remove all calls of agents familiar with D in $\mathbf{c}$ and obtain $\mathbf{c}'$. Due to Lemma 10, $\mathbf{c}'.ad$ is still a valid prefix of a computation. Note that d cannot possibly know C (nor any other secret apart from his own) after $\mathbf{c}'$, because all his calls were removed. At the same time we know that $\mathbf{c}(\text{root})_a = \mathbf{c}'(\text{root})_a$.

Hence, there exists a longer prefix, $\mathbf{c}'.ad.\mathbf{d}.ae$, of this computation such that a finally learns C during ae. Therefore, $\mathbf{c}(\text{root})_a$ is smaller than $\mathbf{c}'.ad.\mathbf{d}(\text{root})_a$, because the later includes at least one more secret (namely D); this is a contradiction with the assumption that a knew the most number of secrets before learning C in the $\mathbf{c}.ad$ prefix of a correct computation. □

This gives us a certain prefix which must be available for all correct propositional protocols. From here we can expand with different cases in order to get our desired result. Before going to case analysis we need one more important result.

From Lemma 12, if we are aiming to create a correct protocol with $2n - 3$ calls or fewer, then all agents must be involved in a call after at most $n - 1$ calls. This gives us a useful cut-off point when looking at how many calls we have remaining before all agents must have been involved in a call.

Lemma 14. *Assume there is a situation in a protocol where r agents have yet to be involved in a call with only $r - 2$ calls remaining before all agents must have been involved in a call. Then no correct protocol exists with this proposed number of calls.*

Proof. Consider an agent not yet involved in a call. If this agent calls an agent already involved in a call then we have $r - 1$ agents and $r - 3$ calls, so this leaves us in the same position, but with fewer uncalled agents. If this continues, we would reach a state with no calls remaining before all agents must have been in at least one call, and yet two agents not yet in a call. We can also make all calls currently available from all agents which have been involved in calls so far.

Again this will at best still leave us in the scenario where there are $r - 1$ agents left and $r - 3$ calls remaining before all must have been involved in a call, but now with no calls directly from or to any agents which already have been involved in a call. If these were the only options we could repeatedly apply them until we are left with two agents and zero calls, in which case we would have failed. Therefore, there must be a call between two agents not yet involved in any call.

Consider any pair of such agents. If after they call each other, one (or both) of these agents could now call an agent already involved in a call then we are again in the scenario where we have $r - 2$ agents and $r - 4$ calls; the exact situation we started, but now with fewer uncalled agents and calls. If these two agents were the last two yet to be involved in a call, then we were already done before this call took place, as we would have two agents left but zero calls. Therefore there must be two agents a and b, such that there is a call between a and b, which cannot be immediately followed by a call to any agent already in a call.

Assume neither a or b now wishes to initiate a call. As there trivially must be more than two agents in total, and this was the first call for both agents, neither a or b is currently an expert, meaning they must be involved in future calls. As neither wishes to initiate a call, this means they must be called, say by an agent c after a call sequence $\mathbf{c}$.

By relabelling, let c call a, i.e. $\mathbf{c}.ca$ is a prefix of a computation. In this situation, by Lemma 11, c did not know A, hence, by Lemma 10, there exists a call sequence $\mathbf{c}'.ac$ where $\mathbf{c}'$ is $\mathbf{c}$ where all calls that involve an agent familiar with A are removed. But this means either a is called by an agent which has already been involved in a call, or we can create the CC situation.

Therefore, either a or b wishes to initiate a call with another agent c, which has yet to be involved in a call. Hence, every agent which knows C also knows A. Therefore, by Lemma 11, no agent with C will ever initiate a call with a. Therefore a must make the call to learn C.

From Lemma 13 it then follows that there must be a call sequence $\mathbf{c}$ such that after this sequence ac is available. This sequence must involve a, and hence can be formed in such a way as to contain at most p new agents for the p new calls involved. If all agents have now been involved in a call we are done by from Lemma 12, because we have used n calls and yet only two agents know C. But, if more agents are yet to be involved in a call, then after ac we have at most $r - p - 5$ calls remaining for at least $r - p - 3$ agents to be involved in a call. We remain in the exact situation as we started, but now with fewer uncalled agents and calls. We may try to repeat this process, however as there is a finite number of agents and calls, we will eventually be left with no calls remaining and agents not yet involved in a call. □

Note that Lemma 14 already shows that every correct propositional gossip protocol has to use at least $2n - 3$ calls in the worst case, because we begin with $n - 2$ calls remaining for n agents yet to be involved in a call.

Lemma 15. *For a correct propositional gossip protocol with n agents, if there are x calls remaining then each secret must be known by at least $n - x$ agents. If only $n - x$ agents know a secret, say, A, then in every future call one of the agents involved get to know A. Furthermore, in such a situation, if y agents are experts, then at least $n - x - y$ agents must be active.*

Proof. As each call can increase the number of agents which know a secret by at most one, if there are x calls remaining then each secret must be known by at least $n - x$ agents.

If we have x calls remaining and only $n - x$ agents know A, then in the remaining x calls, x agents must learn A. At most one agent may learn A in each call, therefore every future call must have an agent learning A. In other words, every call must be between an agent that does not know A and an agent that knows A.

As every call must pass on A, after a call is made both agents involved know A. All agents which are not experts must be involved in at least one more call to become an expert. This means we have at least $n - x - y$ non-expert agents that know A and need to be in at least one more call each. We claim that in this situation all such agents have to be a caller or a callee of an active call which would then imply that at least $n - x - y$ agents are active.

Notice that if fewer than $n - x - y$ agents are active, then not all of the $n - x - y$ non-expert agents that know A may be a caller or a callee of an active call. This is because no agent that knows A may call another agent that knows A, so at most one such agent may be involved in each of these calls.

Suppose, that there is a non-expert agent, denoted by b, that knows A but is not a caller nor a callee in any active call. Let us execute in any order all active calls of agents that do not know A. Note that all these calls are made to agents that know A and they can make at most one such a call, because they get to know A afterwards. Moreover, executing any such call does not activate nor deactivate any calls of other agents that do not know A, because they cannot even observe that such a call was made. Hence, no new calls become active and so none of these calls can be to b, because we assumed he is not a callee in any active call.

Finally, after all these calls are made, agent b knows A and is still not an expert and is still not active, because he was not involved in any call. However, all active agents now know A and therefore cannot call b. Moreover, all active agents in the future must know A, because an agent can only become active by being called. So agent b will never be called nor call anyone to become an expert; a contradiction.   □

3.2   Different Call Scenarios

Let us fix a correct propositional gossip protocol for $n > 4$ agents and analyse its different call scenarios (corresponding to different lemmas in this section). In each of them we will show that at least $2n - 2$ calls can be made by the protocol in the worst case. In all these call scenarios we assume that the call sequence starts as in Lemma 13, i.e., once the first two calls made are between agents a and b and then b and c, ac can occur after some number of calls in order to form CC. Due to space constraints, some of the proofs of these different cases had to be moved to the appendix.

Lemma 16. *Assume ac can occur once a knows all secrets apart from C. Then at least $2n - 2$ calls can be made.*

Proof. As after a and b have had their call, no calls in the sequence leading to ac may involve C, these can occur before b and c have had their call. Therefore, after at least $n-2$ calls we can reach the position where a knows all secrets apart from C, and c has not yet been in any calls. From here, if we are to complete the protocol in $2n - 3$ calls, we have just $n - 1$ calls remaining and $n - 1$ agents do not know C, hence in every call an agent must learn C. As ac is active let us perform this call.

Now a and c are both experts, and the only agents which know C. This means that every call must now involve an agent calling an agent which knows C. However, assume in this state an agent d can call a. If we took da before ac, then we would have used $n - 1$ calls, and therefore $2n - 3$ would not be possible as only one agent knows C from Lemma 12. Hence all calls must be to c. This means that if we go back to the situation before ac, every agent must be able to call c. However, if we go back to the original case now, where b and c have had their call, this means we have used $n - 1$ calls, but the other $n - 2$ agents can now initiate a call with c. This takes us to $2n - 3$ calls yet b is not an expert. □

Lemma 17. *Assume ac can occur once agent a knows all secrets apart from C and one other, say, D. Then at least $2n - 2$ calls can be made.*

Proof. Let us follow this until after ca, whilst using Lemma 10 to remove all calls involving d. This leaves just $n - 2$ calls, yet there are still $n - 1$ agents which do not know D.   □

We can extend Lemma 17 to get an even stronger result.

Lemma 18. *Assume ac can occur after some amount of calls to form CC, leaving at least one agent uncalled, say, d.*
Assume further that CC can be extended with calls until all but one agent is now connected to CC in the graph of calls made. Then at least $2n - 2$ calls can be made.

Proof. In this situation, CC has $n-1$ agents, and hence at least $n-1$ calls. This leaves just $n - 2$ calls, yet there are still $n - 1$ agents which do not know D. □

Lemma 19. *Assume ac can occur once agent a knows all secrets apart from C and two others, say, D and E. Then at least $2n - 2$ calls can be made.*

Lemma 20. *Assume ac can occur after some amount of calls to form CC, leaving at least three agents uncalled.*
*Assume further that for agents not yet in a call (which will now be referred to as **NCC**), they are willing to form a connected component of their own, using all agents, beginning with xy followed by a call between y and z, and finally ending with xz. Then at least $2n - 2$ calls can be made.*

Proof. In this scenario, exactly n calls have been used. This means every secret must be known by at least three agents, if we were to complete in $2n - 3$ calls from Lemma 12. We find that both C and Z are known by exactly 3 agents, and hence must be learned in all future calls. Hence, the next call must be from and to one of a, b, c and x, y, z.

Furthermore, these 3 calls must all be available. Assume there is no call between x, y, z and a. Every call must have an agent learn both C and Z, so any agent which knows exactly one of these secrets must call an agent which knows the other. Therefore, if there is no call between x, y, z and a, then a may not be in any future calls, as these are the only 3 agents which will have have Z and not C, else another call has been made to an agent and C has not been learned. So, in this state these three calls must be available and no others, all calls must be between a, b, c and x, y, z, with each involved exactly once.

This means that either, at least two of these calls are initiated from CC, or at least two of these calls are initiated from NCC. As these are independent, we do not know which occurs first, and hence, due to relabelling, we can say that at least two of these calls are initiated by CC. But assume NCC is still in the position where only two calls have been made, between x and y and then between y and z. Now let the two calls from a, b, c to x, y, z happen. In this position t agents have not yet been involved in a call after $n - t + 1$ calls. Hence $t - 2$ calls remain before all these t agents must have been involved in a call. The result follows from Lemma 14.   □

Lemma 21. *Assume ac can occur after a call sequence forming CC that leaves at least three agents uncalled.*

*Assume further that for agents not yet in a call, they are willing to form a connected component of their own, beginning with xy followed by a call between y and z, and finally ending with xz, however without all agents from NCC included. Assume also from this NCC connected component (now referred to as **NCC-CC**) an agent wishes to initiate a call with an agent in CC (or be called by an agent in CC). Then at least $2n - 2$ calls can be made.*

Proof. Let there be t agents not yet in a call. After the call from NCC-CC to CC (or from CC to NCC-CC), $n - t + 1$ calls have been made, yet t agents have yet to be involved in a call. Hence $t - 2$ calls remain before all these t agents must have been involved in a call. The result follows from Lemma 14.   □

Lemma 22. *Assume ac can occur after some amount of calls to form CC. Continue making all calls possible which can be initiated by the agents in CC, to form a larger CC, until all these calls are used, leaving at least 3 agents uncalled.*

Assume further that for agents not yet in a call (which will now be referred to as NCC), they are willing to form a connected component of their own, beginning with xy followed by a call between y and z, and finally ending with xz, however without all agents from NCC included.

Assume also that no agent from NCC wishes to initiate a call with CC until it knows all secrets of agents in NCC. Then at least $2n - 2$ calls can be made.

Lemma 23. *Assume ac can occur after some amount of calls to form CC, leaving at least 3 agents uncalled.*

Assume further that for agents not yet in a call, NCC, no cycle can be formed without a call to or from CC. Then at least $2n - 2$ calls can be made.

Lemma 24. *Assume ac can occur after some amount of calls to form CC, leaving at least 3 agents uncalled.*

Assume further that in NCC at least two further instances of this can form, all disconnect from each other. Then at least $2n - 2$ calls can be made.

Proof. As eventually the protocol must connect all agents, these three (or more) cycles must join each other. However, two of these must be able to join to form a bigger connected component without the others being involved initially. Hence we could do this before any calls have been made in the other components at all. This takes us to the same position as in Lemma 21. □

Lemma 25. *Assume ac can occur after some amount of calls to form CC, leaving at least 3 agents uncalled.*

Assume further that in NCC a further instances of this can form. Assume that after this, we can reach a situation where these components remain disconnected, but possibly more calls have been made until we are left with these two connected components, and finally two agents not yet in a call. Then at least $2n - 2$ calls can be made.

3.3   The Main Result

We are finally ready to prove Theorem 8, which establishes $2n - 2$ lower bound on the number of calls needed by a correct propositional protocol.

Proof (of Theorem 8). In Lemma 13 we have shown a necessary possible structure for all correct propositional protocols, in where CC is formed. We then examined every possibility that can take place from this structure.

In Lemma 16 we showed that should CC contain all agents then no correct propositional protocol may exist with fewer than $2n-2$ calls. This meant at least one agent must not have been involved in the calls leading up to ac, and hence it must be possible that after ac at least one agent has not yet been involved in a call.

By Lemma 17 and Lemma 19 we see that it must be possible for there to be at least three agents not yet in a call at this stage.

In Lemma 20 we showed that these remaining agents cannot form a complete cycle component using all remaining agents themselves. We also show in Lemma 21 that if an agent remains which has still not been involved in a call after this second cycle component has formed, then these two cycle components cannot immediately call each other. In Lemma 22 we also showed that once the second cycle component is formed, waiting for an expert in NCC does not work either. In Lemma 23 we showed that there must be a connected cycle component in NCC which does not call CC before it is completed.

We have shown a connected cycle component must form in NCC, but not yet be able to call or be called by CC. In Lemma 24 we showed that we could not form three (or more) independent cycle components, so the remaining agents may not form another connected cycle component themselves. If there was just one agent left we would be done by Lemma 11. Finally in Lemma 25 we showed that once two cycle components are formed, if we have two additional agents which have only been involved in a call with each other then this will not give us a protocol with fewer than $2n - 2$ calls either.

Together, this shows that in no case is a correct propositional gossip protocol that uses less than $2n - 2$ calls in the worst case is possible. $\qquad\square$

4   Conclusions

In this paper we showed that any correct propositional gossip protocol in the worst case needs $2n - 2$ calls to terminate in an all-expert situation and thus solving an open Problem 7 from [9]. One may try to increase this lower bound further as not even a linear upper bound is known at the moment (note that LNS, LXS, and LNSwS1 protocols all require $\mathcal{O}(n^2)$ calls in the worst case). However, given how complex analysis was required to increase this lower bound from $2n - 3$ to $2n - 2$, this problem seems very difficult. Nevertheless, we conjecture that this is possible and the different structures of how sequences of calls of a correct protocol may look like that we established in this paper would be crucial in proving such a result and any future analyses of such protocols.

Another interesting problem still open is Problem 6 of [9], which conjectures that $2n - 3$ calls are needed by any gossip protocol (with arbitrary nesting of knowledge modalities). Already [9] demonstrates a (non-propositional) gossip protocol that always terminates in $2n - 3$ steps for $n > 3$ agents, but showing this number of calls is necessary is highly non-trivial.

References

1. Anderson, C.J., et al.: NetKAT: semantic foundations for networks. In: The 41st Annual ACM SIGPLAN-SIGACT Symposium on Principles of Programming Languages, POPL 2014, pp. 113–126. ACM (2014)
2. Apt, K.R., Grossi, D., van der Hoek, W.: Epistemic protocols for distributed gossiping. In: Proceedings of the 15th Conference on Theoretical Aspects of Rationality and Knowledge (TARK 2015), volume 215 of EPTCS, pp. 51–66 (2016)
3. Apt, K.R., Grossi, D., van der Hoek, W.: When are two gossips the same? In: Barthe, G., Sutcliffe, G., Veanes, M. (eds.) LPAR-22. 22nd International Conference on Logic for Programming, Artificial Intelligence and Reasoning, volume 57 of EPiC Series in Computing, pp. 36–55. EasyChair (2018)
4. Apt, K.R., Kopczyński, E., Wojtczak, D.: On the computational complexity of gossip protocols. In: Proceedings of the Twenty-Sixth International Joint Conference on Artificial Intelligence, IJCAI 2017, pp. 765–771 (2017)
5. Apt, K.R., Wojtczak, D.: On decidability of a logic of gossips. In: Michael, L., Kakas, A. (eds.) JELIA 2016. LNCS (LNAI), vol. 10021, pp. 18–33. Springer, Cham (2016). https://doi.org/10.1007/978-3-319-48758-8_2

6. Apt, K.R., Wojtczak, D.: Common knowledge in a logic of gossips. In: Proceedings of the 16th Conference on Theoretical Aspects of Rationality and Knowledge (TARK 2017), volume 251 of EPTCS, pp. 10–27 (2017)
7. Apt, K.R., Wojtczak, D.: Decidability of fair termination of gossip protocols. In: Proceedings of the 21st International Conference on Logic for Programming, Artificial Intelligence and Reasoning (LPAR 21), volume 1 of Kalpa Publications in Computing, pp. 73–85 (2017)
8. Apt, K.R., Wojtczak, D.: Verification of distributed epistemic gossip protocols. J. Artif. Intell. Res. (JAIR) **62**, 101–132 (2018)
9. Apt, K.R., Wojtczak, D.: Open problems in a logic of gossips. In: Proceedings Seventeenth Conference on Theoretical Aspects of Rationality and Knowledge (TARK 2019), volume 297 of EPTCS, pp. 1–18 (2019)
10. Attamah, M., Van Ditmarsch, H., Grossi, D., van der Hoek, W.: Knowledge and gossip. In: Proceedings of ECAI 2014, pp. 21–26. IOS Press (2014)
11. Bumby, R.T.: A problem with telephones. SIAM J. Algebr. Discrete. Methods **2**(1), 13–18 (1981)
12. Cooper, M.C., Herzig, A., Maffre, F., Maris, F., Régnier, P.: Simple epistemic planning: generalised gossiping. In: Proceedings of ECAI 2016, volume 285 of Frontiers in Artificial Intelligence and Applications, pp. 1563–1564. IOS Press (2016)
13. Cooper, M.C., Herzig, A., Maris, F., Vianey, J.: Temporal epistemic gossip problems. In: Slavkovik, M. (ed.) EUMAS 2018. LNCS (LNAI), vol. 11450, pp. 1–14. Springer, Cham (2019). https://doi.org/10.1007/978-3-030-14174-5_1
14. Fagin, R., Halpern, J.Y., Moses, Y., Vardi, M.Y.: Knowledge-based programs. Distrib. Comput. **10**(4), 199–225 (1997)
15. Gattinger, M., Wagemaker, J.: Towards an analysis of dynamic gossip in NetKAT. In: Desharnais, J., Guttmann, W., Joosten, S. (eds.) RAMiCS 2018. LNCS, vol. 11194, pp. 280–297. Springer, Cham (2018). https://doi.org/10.1007/978-3-030-02149-8_17
16. Harary, F., Schwenk, A.J.: The communication problem on graphs and digraphs (1974)
17. Hedetniemi, S.M., Hedetniemi, S.T., Liestman, A.L.: A survey of gossiping and broadcasting in communication networks. Networks **18**(4), 319–349 (1988)
18. Herzig, A., Maffre, F.: How to share knowledge by gossiping. In: Rovatsos, M., Vouros, G., Julian, V. (eds.) EUMAS/AT -2015. LNCS (LNAI), vol. 9571, pp. 249–263. Springer, Cham (2016). https://doi.org/10.1007/978-3-319-33509-4_20
19. Herzig, A., Maffre, F.: How to share knowledge by gossiping. AI Commun. **30**(1), 1–17 (2017)
20. Hromkovič, J., Klasing, R., Pelc, A., Ruzicka, P., Unger, W.: Dissemination of Information in Communication Networks - Broadcasting, Gossiping, Leader Election, and Fault-Tolerance. Texts in Theoretical Computer Science. An EATCS Series. Springer, Heidelberg (2005)
21. Kempe, D., Dobra, A., Gehrke, J.: Gossip-based computation of aggregate information. In: Proceedings of the 44th Annual IEEE Symposium on Foundations of Computer Science, FOCS 2003, pp. 482–491. IEEE (2003)
22. Kermarrec, A., van Steen, M.: Gossiping in distributed systems. Oper. Syst. Rev. **41**(5), 2–7 (2007)
23. Ladin, R., Liskov, B., Shrira, L., Ghemawat, S.: Providing high availability using lazy replication. ACM Trans. Comput. Syst. (TOCS) **10**(4), 360–391 (1992)
24. Livesey, J., Wojtczak, D.: Propositional gossip protocols. In: Proceedings of the 23rd International Symposium on Fundamentals of Computation Theory (FCT 2021), (to appear) (2021)

25. Tijdeman, R.: On a telephone problem. Nieuw Archief voor Wiskunde **3**(XIX), 188–192 (1971)
26. Ditmarsch, H., Grossi, D., Herzig, A., van der Hoek, W., Kuijer, L. B.: Parameters for epistemic gossip problems. In: Proceedings of the 12th Conference on Logic and the Foundations of Game and Decision Theory (LOFT 2016) (2016)
27. van Ditmarsch, H., Kokkinis, I.: The expected duration of sequential gossiping. In: Belardinelli, F., Argente, E. (eds.) EUMAS/AT -2017. LNCS (LNAI), vol. 10767, pp. 131–146. Springer, Cham (2018). https://doi.org/10.1007/978-3-030-01713-2_10
28. van Ditmarsch, H., Kokkinis, I., Stockmarr, A.: Reachability and expectation in gossiping. In: An, B., Bazzan, A., Leite, J., Villata, S., van der Torre, L. (eds.) PRIMA 2017. LNCS (LNAI), vol. 10621, pp. 93–109. Springer, Cham (2017). https://doi.org/10.1007/978-3-319-69131-2_6
29. van Ditmarsch, H., van Der Hoek, W., Kuijer, L.B.: The logic of gossiping. Artif. Intell. **286**, 103306 (2020)
30. van Ditmarsch, H., van Eijck, J., Pardo, P., Ramezanian, R., Schwarzentruber, F.: Epistemic protocols for dynamic gossip. J. Appl. Log. **20**(C), 1–31 (2017)
31. van Ditmarsch, H., van Eijck, J., Pardo, P., Ramezanian, R., Schwarzentruber, F.: Dynamic gossip. Bull. Iran. Math. Soc. 1–28 (2018)

Reachability is NP-Complete Even for the Simplest Neural Networks

Marco Sälzer[✉][iD] and Martin Lange[iD]

School of Electr. Eng. and Computer Science, University of Kassel, Kassel, Germany
{marco.saelzer,martin.lange}@uni-kassel.de
https://www.uni-kassel.de/eecs/fmv

Abstract. We investigate the complexity of the reachability problem for (deep) neural networks: does it compute valid output given some valid input? It was recently claimed that the problem is NP-complete for general neural networks and conjunctive input/output specifications. We repair some flaws in the original upper and lower bound proofs. We then show that NP-hardness already holds for restricted classes of simple specifications and neural networks with just one layer, as well as neural networks with minimal requirements on the occurring parameters.

Keywords: Machine learning · Computational complexity · Formal specification and verification

1 Introduction

Deep learning has proved to be very successful for highly challenging or even otherwise intractable tasks in a broad range of applications such as image recognition [11] or natural language processing [5] but also safety-critical applications like autonomous driving [4], medical applications [12], or financial matters [2]. These naturally come with safety concerns and the need for certification methods. Recent such methods can be divided into (I) Adversarial Attack and Defense, (II) Testing, and (III) Formal Verification. A comprehensive survery about all three categories is given in [6].

The former two cannot guarantee the absence of errors. Formal verification of neural networks (NN) is a relatively new area of research which ensures completeness of the certification procedure. Recent work on sound and complete verification algorithms for NN are mostly concerned with efficient solutions to their reachability problem NNREACH [1,3,8,13]: given an NN and symbolic specifications of valid inputs and outputs, decide whether there is some valid input such that the corresponding output is valid, too. This corresponds to the understanding of reachability in classical software verification: valid sets of inputs and outputs are specified and the question is whether there is a valid input that leads to a valid output. Put differently, the question is whether the set of valid outputs is reachable from the set of valid inputs. The difference to classical reachability problems in discrete state-based programs is that there reachability is a matter

© Springer Nature Switzerland AG 2021
P. C. Bell et al. (Eds.): RP 2021, LNCS 13035, pp. 149–164, 2021.
https://doi.org/10.1007/978-3-030-89716-1_10

of *lengths* of a connection. In NN this is given by the number of layers, and it is rather the *width* of the continuous state space which may cause unreachability.

Solving NNREACH is interesting for practical purposes. An efficient algorithm can be used to ensure that no input from some specified set of inputs is misclassified or that some undesired class of outputs is never reached. In applications like autonomous-driving, where classifiers based on neural networks are used to make critical decisions, such safeguards are indispensable.

However, all known algorithms for NNREACH show the same drawback: a lack of scalability to networks of large size which, unfortunately, are featured typically in real-world applications [10]. This is not a big surprise as the problem is NP-complete. This result was proposed by Katz et al. [8] for NN with ReLU and identity activations, and later also by Ruan et al. [14]. While there is no reason to doubt the NP-completeness claim, the proofs are not stringent and contain flaws.

The argument for the upper bound in [8] misses the fact that real inputs are not necessarily polynomially bounded in size. In fact, guessing values in $\mathbb{R}$ is not even effective without a bound on the size of their representation. Such a bound is closely linked to the question whether such values can be approximated upto some precision. The proof by Katz et al. makes no argument for any bound on the representation of such values, let alone a polynomial one.[1]

The arguments for the lower bound by a reduction from 3SAT in [8] and [15] rely on a discretisation of real values to model Boolean values. This does not work for the signum function σ used by Ruan et al. as it is not congruent for sums: e.g. $\sigma(-3) = \sigma(-1)$ but $\sigma(2 + (-3)) \neq \sigma(2 + (-1))$, showing that one cannot simply interpret any negative number as the Boolean value *false* etc. As a consequence, completeness of the construction fails as there are (real) solutions to NNREACH which do not correspond to (discrete) satisfying 3SAT assignments. Katz et al. seem to be aware of this and use a slightly more elaborate discretisation in their reduction, but unfortunately it still suffers from similar problems.[2]

We start our investigations into the complexity of NNREACH by fixing these issues in Sect. 3. We provide a different argument for membership in NP which shows that the need for nondeterminism is not to be sought in the input values but in the use of ReLU nodes. As a corollary we obtain polynomial decidability for NN with a bounded number of such nodes. We also address the issue of discretisation of real values in the lower bound proof, fixing the construction given by Katz et al. We do not address the one by Ruan et al. further, as this does not provide any further insights or new results.

We then observe that the reduction from 3SAT constructs a very specific class of NNREACH instances which we call $\mathcal{C}(3SAT)$. NN from this class have a fixed amount of layers but scaling input and output dimension as well as layer size. This raises the question whether, in comparison to the networks from $\mathcal{C}(3SAT)$,

---

[1] While this paper was being processed, Katz et al. published an extended version of their original paper [9]. Unfortunately, the flaws concerning the upper bound are still present in this version.

[2] These problems are repaired in [9], but in a slightly different way than we do.

reducing the amount of layers or fixing dimensionality leads to a class of networks for which NNREACH is efficiently solvable. In Sect. 4 we show that the answer to this is mostly negative: NP-hardness of NNREACH holds for NN with just one layer and an output dimension of one. While this provides minimal requirements on the structure of NN for NNREACH to be NP-hard, we also give minimal criteria on the weights and biases in NN for NP-hardness to hold. Thus, the computational difficulty of NNREACH in the sense of NP-completeness is quite robust. The requirements on the structure or parameters of an NN that are needed for NP-hardness to occur are easily met in practical applications. Due to space restrictions, some technical proof details are deferred to the appendix.

We conclude in Sect. 5 with references to possible future work.

2 Preliminaries

Definition 1. *A neural network (NN) N is a layered graph that represents a function of type $\mathbb{R}^n \to \mathbb{R}^m$.*

The first layer $l = 0$ is called the input layer *and consists of n nodes. The i-th node computes the output $y_{0i} = x_i$ where x_i is the i-th input to the overall network. Thus, the output of the input layer $(y_{00}, \ldots, y_{0(n-1)})$ is identical to the input of N.*

A layer $1 \leq l \leq L - 2$ is called hidden *and consists of k nodes. Note that k must not be uniform across the hidden layers of N. Then, the i-th node of layer l computes the output $y_{li} = \sigma_{li}(\sum_j c_{ji}^{(l-1)} y_{(l-1)j} + b_{li})$ where j iterates over the output dimensions of the previous layer, $c_{ji}^{(l-1)}$ are real constants which are called* weights, *b_{li} is a real constant which is called* bias *and σ_{li} is some (typically nonlinear) function called* activation. *The outputs of all nodes of layer l combined gives the output $(y_{l0}, \ldots, y_{l(k-1)})$ of the hidden layer.*

The last layer $l = L - 1$ is called the output layer *and consists of m nodes. The i-th node computes an output $y_{(L-1)i}$ in the same way as a node in a hidden layer. The output of the output layer $(y_{(L-1)0}, \ldots, y_{(L-1)(m-1)})$ is considered as the output of the network N.*

The output of a neural network N under input x is denoted $N(x)$. If a node in a layer $l > 0$ has less inputs than there are outputs in layer $l - 1$ then we assume that the unconsidered outputs of $l - 1$ are weighted with zero. We only consider networks where nodes in hidden layers have the identity or the ReLU function, and nodes in the output layer have the identity as activation. The *ReLU function* is defined as $x \mapsto \max(0, x)$. Nodes with ReLU or identity activation are called ReLU nodes or identity nodes, respectively. Given some input to the NN, we say that a ReLU node is *active*, resp. *inactive* if the input for its activation function is greater, resp. less than or equal to 0. We visualize an NN as a directed graph with weighted edges. An example is given in Fig. 1.

Our main interest lies in the validity of specifications over the output values of NN given specifications over their input values. These specifications are expressed as conjunctions of linear constraints on the input and output variables of a network.

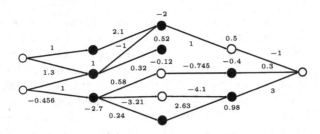

Fig. 1. Schema of a neural network with five layers, input dimension of two and output dimension of one. Filled nodes are ReLU nodes, empty nodes are identity nodes. An edge between two nodes u and v with label w denotes that the output of u is weighted with w in the computation of v. No edge between u and v implies $w = 0$. The bias of a node is depicted by a value above or below the node. If there is no such value then the bias is zero.

Definition 2. *A* specification *φ for a given set of variables X is defined by the following grammar:*

$$\varphi ::= \varphi \wedge \varphi \mid t \leq b \qquad\qquad t ::= c \cdot x \mid t + t$$

where b, c are rational constants and $x \in X$ is a variable.

We use $t \geq b$ and $t = b$ as syntactic sugar for $-t \leq -b$ and $t \leq b \wedge -t \leq -b$. Furthermore, we use $\top$ for $x + (-x) = 0$ and $\bot$ for $x + (-x) = 1$ where x is some variable. We call a specification φ *simple* if for all $t \leq b$ it holds that $t = c \cdot x$ for some rational constant c and variable x.

Definition 3. *Specification $\varphi(x_0, \ldots, x_{n-1})$ is true under $\boldsymbol{x} = (r_0, \ldots, r_{n-1}) \in \mathbb{R}^n$ if each inequality in φ is satisfied in real arithmetic with each x_i set to r_i.*

We write $\varphi(\boldsymbol{x})$ for the application of $\boldsymbol{x}$ to the variables of φ. If there are less variables in φ than dimensions in $\boldsymbol{x}$ we ignore the additional values of $\boldsymbol{x}$. If we consider a specification φ in context of a neural network N we call it an *input or output specification* and assume that the set of variables occurring in φ is a subset of the input respectively output variables of N.

Definition 4. *The decision problem NNREACH is the following: given a neural network N, input specification $\varphi_{in}(x_0, \ldots, x_{n-1})$ and output specification $\varphi_{out}(y_0, \ldots, y_{m-1})$, is there $\boldsymbol{x} \in \mathbb{R}^n$ such that $\varphi_{in}(\boldsymbol{x})$ and $\varphi_{out}(N(\boldsymbol{x}))$ are true?*

3   NNReach is NP-Complete

3.1   Membership in NP

The argument used by Katz et al. to show membership of NNREACH in NP can be summarized as follows: nondeterministically guess an input vector $\boldsymbol{x}$ as a witness, compute the output $N(\boldsymbol{x})$ of the network and check that $\varphi_{in}(\boldsymbol{x}) \wedge$

$\varphi_{out}(N(\boldsymbol{x}))$ holds. It is indisputable that the computation and check of this procedure are polynomial in the size of N, φ_{in}, φ_{out} *and* the size of $\boldsymbol{x}$. However, for inclusion in NP we also need the size of $\boldsymbol{x}$ to be polynomially bounded in the size of the instance given as $(N, \varphi_{in}, \varphi_{out})$. There may be an argument for this, for instance based on the correspondence between size of $\boldsymbol{x}$ and required approximation precision for such values. However, we are not aware of such an argument, let alone a striking one, and there is also a simpler way of obtaining the upper bound.

Definition 5. *A* ReLU-linear program *over a set* $X = \{x_0, \ldots, x_{n-1}\}$ *of vari- ables is a set* Φ *of (in-)equalities of the form*

$$b_j + \sum_{i=1}^{m} c_{ji} \cdot x_{ji} \leq x_j \quad or \quad ReLU\left(b_j + \sum_{i=1}^{m} c_{ji} \cdot x_{ji}\right) = x_j$$

where $x_{ji}, x_j \in X$ *and* $c_{ji}, b_j \in \mathbb{Q}$. *Equations of the second form are called* ReLU-*equations. A solution to* Φ *is a vector* $\boldsymbol{x} \in \mathbb{R}^n$ *which satisfies all (in-)equalities when each variable* $x_i \in X$ *is replaced by* $\boldsymbol{x}(i)$. *A* ReLU-equality $ReLU(b_j + \sum_{i=1}^{m} c_{ji} \cdot x_{ji}) = x_j$ *is satisfied by* $\boldsymbol{x}$ *if*

- $b_j + \sum_{i=1}^{m} c_{ji} \cdot x_{ji} \geq 0$ *and* $x_j = b_j + \sum_{i=1}^{m} c_{ji} \cdot x_{ji}$, *or*
- $b_j + \sum_{i=1}^{m} c_{ji} \cdot x_{ji} \leq 0$ *and* $x_j = 0$.

The problem of solving a ReLU-linear program *is: given* Φ, *decide whether there is a solution to it.*

Any ReLU-linear program without ReLU-equalities is a linear program in the usual sense, and linear programs are known to be solvable in polynomial time [7].

Lemma 1. *The problem of solving a ReLU-linear program is in NP.*

Proof. Suppose a ReLU-linear program Φ with l ReLU-equalities is given. Existence of a solution can be decided as follows. Guess, for each ReLU-equation χ_k of the form $ReLU(b_j + \sum_{i=1}^{m} c_{ji} \cdot x_{ji}) = x_j$, some $a_k \in \{0, 1\}$. Let $\boldsymbol{a} = (a_0, \ldots, a_{l-1})$. Next, let $\Phi_{\boldsymbol{a}}$ result from Φ by replacing each χ_k by the following (in-)equalities.

$$b_j + \sum_{i=1}^{m} c_{ji} \cdot x_{ji} \geq 0 \ , \ b_j + \sum_{i=1}^{m} c_{ji} \cdot x_{ji} = x_j \qquad \text{if } a_k = 1$$

$$b_j + \sum_{i=1}^{m} c_{ji} \cdot x_{ji} \leq 0 \ , \ x_j = 0 \qquad \text{if } a_k = 0$$

The following is not hard to see: (I) Using standard transformations, $\Phi_{\boldsymbol{a}}$ can be turned into a linear program of size linear in Φ. (II) Any solution to $\Phi_{\boldsymbol{a}}$ is also a solution to Φ, (III) If Φ has a solution, then there is $\boldsymbol{a} \in \{0, 1\}^l$ such that $\Phi_{\boldsymbol{a}}$ has a solution. This can be created as follows. Let $\boldsymbol{x}$ be a solution to Φ. For each ReLU-equation χ_k as above, let $a_k = 1$ if the corresponding sum is non-negative, otherwise let $a_k = 0$. Then $\boldsymbol{x}$ is also a solution for Φ_a. Thus, ReLU-linear programs can be solved in nondeterministic polynomial time by guessing $\boldsymbol{a}$, and then constructing the linear program Φ_a and solving it.   □

With this definition of a ReLU-linear program and the corresponding lemma at hand, we are set to prove NP-membership of NNREACH.

Theorem 1. NNREACH *is in NP.*

Proof. Let $\mathcal{I} = (N, \varphi_{\text{in}}, \varphi_{\text{out}})$. We construct a ReLU-linear program $\Phi_{\mathcal{I}}$ of size linear in $|N| + |\varphi_{\text{in}}| + |\varphi_{\text{out}}|$ which is solvable iff there is a solution for $\mathcal{I}$. The ReLU-linear program $\Phi_{\mathcal{I}}$ contains the following (in-)equalities.

- φ_{in} and φ_{out} (with each conjunct seen as one (in-)equality),
- for each non-ReLU node v_{li} computing $\sum_j c_{ji}^{(l-1)} y_{(l-1)j} + b_{li}$ add the equality $\sum_j c_{ji}^{(l-1)} y_{(l-1)j} + b_{li} = y_{li}$ (in the form of two inequalities of appropriate form),
- for each ReLU node v_{li} computing $ReLU(\sum_j c_{ji}^{(l-1)} y_{(l-1)j} + b_{li})$ add the ReLU-equality $ReLU(\sum_j c_{ji}^{(l-1)} y_{(l-1)j} + b_{li}) = y_{li}$.

The claim on the size of $\Phi_{\mathcal{I}}$ should be clear. Moreover, note that a solution $\boldsymbol{x}$ to $\mathcal{I}$ can be extended to an assignment $\boldsymbol{x}'$ of real values at every node of N, including values $\boldsymbol{y}$ for the output nodes of N s.t., in particular $N(\boldsymbol{x}) = \boldsymbol{y}$. Then $\boldsymbol{x}'$ is a solution to $\Phi_{\mathcal{I}}$. Likewise, a solution to $\Phi_{\mathcal{I}}$ can be turned into a solution to $\mathcal{I}$ by projection to the input variables.

Hence, NNREACH polynomially reduces to the problem of solving ReLU-linear programs which, by Lemma 1 is in NP.   □

It is interesting to point out the role of witnesses for positive instances of the NNREACH problem: it is tempting to regard values to the input nodes of the NN as potential witnesses as done by Katz et al. but, as mentioned before, for as long as there is no argument for their polynomial boundedness these are *not* suitable witnesses in an NP procedure. Instead, Theorem 1 above shows that an assignment to the ReLU nodes as being in-/active can serve as such a witness. This immediately yields a polynomial fragment of NNREACH.

Corollary 1. *The reachability problem for NN with a bounded number of ReLU nodes is decidable in polynomial time.*

3.2   NP-Hardness

Katz et al. try to build a polynomial-time reduction from 3SAT to NNREACH. The underlying idea is to encode the structure of a 3SAT formula in a neural network and the existence of a satisfying assignment for this formula in the corresponding input- and output-specifications. Consider the 3SAT instance

$$\psi = (X_0 \vee X_1 \vee X_1) \wedge (\neg X_0 \vee X_1 \vee \neg X_2) \wedge (\neg X_1 \vee X_2 \vee X_3)$$

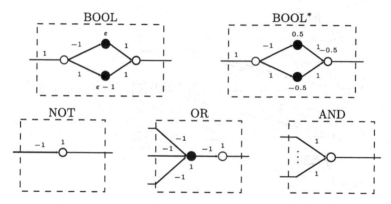

Fig. 2. Gadgets used in the reduction from 3SAT to NNREACH. A non-weighted outgoing edge of a gadget is connected to a weighted incoming edge of another gadget in the actual construction or is considered an output of the overall neural network.

with four propositional variables and three clauses, and let $(N, \varphi_{\text{in}}, \varphi_{\text{out}})$ be the NNREACH instance resulting from the mapping of ψ according to the reduction. To understand the structure of N we make use of so-called *gadgets*, specified in Fig. 2. Each gadget is a compact NN and is used to describe a functional subcomponent of N. Using these gadgets, the network N is depicted in Fig. 3.

Ignoring the BOOL-gadgets for the moment, assume that input values are taken from $\{0, 1\}$ instead of $\mathbb{R}$. The function computed by N is described as follows. Each of the three OR-gadgets together with their connected NOT-gadgets represent one of the clauses in ψ. From Fig. 2 we can infer that the NOT-gadgets negate their inputs and that the OR-gadgets output 1 if at least one input is 1 and 0 otherwise. Hence, if an OR-gadget outputs 1 then the current input, viewed as an assignment to the propositional variables in ψ, satisfies the corresponding clause. The AND-gadget simply sums up all of its inputs and, thus, we get that y is equal to 3 iff each OR-gadget outputs one. Therefore, with the output specification $\varphi_{\text{out}} := y = 3$, we get a reduction from 3SAT to NNREACH, provided that input values are externally restricted to $\{0, 1\}$.

But NN are defined for all real-valued inputs, so we need further adjustments to make the reduction complete. First, note that it is impossible to write an input specification $\varphi_{\text{in}}(\boldsymbol{x})$ which is satisfied by $\boldsymbol{x}$ iff $\boldsymbol{x} \in \{0, 1\}^n$ because $\{0, 1\}^n$ is not a hyperrectangle in $\mathbb{R}^n$ but conjunctions of inequalities only specify hyperrectangles. This is where we make use of BOOL-gadgets. Let ε be a very small constant. A BOOL-gadget with input x and output z computes $z = \max(0, \varepsilon - x) + \max(0, x - 1 + \varepsilon)$. Now, Katz et al. claim the following: if $x \in [0; 1]$ then we have $z \in [0; \varepsilon]$ iff $x \in [0; \varepsilon]$ or $x \in [1 - \varepsilon; 1]$. Thus, by connecting a BOOL-gadget to each input x_i in N and using the simple specifications

$$\varphi_{\text{in}} := \bigwedge_{i=0}^{3} x_i \geq 0 \wedge x_i \leq 1 \qquad \varphi_{\text{out}} := \bigwedge_{i=0}^{3} z_i \geq 0 \wedge z_i \leq \varepsilon \wedge y \geq 3(1 - \varepsilon) \wedge y \leq 3$$

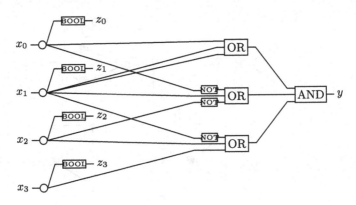

Fig. 3. Schema of a neural network resulting from the reduction of the 3SAT-formula $(X_0 \vee X_1 \vee X_1) \wedge (\neg X_0 \vee X_1 \vee \neg X_2) \wedge (\neg X_1 \vee X_2 \vee X_3)$. Note that no weights are depicted as these are specified inside the gadgets.

we would get a correct translation of ψ. Note that the constraint on y is no longer $y = 3$ as the valid inputs to N, determined by the BOOL-gadgets and their output constraints, are not exactly 0 or exactly 1. However, the claim about BOOL-gadgets is wrong. Consider a BOOL-gadget with very small ε such that it is safe to assume $\varepsilon < 2\varepsilon < 1 - \varepsilon$. Then, for $x = 2\varepsilon$ we have $z = 0$, which contradicts the claim. In fact, it can be shown that for each $\varepsilon \leq \frac{1}{2}$ and each input $x \in [0; 1]$ the output z is an element of $[0; \varepsilon]$. Clearly, this is not the intended property of these gadgets. But with some adjustments to the BOOL-gadgets we can make the reduction work.

A BOOL*-*gadget* is a neural network with functional form $\mathbb{R} \to \mathbb{R}$ shown in Fig. 2. It computes the function

$$ z = \max\left(0, \frac{1}{2} - x\right) + \max\left(0, x - \frac{1}{2}\right) - \frac{1}{2}, $$

where x is the input variable and z is the output variable. For this BOOL*-gadget we can show a similar statement as it was intended for the BOOL-gadgets in the original proof.

Lemma 2. *In a BOOL*-gadget with input x and output z we have $z = 0$ if and only if $x = 0$ or $x = 1$.*

Proof. Note that $z = \max\left(0, \frac{1}{2} - x\right) + \max\left(0, x - \frac{1}{2}\right) - \frac{1}{2}$ is equivalent to

$$ z = \begin{cases} -x & \text{if } x < \frac{1}{2}, \\ x - 1 & \text{otherwise.} \end{cases} $$

From this we immediately get that $z = 0$ if $x = 0$ or $x = 1$, and $z \neq 0$ for all other values of x. $\square$

Now, replacing all BOOL-gadgets with BOOL*-gadgets in the construction and using the simple specifications $\varphi_{\text{in}} = \top$ and $\varphi_{\text{out}} = \bigwedge_{i=0}^{n-1} z_i = 0 \wedge y = m$ for a 3SAT-instance with n propositional variables and m clauses, we get a correct reduction from 3SAT to NNREACH.

Theorem 2. NNREACH *is NP-hard.*

One could argue that the networks resulting from the reduction of 3SAT are not typical feed-forward neural networks as they do not follow a layerwise structure. A reason for this is that some inputs are connected to NOT-gadgets where some are not and that the outputs z_i are not in the same layer as the output y. This can of course be fixed by introducing additional dummy nodes.

4 NP-Hardness Holds in Very Restricted Cases Already

Let $\mathcal{C}(\text{3SAT})$ be the class of NNREACH instances which are obtained as images under the reduction presented in the previous section. Note that the NN of $\mathcal{C}(\text{3SAT})$ are already quite restricted; they possess only a fixed number of layers. In this section we strengthen the NP-hardness result by constructing even simpler classes of NN for which NNREACH is NP-hard already. Section 4.1 studies the possibility to make these NN structurally as simple as possible; Sect. 4.2 shows that requirements on weights and biases can be relaxed whilst retaining NP-hardness.

4.1 Neural Networks of a Simple Structure

We consider NN with just one hidden layer of ReLU nodes and an output dimension of one. As before, we can establish a reduction from 3SAT.

Theorem 3. NNREACH *is NP-hard for NN with output dimension one, a single hidden layer and simple specifications.*

Proof. Let ψ be a 3SAT formula with n propositional variables X_i and m clauses l_j. We slightly modify the construction of a network N in the proof of Theorem 2. First, we remove the last identity node of all BOOL*-gadgets in N and directly connect the two outputs of their ReLU nodes to the AND-gadget, weighted with 1. Additionally, we merge NOT-gadgets and OR-gadgets in N. Consider the OR-gadget corresponding to some clause l_j. The merged gadget has three inputs $x_{j_0}, x_{j_1}, x_{j_2}$ and computes $\max\left(0, 1 - \sum_{k=0}^{2} f_j(x_{j_k})\right)$ where $f_j(x_{j_k}) = x_{j_k}$ if X_{j_k} occurs positively in l_j and $f_j(x_{j_k}) = 1 - x_{ij}$ if it occurs negatively. It is straightforward to see that the output of such a gadget is 0 if at least one positively (resp. negatively) weighted input is 0, resp. 1, and that the output is 1 if all positively weighted inputs are 1 and all negatively weighted inputs are 0. These merged gadgets are connected with weight -1 to the AND-gadget. Once done for all BOOL*-, NOT- and OR-gadgets, the overall output y of N is given by

$$\sum_{i=0}^{n-1} \max\left(0, \frac{1}{2} - x_i\right) + \max\left(0, x_i - \frac{1}{2}\right) - \sum_{i=0}^{m-1} \max\left(0, 1 - \sum_{j=0}^{2} f_i(x_{ij})\right).$$

Note that N has input dimension n, a single hidden layer of $2n + m$ ReLU nodes and output dimension 1.

Now take the simple specifications $\varphi_{in} = \bigwedge_{i=0}^{n-1} x_i \geq 0 \wedge x_i \leq 1$ and $\varphi_{out} = y = \frac{n}{2}$. We argue that the following holds for a solution to $(N, \varphi_{in}, \varphi_{out})$: (I) all x_i are either 0 or 1, and (II) the output of each merged OR-gadget is 0. To show (I), we assume the opposite, i.e. there is a solution with $x_k \in (0; 1)$ for some k. This implies that $\sum_{i=0}^{n-1} \max(0, \frac{1}{2} - x_i) + \max(0, x_i - \frac{1}{2}) < \frac{n}{2}$ as for all $x_i \in [0; 1]$ we have $\max(0, \frac{1}{2} - x_i) + \max(0, x_i - \frac{1}{2}) \leq \frac{1}{2}$, and for x_k we have $\max(0, \frac{1}{2} - x_k) + \max(0, x_k - \frac{1}{2}) < \frac{1}{2}$. Furthermore, we must have $-\sum_{i=0}^{m-1} \max(0, 1 - \sum_{j=0}^{2} f(x_{ij})) \leq 0$. Therefore, this cannot be a solution for $(N, \varphi_{in}, \varphi_{out})$ as it does not satisfy $y = \frac{n}{2}$.

To show (II), assume there is a solution such that one merged OR-gadget outputs a value different from 0. Then, $-\sum_{i=0}^{m-1} \max(0, 1 - \sum_{j=0}^{2} f(x_{ij})) < 0$ which in combination with (I) yields $y < \frac{n}{2}$. Again, this is a contradiction.

Putting (I) and (II) together, a solution for $(N, \varphi_{in}, \varphi_{out})$ implies the existence of a model for ψ. For the opposite direction assume that ψ has a model I. Then, a solution for $(N, \varphi_{in}, \varphi_{out})$ is given by $x_i = 1$ if $I(X_i)$ is true and $x_i = 0$ otherwise. □

In the previous section, especially in the arguments of Corollary 1, we pointed out that the occurrence of ReLU nodes is crucial for the NP-hardness of NNREACH. Thus, it is tempting to assume that any major restriction to these nodes leads to efficiently solvable classes.

Theorem 4. NNREACH *is NP-hard for NN where all ReLU nodes have at most one non-zero weighted input and simple specifications.*

Proof. We prove NP-hardness via a reduction from 3SAT. The reduction works in the same way as in the proof of Theorem 2, but with the following adjustments. We replace the OR-gadgets with simple identity-nodes, we do not include the AND-gadget, and we set the output specification to $\varphi_{out} = \bigwedge_{i=0}^{n-1} z_i = 0 \wedge \bigwedge_{i=0}^{m} y_i \geq 1$, where y_i is the output of the i-th identity-node replacing the former i-th OR-gadget, z_i is the output of the i-th BOOL-gadget, n is the number of propositional variables and m the number of clauses in the considered 3SAT-instance. Note that this is a simple specification and that the only ReLU nodes in this network are inside the BOOL*-gadgets, which have only one non-zero input. Now, if each $z_i = 0$ then the value of an output y_i is equivalent to the number of inputs equal to 1. The correctness of this reduction is argued int the exaxt same way as in in the original one. □

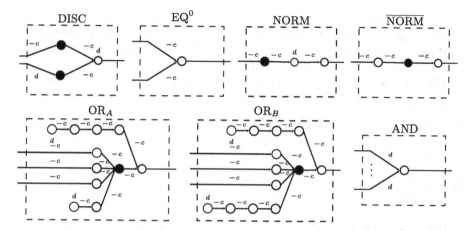

Fig. 4. Gadgets used to show that NNREACH is NP-hard if restricted to $\mathcal{C}(\{-c, 0, d\})$. A non-weighted outgoing edge of a gadget is connected to a weighted incoming one of another gadget in the actual construction or are considered as outputs of the overall neural networks.

4.2   Neural Networks with Simple Parameters

One could argue that the NP-hardness results in Theorem 2 and 3 are only partially applicable to real world problems as the constructed NN use very specific combinations of weights and biases, namely $-1, 0, \frac{1}{2}$ and 1, which may be unlikely to occur in this exact combination in real-world applications. We show that NNREACH is already NP-hard in cases where only very weak assumptions are made on the set of occurring weights and biases.

For $P \subseteq \mathbb{Q}$ let $\mathcal{C}(P)$ be the class of NNREACH instances whose NN only use weights and biases from P and simple specifications. We will show that NP-hardness already occurs when P contains three values: 0, some positive and some negative value. We make use of the same techniques as in Sect. 3 and assume that the general idea of gadgets and the reduction from 3SAT to NNREACH are known.

Definition 6. *Let $c, d \in \mathbb{Q}^{>0}$ and ψ be a 3SAT-formula with n propositional variables X_i and m clauses l_j. The network $N_{-c,d,\psi}$ is a network with $2n$ inputs, two for each X_i, called x_i and $\overline{x_i}$. We describe the structure of $N_{-c,d,\psi}$ using the gadgets from Fig. 4:*

- *Each input x_i is connected to both inputs of a DISC-gadget and this gadget is connected with weight $-c$ to a chain of five identity nodes interconnected with weight $-c$. We call the output of the last node of this chain z_i.*
- *Each pair x_i and $\overline{x_i}$ is connected to an EQ^0-gadget and this gadget is connected with weight $-c$ to a chain of six identity nodes interconnected with weight $-c$. We call the output of the last node of this chain e_i.*
- *Each input x_i is connected to a NORM-gadget. Analogously, each $\overline{x_i}$ is connected to a $\overline{\text{NORM}}$-gadget.*

- If $c \geq 1$ (resp. $c < 1$) then there are m OR$_A$-gadgets (resp. OR$_B$-gadgets), one for each l_j s.t. if X_i occurs positively in l_j then the output of the NORM-gadget connected to x_i is connected and if X_i occurs negatively the output of the $\overline{\text{NORM}}$-gadget connected to $\overline{x_i}$ is connected.
- The outputs of all OR$_A$-gadgets respectively OR$_B$-gadgets are connected to a single AND-gadget. We denote the output of this AND-gadget with y.

Note that each $N_{-c,d,\psi}$ has eight layers and output dimension $2n + 1$. Moreover, $N_{-c,d,\psi} \in \mathcal{C}(\{-c, 0, d\})$. Next, we need to clarify some properties of the used gadgets.

Lemma 3. Let x_0, x_1, x_2 denote inputs for some gadget. The following statements hold:

1. If $x_0 = x_1$ then the output of a DISC-gadget is 0 if and only if $x_0 = x_1 = -\frac{d}{c^2}$ or $x_0 = x_1 = \frac{1}{c}$.
2. If $x_0 = -\frac{d}{c^2}$ then the output of a NORM-gadget is 0 and if $x_0 = \frac{1}{c}$ then the output is $-dc$.
3. If $x_0 = \frac{d}{c^2}$ then the output of $\overline{\text{NORM}}$-gadget is $-dc$ and if $x_0 = -\frac{1}{c}$ then the output is 0.
4. If $x_0 = x_1 = x_2 = 0$ then the output of an OR$_A$-gadget is $dc^4 - dc^3$. If at least one input is $-dc$ while the others are 0 then the output is dc^4. The same holds for an OR$_B$-gadget with the difference that if $x_0 = x_1 = x_2 = 0$ then the output is $dc^4 - dc^5$.

Proof. We start with Property 3.1 and assume that the inputs x_0, x_1 are equal. We can infer from the depiction in Fig. 4 that the output of a DISC-gadget is given by $d - c\max(0, dx_0) - c\max(0, -cx_1)$. At this point we make a case distinction. If $x_0 = x_1 < 0$ then the output is given by $d + c^2 x_1$ and equal to zero if and only if $x_1 = -\frac{d}{c^2}$. If $x_0 = x_1 > 0$ then the output is given by $d - cdx_0$ and equal to zero if and only if $x_0 = \frac{1}{c}$. The last case, namely $x_0 = x_1 = 0$, leads to an output of d.

The Properties 3.2, 3.3 and 3.4 are easily argued. We can infer from Fig. 4 that the output of a NORM-gadget is given by $-c(d - c\max(0, -cx_0))$, the output of a $\overline{\text{NORM}}$-gadget given by $-c\max(0, c^2 x_0)$, the output of an OR-A-gadget given by $dc^4 - c\max(0, dc^2 + c^2 \sum_{i=0}^{2} x_i)$ and the output of an OR-B-gadget given by $dc^4 - c\max(0, dc^4 + c^2 \sum_{i=0}^{2} x_i)$. Then the statements about these gadgets follow by inserting the mentioned values and solving the equations. $\square$

With these properties at hand, we are suited to prove our main statement of this section.

Theorem 5. Let $c, d \in \mathbb{Q}^{>0}$. NNREACH restricted to $\mathcal{C}(\{-c, 0, d\})$ is NP-hard.

Proof. Let $c, d \in \mathbb{Q}^{>0}$. Take a 3SAT-formula ψ and consider $(N_{-c,d,\psi}, \varphi_{\text{in}}, \varphi_{\text{out}})$ with $N_{-c,d,\psi}$ defined above, $\varphi_{\text{in}} = \top$ and $\varphi_{\text{out}} = \bigwedge_{i=0}^{n-1} z_i = 0 \wedge e_i = 0 \wedge y = m \cdot d^2 c^4$. Obviously, these specifications are simple.

Clearly, $(N_{-c,d,\psi}, \varphi_{\text{in}}, \varphi_{\text{out}})$ can be constructed in time polynomial in the size of ψ. For the correctness of the construction assume that ψ has a model I. We claim that $(N_{-c,d,\psi}, \varphi_{\text{in}}, \varphi_{\text{out}})$ is solved with $x_i = \frac{1}{c}$ if $I(X_i)$ is true, $x_i = -\frac{d}{c^2}$ otherwise, and $\overline{x_i} = -x_i$. Note that φ_{in} is trivially satisfied.

So apply these inputs to $N_{-c,d,\psi}$. According to Lemma 3.1, all outputs z_i are 0. It is easily verified that all outputs e_i are 0 as well. Thus, it is left to argue that $y = m \cdot d^2 c^4$. Consider one of the $\text{OR}_{\text{A}|\text{B}}$-gadgets occurring in $N_{-c,d,\psi}$, corresponding to a clause l_j. Its inputs are given by the NORM- and $\overline{\text{NORM}}$-gadgets connected to the inputs x_i, resp. $\overline{x_i}$ corresponding to the X_i occurring in l_j. According to Lemma 3.2 and 3 these inputs are either 0 or $-dc$. If l_j is satisfied by I then there is at least one input to the $\text{OR}_{\text{A}|\text{B}}$-gadget that is equal to $-dc$. From the fact that ψ is satisfied by I and Lemma 3.4 it follows that each $\text{OR}_{\text{A}|\text{B}}$-gadget outputs dc^4. Therefore, the output y of $N_{-c,d,\psi}$ is $m \cdot d^2 c^4$. This means that φ_{out} is valid as well.

Consider now the converse direction. A solution for $(N_{-c,d,\psi}, \varphi_{\text{in}}, \varphi_{\text{out}})$ must yield that all x_i are $\frac{1}{c}$ or $-\frac{d}{c^2}$ and $x_i = \overline{x_i}$ as all z_i and e_i have to equal 0. Therefore, all m $\text{OR}_{\text{A}|\text{B}}$-gadgets have to output dc^4 as y must equal $m \cdot d^2 c^4$. This implies that each $\text{OR}_{\text{A}|\text{B}}$-gadget has at least one input that is $-dc$ which in turn means that there is at least one indirectly connected x_i or $\overline{x_i}$ that is $\frac{1}{c}$ resp. $\frac{d}{c^2}$. Thus, ψ is satisfied by setting X_i true if $x_i = \frac{1}{c}$ and false if $x_i = -\frac{d}{c^2}$. $\square$

If $d = c$ and we allow arbitrary specifications we can show that 0 as a value for weights or biases is unnecessary to keep the lower bound.

Theorem 6. *Let $c \in \mathbb{Q}^{>0}$. NNREACH is NP-hard for NN in $C(\{-c, c\})$ and arbitrary specifications.*

Proof. This is done in the same way as the proof of Theorem 5 with some slight modifications. We only sketch this reduction by describing the differences compared to the instances $(N_{-c,c,\psi}, \varphi_{\text{in}}, \varphi_{\text{out}})$ resulting from the reduction used in Theorem 5.

We do not use EQ^0-gadgets in the network but add for each input x_i the conjunct $x_i = -\overline{x_i}$ to the input specification φ_{in}. This also means that we do not include $\bigwedge_{i=0}^{n-1} e_i = 0$ in the output specification φ_{out}. Consider the weights between the input and the first hidden layer. If the inputs x_i and $\overline{x_i}$ were originally weighted with zero we set the weights corresponding to x_i and $\overline{x_i}$ to be c. In combination with the input constraint $x_i = -\overline{x_i}$ this is equal to weighting x_i and $\overline{x_i}$ with zero. If x_i ($\overline{x_i}$) was originally weighted with c we have to set the weight of $\overline{x_i}$ (x_i) to be $-c$. If it was weighted with $-c$ we have to set the weight of its counterpart to be c. This leads to the case that all non-zero inputs of a node in the first hidden layer are doubled compared to the same inputs in a network $N_{-c,c,\psi}$. Consider now the weights between two layers l and $l+1$ with $l > 0$. For each node in l we add a node in the same layer with the same input weights. If the output of a node in layer l was originally weighted with zero then we weight it with c and the corresponding output of its copy with $-c$. If the output was originally weighted with weight c $(-c)$ then we weight the output of the copy node with c $(-c)$, too. As before, this doubles the input values at the nodes in layer $l+1$, which means that compared to a network $N_{-c,c,\psi}$ the output value of our modified network is multiplied by 2^7. Thus, we have to change the output constraint of y to be $y = 2^7(m \cdot c^6)$. Note that these modifications give a network using only the weights $-c$ and c.

To get rid of zero bias, we add the inputs $x_{\text{bias},1}, \overline{x_{\text{bias},1}}, \ldots, x_{\text{bias},7}, \overline{x_{\text{bias},7}}$ to the network and add the input constraints $x_{\text{bias},i} = -\sum_{j=0}^{i-1} \frac{1}{2^{j+1}c^j}$ and $x_{\text{bias},i} = -\overline{x_{\text{bias},i}}$ to φ_{in}. Then, we set the bias of all nodes which originally had a zero bias to be c. For $x_{\text{bias},i}$ with $i > 1$ we add a chain of $i-1$ identity nodes each with bias c and interconnected with weight c and connect this chain with weight c to $x_{\text{bias},i}$ and $-c$ to $\overline{x_{\text{bias},i}}$. All other weights are assumed to be zero which is realized using the same techniques as described in the previous paragraph. If a node in the first hidden layer originally had a zero bias we weight the input $x_{\text{bias},1}$ with c and $\overline{x_{\text{bias},i}}$ with $-c$. If the input specification holds then the bias plus these inputs sums up to zero. If a node in some layer $l \in \{2, \ldots, 7\}$ originally had a zero bias we weight the output of the last node of the chain corresponding to $x_{\text{bias},l}$ and its copy with c. Again, if the input specification holds, the bias value of this node is nullified. This modification ensures that the network is from $\mathcal{C}(\{-c, c\})$. $\qquad\square$

5 Conclusion

We investigated the computational complexity of the reachability problem for NN with ReLU and identity activations. We revised the original proof of its NP-completeness, fixing flaws in both the upper and lower bound, and showed that the parameter driving NP-hardness is the number of ReLU nodes. Furthermore, we showed that NNREACH is difficult for very restricted classes of small NN already, respectively that three parameters of different signum occurring as weights and biases suffice for NP-hardness. This indicates that finding non-trivial classes of NN with practical relevance and polynomial NNREACH is unlikely.

It remains to be seen whether NP-hardness can be strengthened, for instance for classes of NN with a single hidden layer and a maximum of two non-zero inputs to ReLU nodes, or only one arbitrary positive and only one arbitrary negative weight and bias value. However, possible results here are only of theoretical interest.

From a practical perspective, it would be interesting to see if pure ReLU networks, where every node in a hidden layer has a ReLU activation, lead to similar results as these are more common in practice. Also, investigating the fixed-parameter tractability of the problem more broadly could be promising. It remains to be seen whether there are parameters other than the number of ReLU nodes, like structural properties or dimensionality, whose fixing leads to polynomial decidability. This could yield efficiently solvable classes of NN that are also of practical interest.

References

1. Bunel, R., Turkaslan, I., Torr, P.H.S., Kohli, P., Mudigonda, P.K.: A unified view of piecewise linear neural network verification. In: Bengio, S., Wallach, H.M., Larochelle, H., Grauman, K., Cesa-Bianchi, N., Garnett, R. (eds.) Advances in Neural Information Processing Systems 31: Annual Conference on Neural Information Processing Systems 2018, NeurIPS 2018, 3–8 December 2018, Montréal, Canada, pp. 4795–4804 (2018). https://proceedings.neurips.cc/paper/2018/hash/be53d253d6bc3258a8160556dda3e9b2-Abstract.html
2. Dixon, M., Klabjan, D., Bang, J.H.: Classification-based financial markets prediction using deep neural networks. Algorithmic Finance **6**(3–4), 67–77 (2017). https://doi.org/10.3233/AF-170176
3. Ehlers, R.: Formal verification of piece-wise linear feed-forward neural networks. In: D'Souza, D., Narayan Kumar, K. (eds.) ATVA 2017. LNCS, vol. 10482, pp. 269–286. Springer, Cham (2017). https://doi.org/10.1007/978-3-319-68167-2_19
4. Grigorescu, S.M., Trasnea, B., Cocias, T.T., Macesanu, G.: A survey of deep learning techniques for autonomous driving. J. Field Robot. **37**(3), 362–386 (2020). https://doi.org/10.1002/rob.21918
5. Hinton, G., et al.: Deep neural networks for acoustic modeling in speech recognition: the shared views of four research groups. IEEE Signal Process. Mag. **29**(6), 82–97 (2012). https://doi.org/10.1109/MSP.2012.2205597
6. Huang, X., et al.: A survey of safety and trustworthiness of deep neural networks: verification, testing, adversarial attack and defence, and interpretability. Comput. Sci. Rev. **37**, 100270 (2020). https://doi.org/10.1016/j.cosrev.2020.100270
7. Karmarkar, N.: A new polynomial-time algorithm for linear programming. Comb. **4**(4), 373–396 (1984). https://doi.org/10.1007/BF02579150
8. Katz, G., Barrett, C., Dill, D.L., Julian, K., Kochenderfer, M.J.: Reluplex: an efficient SMT solver for verifying deep neural networks. In: Majumdar, R., Kunčak, V. (eds.) CAV 2017. LNCS, vol. 10426, pp. 97–117. Springer, Cham (2017). https://doi.org/10.1007/978-3-319-63387-9_5
9. Katz, G., Barrett, C.W., Dill, D.L., Julian, K., Kochenderfer, M.J.: Reluplex: a calculus for reasoning about deep neural networks. Form Methods Syst. Des. (2021). https://doi.org/10.1007/s10703-021-00363-7
10. Khan, A., Sohail, A., Zahoora, U., Qureshi, A.S.: A survey of the recent architectures of deep convolutional neural networks. Artif. Intell. Rev. **53**(8), 5455–5516 (2020). https://doi.org/10.1007/s10462-020-09825-6
11. Krizhevsky, A., Sutskever, I., Hinton, G.E.: Imagenet classification with deep convolutional neural networks. Commun. ACM **60**(6), 84–90 (2017). https://doi.org/10.1145/3065386
12. Litjens, G., et al.: A survey on deep learning in medical image analysis. Med. Image Anal. **42**, 60–88 (2017). https://doi.org/10.1016/j.media.2017.07.005
13. Narodytska, N., Kasiviswanathan, S.P., Ryzhyk, L., Sagiv, M., Walsh, T.: Verifying properties of binarized deep neural networks. In: McIlraith, S.A., Weinberger, K.Q. (eds.) Proceedings of the Thirty-Second AAAI Conference on Artificial Intelligence, (AAAI-18), the 30th innovative Applications of Artificial Intelligence (IAAI-18), and the 8th AAAI Symposium on Educational Advances in Artificial Intelligence (EAAI-18), New Orleans, Louisiana, USA, 2–7 February 2018, pp. 6615–6624. AAAI Press (2018). https://www.aaai.org/ocs/index.php/AAAI/AAAI18/paper/view/16898

14. Ruan, W., Huang, X., Kwiatkowska, M.: Reachability analysis of deep neural networks with provable guarantees. In: Lang, J. (ed.) Proceedings of the Twenty-Seventh International Joint Conference on Artificial Intelligence, IJCAI 2018, 13–19 July 2018, Stockholm, Sweden, pp. 2651–2659. ijcai.org (2018). https://doi.org/10.24963/ijcai.2018/368

15. Ruan, W., Huang, X., Kwiatkowska, M.: Reachability analysis of deep neural networks with provable guarantees. CoRR abs/1805.02242 (2018). http://arxiv.org/abs/1805.02242

Author Index

Printed in the United States
by Baker & Taylor Publisher Services

Printed in the United States
by Baker & Taylor Publisher Services